IMAGINING
THE ANGLO-SAXON PAST

THE SEARCH FOR
ANGLO-SAXON PAGANISM
AND
ANGLO-SAXON TRIAL BY JURY

ERIC STANLEY has an international reputation as a leading Anglo-Saxonist, and his perceptive and original contributions to the field continue to offer valuable correctives to prevailing views and to show how scholarly predilection can easily become prejudice and orthodoxy. The two issues under scrutiny in this book are the tendency among some writers to exalt whatever is primitive and supposedly pagan or crypto-pagan in the surviving Old English texts of the early Christian Middle Ages (for example, Tolkien on monsters or Jacob Grimm on everything Germanic), and the idealism of some advocates of political and legal reform that leads them to identify the beginnings of trial by jury (and hence the first step on the way to democratic rule by law), in Germanic or Alfredian institutions.

ERIC GERALD STANLEY is Rawlinson and Bosworth Professor Emeritus of Anglo-Saxon in the University of Oxford.

IMAGINING THE ANGLO-SAXON PAST

THE SEARCH FOR
ANGLO-SAXON PAGANISM

AND

ANGLO-SAXON TRIAL BY JURY

Eric Gerald Stanley

D. S. BREWER

© Eric Gerald Stanley 1975, 2000

All Rights Reserved. Except as permitted under current legislation no part of this work may be photocopied, stored in a retrieval system, published, performed in public, adapted, broadcast, transmitted, recorded or reproduced in any form or by any means, without the prior permission of the copyright owner

The Search for Anglo-Saxon Paganism
First published in book form 1975
Reprinted 2000

Anglo-Saxon Trial by Jury
First published 2000

D. S. Brewer, Cambridge

ISBN 0 85991 588 3

D. S. Brewer is an imprint of Boydell & Brewer Ltd
PO Box 9, Woodbridge, Suffolk IP12 3DF, UK
and of Boydell & Brewer Inc.
PO Box 41026, Rochester, NY 14604–4126, USA
website: http://www.boydell.co.uk

A catalogue record for this book is available
from the British Library

Library of Congress Cataloging-in-Publication Data

Stanley, Eric Gerald
 [Search for Anglo-Saxon paganism]
 Imagining the Anglo-Saxon past / Eric Gerald Stanley
   p. cm.
 First work previously published in 1975; second work published now for the first time.
 Includes bibliographical references and index.
 Contents: The Search for Anglo-Saxon paganism – Anglo-Saxon trial by jury.
 ISBN 0-85991-588-3 (alk. paper)
   1. English literature – Old English, ca. 450–1100 – History and criticism. 2. Paganism – England – History – To 1500. 3. Jury – England – History – To 1500. 4. Mythology, Germanic, in literature 5. Anglo-Saxons – Religion. 6. Law, Anglo-Saxon. I. Stanley, Eric Gerald. Anglo-Saxon trial by jury. II. Title.
PR176.S68   2001
829.00–dc21   00–057203

This publication is printed on acid-free paper

Typeset by Joshua Associates Ltd, Oxford
Printed in Great Britain by
St Edmundsbury Press Ltd, Bury St Edmunds, Suffolk

CONTENTS

Preface to the new edition, AD 2000	vii
Introduction to the 1975 edition of *The Search for Anglo-Saxon Paganism*	xiii

PART I
THE SEARCH FOR ANGLO-SAXON PAGANISM

1.	The Romantic background	3
2.	The English branch of the German tree	7
3.	Christianity puts an end to folk-poetry	10
4.	'Half-veiled remains of pagan poetry'	14
5.	English and German views on the conversion of the English	24
6.	J.M. Kemble	29
7.	The views of the founders seen through the writings of their lesser contemporaries	33
8.	English views of the late nineteenth century and after	38
9.	Stock views disintegrating Old English poems and finding Germanic antiquities in them	40
	A. Disintegration	40
	i. *Beowulf*	41
	ii. The elegies	50
	iii. Gnomic Poems	61
	B. The search for Germanic antiquities	63
10.	The gods Themselves	77
	A. Appearances veiled by Christianity	77
	B. Overt appearances	80
11.	*Wyrd*	85
	A. 'Event' or 'fate', Norn or Fortune	85

	B.	Early interpretations of *wyrd*	88
	C.	*Wyrd* in a Leipzig Ph.D. thesis	92
	D.	Germanic fatalism accommodated in Anglo-Saxon Christianity	93
	E.	Germanic fatalism: a key to Anglo-Saxon melancholy	94
	F.	*Wyrd*: the mark of heathenism	96
	G.	Fate and Providence	98
	H.	*Metod*	101
	I.	More recent pagan interpretations of *wyrd*	102
	J.	Wyrd in *Solomon and Saturn*	105
	K.	Current views on *wyrd*	106
12.	Conclusion		110

PART II

ANGLO-SAXON TRIAL BY JURY
Trial by Jury and how Later Ages Perceive its Origins perhaps in Anglo-Saxon England

1.	Jury: this *palladium* of our liberties, sacred and inviolate	111
2.	Delivering the truth not the same as judging	123
3.	Guilt and innocence a matter of conscience	128
4.	'England's great and glorious Revolution' (1688), its debt to Henry II's revival of ancient institutions fostering liberty	132
5.	Trial by jury not a Proto-Germanic nor perhaps an Anglo-Saxon institution; but what of the twelve leading thegns of the wapentake?	136
6.	Why promulgated at Wantage?	140
7.	The twelve of the wapentake probably an institution for the Danelaw only	142
8.	Conclusion	146
I.	Index of sources	149
II.	Index of scholars, critics, and authors	152
III.	General Index	155

PREFACE TO THE NEW EDITION, AD 2000

Fifty years have passed since I started to collect quotations from scholarly writings that struck me, at that time an undergraduate, as wholly unfounded in claiming to have found in the Christian literature of the Anglo-Saxons indelible vestiges of Germanic paganism, or in claiming to have discovered the paganisms the Anglo-Saxon authors appeared to have striven to conceal. Those teaching at Oxford, and among them those whose teaching I attended regularly were, however, not guilty of these misguided scholarly endeavours: my tutor, E. Stefanyja Olszewska (Mrs Alan S.C. Ross), a brilliantly sensitive and wide-ranging reader of Old and Middle English literature and of Icelandic literature, from whom I learnt everything that I was capable of learning, J.R.R. Tolkien, and Alistair Campbell.

I began reading widely in the scholarly writings on the Anglo-Saxon laws only in the last few years. I had noticed long ago that the Saxonists of Archbishop Matthew Parker's time and those who followed him looked back to their ancestors before the Norman Conquest for the civil liberty extinguished, as they thought, under the Normans and only slowly restored.[1] King Alfred and the institution of trial by jury, supposedly in his reign, played a part in a venerative view of the Anglo-Saxon heritage and King Alfred's place in it.[2] I did not know till fairly recently the range of reference to the supposed debt to the Anglo-Saxons for the institution of trial by jury, and not at all that it played a part in the politics of nineteenth-century Germany. When it was suggested to me that I might read a paper to the Bayerische Akademie der Wissenschaften, which had honoured me by making me a corresponding member, it seemed appropriate to take as my subject the law of the Anglo-Saxons and how it was perceived in later ages. An expanded version of that paper, read 5 July 1996, forms a Sitzungsbericht of the

---

[1] See E.G. Stanley, 'The Scholarly Recovery of the Significance of Anglo-Saxon Records in Prose and Verse: A New Bibliography', *Anglo-Saxon England* 9 (1981), pp. 231–2; reprinted in E.G. Stanley, *A Collection of Papers with Emphasis on Old English Literature* (Toronto, 1987), p. 13.

[2] See E.G. Stanley, 'The Glorification of Alfred King of Wessex (from the Publication of Sir John Spelman's *Life*, 1678 and 1709, to the Publication of Reinhold Pauli's, 1851)', *Poetica* (Tokyo) xii (1981), p. 113; reprinted in Stanley, *A Collection of Papers*, p. 420.

Philosophisch-historische Klasse of the Akademie, and the institution of trial by jury is a part of that. A somewhat different, English version was read to members of a conference at Western University, London (Ontario), in April 1997, and that underlies the part on jury contained in this book. I wish to thank Professor Jane Toswell for inviting me to participate in the conference.

There are good reasons for presenting the material on trial by jury in a volume in which 'The Search for Anglo-Saxon Paganism' is reprinted, not just because both involve scholarly mythographies about the Anglo-Saxon past, but because these mythographies share in the same political origins from the early nineteenth century till much later. Jacob Grimm plays a major rôle in the creation of both myths,[3] and it is important to understand the politics of Germany at the beginning of the nineteenth century when he began to publish. *Vaterlandsliebe*, German patriotism, underlies it all. The German states were, of course, not yet united, but the Napoleonic defeats, culminating in Jena and followed by victories at Leipzig and Waterloo, in both of which German arms were significantly involved, shaped attitudes. Not that all Germans were of one mind about Napoleon himself; some were conservatives, others were not unsympathetic to republican notions: but defeat is bitter, and forged a united, patriotic spirit in scholars and poets who were, in other respects, of varied outlook. And Jacob Grimm was among the patriotic scholars.

Grimm's primary interests were not only philological. The most literary president of the Philological Society in more than a century-and-a-half of its history, William Paton Ker, understood Grimm's literary motivation well, and he portrayed him sympathetically in 1915, a time when the Kaiser's war would not have made a glowing reference to *Vaterlandsliebe* an acceptable subject of praise to a London audience or British readership.[4] Ker draws attention to Grimm's statement on how his interest in philology developed:[5]

---

[3] A succinct account of Jacob and Wilhelm Grimm, with excellent bibliographical information is E. Ebel's entry, s.v. Grimm, in the 2nd edition of Johannes Hoops, founder, *Reallexikon der Germanischen Altertumskunde*, XIII (Berlin and New York, 1999), pp. 40–5. It is to be regretted that Ebel had no more than about nine-and-a-half columns for his entry; that is to be contrasted with the entry Heusler by the general editor, Heinrich Beck, *Reallexikon*, XIV (1999), pp. 533–43, nearly twenty columns, and the reader is directed further to Beck's own entry Ethik § 6, *Reallexikon*, VII (1989), pp. 609–11, not quite five columns long, in which Heusler plays a major part. I am not arguing that Heusler should have had less space, but that the Brothers Grimm could valuably have been given more.

[4] W.P. Ker, *Jacob Grimm – An address delivered at the annual meeting of the Philological Society on Friday, May 7, 1915*, Publications of the Philological Society VII (1915).

[5] J. Grimm, *Deutsche Grammatik*, I, 2nd edn (Göttingen, 1822), p. viii: 'Das einladende studium mittelhochdeutscher poesie führte mich zuerst auf grammatische untersuchungen; die übrigen älteren mundarten mit voller ausnahme der

PREFACE TO THE NEW EDITION

The inviting study of Middle High German poetry led me first to grammatical investigations. The other older dialects offer little by way of poetry, with the full exception of the Old Norse dialect, and the more partial exception of the Anglo-Saxon dialect. A considerable volume of Middle Dutch and early Middle English works can hardly be compared with the aforementioned verse.

That was published ten years after the Battle of the Nations at Leipzig, seven years after Waterloo. Glorious victories had been achieved, and after the earlier defeats there was a sense not so much of exultation but, as there had been after the Thirty Years War concluded in 1648, a sense of gratitude that the country had come through. Some years earlier, the poet Friedrich Hölderlin, with a very different political outlook from that of the Brothers Grimm, had expressed well that sense of gratitude for a national survival in the very turbulent times of his own sickness and of humiliating, multiple defeat at the turn of the century, when, after a long absence, he returned home:[6] 'But thou, my fatherland, sacred in thy suffering, behold, thou hast endured!' There were more calamities to come for Germany, and these youthful years of the Brothers Grimm – Jacob was born in 1785 and Wilhelm a year later – were formative.

Early in their lives the Brothers Grimm were imbued with a love of all aspects of the Germanic past. Jacob Grimm's first academic study was Law; at the University of Marburg F.C. von Savigny was an inspiring teacher, and the legal institutions of the Germanic peoples before they were imbrued with alien legal systems were of a kind with the ancient Germanic literatures and with the sister dialects of the Germanic peoples: that kind was seen by him as 'our kind', *unsere Art*, the national character. German patriotism was sentimentally affectionate of the German past and not yet aggressively expansionist.

There was a vigorously imaginative side to Jacob Grimm's scholarship, leading quite often to conclusions based on wishful thinking, about half-concealed manifestations of paganism and about Proto-Germanic origins of legal institutions. W.P. Ker ends his account of Grimm with a wonderful play on words: 'the cloud of his fancies and aspirations had fire and life in it; and the history of Jacob Grimm, his progress and his

---

altnordischen, theilweise der angelsächsischen, bieten wenig dichterisches; eine ansehnliche maße mittelniederländischer und altenglischer werke läßt sich jenen kaum vergleichen.'

[6] N. von Hellingrath, F. Seebass and L. von Pigenot (eds), *Hölderlin: Sämtliche Werke*, IV Gedichte 1800–06, 3rd edn (Berlin, 1943), p. 32, 'Rükkehr in die Heimath' lines 11–12 (and cf. pp. 285–6, notes on the poem):
  Doch du mein Vaterland! du heilig-
  Duldendes! siehe, du bist geblieben.
It might be possible to take *geblieben* as meaning 'stayed (behind)' rather than 'endured', but I think hardly here with *duldend*; perhaps both senses are present.

conquests, is a demonstration of the power of that great god *Wish* whom Jacob Grimm was the first to name.' Carlyle had noted that:[7]

> But perhaps the notablest god we hear tell of is one of whom Grimm the German Etymologist finds trace: the God *Wünsch*, or Wish. The God *Wish*; who would give us all that we *wished!* Is not this the sincerest and yet rudest voice of the spirit of man?

Grimm's account of the god Wish does not relate him to wishful thinking, but to wish-fulfilment:[8]

> The essence of prosperity and happiness, the fulfilment of all endowments appears to have been expressed in the ancient language by one single word, the semantic range of which was subsequently narrowed: it was called *der Wunsch* 'wish'. This word is probably derived from *wunnia*, *Wonne* 'joy', [*]*wunisc*,[9] *wunsc*, 'perfection in all respects' such as we would call 'ideal'. . . . The sense 'desire of, longing for such perfection' may have been connected adventitiously with the word *wunsc*, Old Norse *ôsk*. Among the Eddaic names of Othin, *Osci* does indeed occur . . ., *i.e.* the one who grants to mankind to participate in the wish, in the highest gift.

Jacob Grimm on the word *wish* and its extension into Germanic myth, the ideal and the divinity of that ideal, and how it all hangs on a shared heritage going back to a Proto-Germanic age when the various peoples had not yet been scattered and diversified. Early in his scholarly career and in that of his brother Wilhelm, the Brothers had shown themselves vehement in pursuance and defence of ideas and Germanic ideals they had not yet fully formulated, especially when some part of the Germanic

---

[7] T. Carlyle, *On Heroes, Hero-Worship, and the Heroic in History: Six Lectures* (London, 1841), p. 29.

[8] J. Grimm, *Deutsche Mythologie* (Göttingen, 1835), p. 99 (and see 2nd edn [Göttingen, 1844], p. 126): 'Den inbegrif von heil und seligkeit, die erfüllung aller gaben, scheint die alte sprache mit einem einzigen worte, dessen bedeutung sich nachher verengerte, auszudrücken, es hieß der *wunsch*. dieses wort ist wahrscheinlich von wunja, wunnja, wonne, freude abstammend, wunisc, wunsc, vollkommenheit in jeder art, was wir ideal nennen würden. . . . die bedeutung des begehrens und verlangens nach solchen vollkommenheiten mag sich erst zufällig mit dem worte *wunsc*, altn. *ôsk* verbunden haben. Unter den eddischen namen Odhins kommt nun auch vor *Osci* . . . d. h. der die menschen des wunsches, der höchsten gabe theilhaftig machende.'

Grimm's god *Wish* is now regarded as a misconception; see E.A. Philippson, *Germanisches Heidentum bei den Angelsachsen*, Kölner Anglistische Arbeiten IV (Leipzig, 1929), pp. 14, 162. The relationship of Old High German *wunsc* to *wunna*, Old Saxon *wunnia*, is still accepted; see W. Pfeifer (ed.), *Etymologisches Wörterbuch des Deutschen* (Berlin, 1989), III, s.vv. *wohnen*, *Wonne*, *Wunsch*.

[9] I have not been able to find this Old High German form, and presume it is a form regarded as theoretically ideal by Grimm; see J. Grimm, *Deutsche Grammatik*, II (Göttingen, 1826), p. 276.

foundation on which their ideas rested seemed under attack. When in 1964 and 1965 I published the articles 'The Search for Anglo-Saxon Paganism', and when I republished them in 1975 in book form, I had not read the works of Friedrich Rühs seeking to establish that Old Icelandic poetry was derived from Anglo-Saxon poetry, attempting to prove that derivation by false etymologies because he did not understand the hereditary nature of the shared vocabulary.[10] Since then I have read all of Rühs's work in book and pamphlet form and the two dismissive reviews written separately by Jacob and Wilhelm Grimm that aroused Rühs's ire. I first thought that in this new edition I should quote from Rühs's writings because they strove to show that contact of Germanic peoples in historical times led to borrowing, a process neglected by the Brothers Grimm who believed too readily that Common Germanic features were derived from Proto-Germanic features, linguistic and other. In the end I decided to leave Rühs in well-deserved oblivion, partly because he was so rude – coarse, even by the standards of nineteenth-century German professorial altercations – and so obviously wrong in detail that he could hardly be thought a useful critic of the flawed methods of the Brothers Grimm, and mainly because, though more widely applicable, the criticism as stated by him is not really relevant to either the search for Anglo-Saxon paganism or the myth of trial by jury in Anglo-Saxon England. It could have been made relevant to both: to Ælfric's account of paganism in late Anglo-Saxon times and to the institution in the Danelaw of a group of twelve in legal process, a group that looks remarkably like a jury. For such an extension, however, Rühs's views as stated by him are too feeble a foundation.

Both parts of the new book, the reprinted section on paganism and the account of the historical perception of the origin of trial by jury here published in English for the first time, do not stand alone in academic endeavours. Much of the twentieth-century scholarship on Anglo-Saxon paganism is in tune with what I have written, and in the last third of the century my work is mentioned now and again in agreement rather than disagreement. On jury too my views are symptomatic of current views rather than deviating from them, but I believe that I have traced the history of the scholarship of the subject more fully than others.

More important, I am very conscious of the fact that the scholarship of Anglo-Saxon law and legal institutions has undergone fundamental reappraisal at the hands of Patrick Wormald since the publication of

---

[10] R.P. Wülker was clearly ashamed of F. Rühs's polemics against the young Brothers Grimm, who in separate reviews criticized unfavourably but justly his book *Über den Ursprung der isländischen Poesie aus der Angelsächsischen* (n.p., 1813), when he gave it no more than a footnote with a long abusive quotation in R. Wülker, *Grundriss der Geschichte der angelsächsischen Litteratur* (Leipzig, 1885), p. 47, attached to § 69 on Jacob Grimm's *Deutsche Grammatik*.

his fundamental book on the subject.[11] I am very grateful to him that he has read my work in print-out and has made it better by his comments. That errors, omissions and misconceptions remain is, of course, entirely due to me. The current opinion on how jury may be related to Anglo-Saxon legal institutions is conveniently summarized in his article, 'Jury', in a recent encyclopaedia.[12]

I owe to Simon Keynes my knowledge of a Victorian pictorial representation of King Alfred presiding over the newly instituted trial by jury, referred to in a paper read at Oxford, now published more fully.[13] The original fresco by C.W. Cope adorned the walls of a corridor in the House of Lords; the cartoon for it was well received and awarded a prize, but nothing other than the lithograph seems to have survived.[14] I am grateful to the authorities of the British Museum for permission to reproduce their copy of the lithograph, British Museum 1854–12–11–135. I use it as an illustration of an Alfredian myth, although I do not refer to it in the part of this book dealing with the origins of trial by jury.

It is a pleasure to record my gratitude for kindnesses received: routinely, but always more helpfully than routine requires, from the staff of the Bodleian Library and its Law Library, the English Faculty Library, Oxford, and the British Library. His Honour Judge Paul V. Baker, QC, facilitated my use of the Library of Lincoln's Inn, and its Librarian Mr Guy Holborn allowed me to use it and helped me to find continental sources, rare in England, many of them from the collection Charles Purton Cooper. Professor Helmut Gneuss and Ms Svenja Weidinger, both of Munich, made my visits to the Bayerische Staatsbibliothek possible and profitable. I am indebted to Professor Daniel Donoghue (Harvard University) for making it possible for me to see Ignaz Gundermann's *Geschichte der Entstehung der Jury in England und deren leitender Gedanke. Ein germanistischer Versuch* (Munich, 1847). I am indebted to Dr Nicholas Cronk (St Edmund Hall, Oxford) for guiding me through the labyrinthine Voltaire bibliography.

Eric Stanley

Oxford, January 2000.

---

[11] Patrick Wormald, *The Making of English Law: King Alfred to the Twelfth Century*, I, Legislation and its Limits (Oxford, 1999).

[12] M. Lapidge, J. Blair, S. Keynes and D. Scragg (eds), *The Blackwell Encyclopaedia of Anglo-Saxon England* (Oxford, 1999), p. 267.

[13] S. Keynes, 'The Cult of King Alfred the Great', *Anglo-Saxon England* 28 (1999), pp. 225–356. Plate VIIb has a reproduction of C.W. Cope's 'The First Trial by Jury', a lithograph of 1847.

[14] See T.S.R. Boase, 'The Decoration of the New Palace of Westminster', *Journal of the Warburg and Courtauld Institutes* xvii (1954), p. 328 and Pl. 46c; C.H. Cope, *Reminiscences of Charles West Cope R.A.* (London, 1891), pp. 147 'An Early Trial by Jury', 149, 378 No. 47, and 389.

INTRODUCTION TO THE 1975 EDITION OF
THE SEARCH FOR ANGLO-SAXON PAGANISM

It is difficult to recall a writer who, faced with doubts whether to publish or no –

> *Some said,* John, *print it; others said, Not so:*
> *Some said, It might do good; others said, No* –

came down on the side of 'No', but then it is in the nature of the evidence to reveal only those who acceded when asked to publish, not those who forbore. When the material, here reprinted in the form of a monograph, first appeared in *Notes and Queries* ccix (1964) and ccx (1965) as a series of articles I had no doubt that it was right to print it and even some hopes that it might do good. But republishing is quite another matter, and my excuse must be that the suggestion to do so did not come from me, and that I have had many requests for offprints of the articles which I have not been able to satisfy. Perhaps it was arrogant not to feel the doubts Bunyan felt, but, asked to turn the series into a monograph, I wondered if it should not be extended especially by further examples and the discussion of later work. A series of articles can be selective; a book, large or small enough to be called a monograph, should be systematic and comprehensive, though not necessarily exhaustive. The material for the articles in *Notes and Queries* was collected in haphazard fashion over about fifteen years; the reading was done incidentally, quotations jumping out of pages usually read for some quite different purpose: a book, at least a book intended for academic readers, demands research with only one single aim in mind, the furtherance of the subject of the book.

The quotations and references I give, collected as by-products of reading, could have been increased in bulk and weight at almost every point, and as I turn the series of articles into a monograph I feel more like Mrs Arrowpoint: 'These things I daresay I shall publish eventually: several friends have urged me to do so, and one doesn't like to be obstinate. My Tasso, for example – I could have made it twice the size.' I doubt, however, if the publication of such further material would be of real use in supporting (or refuting) the general conclusion, which is, I think, sufficiently supported by the material here reprinted, that for a long time Old English literature was much read in the hope of discovering in it a lost world of pre-Christian antiquity, for the reconstruction of which the Old English writings themselves do not provide sufficient fragments.

If I were to write about the subject now I should, of course, be able to put in references to new work, much of it very good – like G.W. Weber's book on *Wyrd*, in Frankfurter Beiträge zur Germanistik VIII (1969) – in which the extant literature of the early medieval Germanic vernaculars is discussed without the prejudices to be found in earlier writers. Though it might have been pleasant to have included more quotations from early writers on Old English literature, and though it would not have been difficult to have done so, there is really very little that I now feel I ought to have included because of the central place it occupies in the history of nineteenth- and early twentieth-century Anglo-Saxon scholarship; probably Benjamin Thorpe's introduction to his edition for the Society of Antiquaries of *Codex Exoniensis* (1842) ought not to have been ignored. He runs down, in general and in detail, the Christian matter of his manuscript, especially the poems we now call *Christ* of which he says that he would gladly give them in exchange for the restoration of the damaged parts of *The Ruin*; he has not a good word to say for *Juliana*, but speaks more appreciatively of *Guthlac*; but where the text is secular, and he is able to understand it, he is full of praise. The book was influential, for it was half a century till Gollancz produced his edition for the Early English Text Society of half the Exeter Book with translations into Modern English, and considerably longer till all of the contents of the manuscript was conveniently available in Modern English translations, though Grein's translations into German appeared in 1857 and 1859.

Substantially the monograph is the same as it was when printed as a series of articles in 1964 and 1965. I have, however, tinkered with the wording here and there, especially in my translations, in the hope of improving the wording without altering the spirit of the study. Some misprints have been corrected. Indexes have been provided, and the footnotes have been transferred to the end of the book. If I had really brought the book up to date, I should have wished to alter the emphasis.

I know that something of what I was writing about is still with us, at least in some measure. The book-producing industry has brought into the world reprints of Miss Wardale's and Professor G.K. Anderson's books, for example. Now and again older views are alluded to, as, for example, in the note on line 19 in Dr Pamela O.E. Gradon's excellent edition of *Elene* (1958), where a reference to 'ON *ómi* a *heiti* of Odin' brings back to me, in connection with *wiges woma*, a history of error, even though, as stated by Dr Gradon, there is no error.

In Anglo-Saxon studies as a whole the balance of views has changed. A good number of books and articles, the vast majority, emphasize the fundamentally Christian nature of Old English literature as it is known to us, so much so that the reissue of what was collected early in the present half-century may seem now to be making heavy weather of discovering the obvious. Perhaps I should go further than that. After reading some works on what seem to me to be non-religious Old English poems, and I include *Beowulf* among them, I should now wish to protest their secularity. Of course, it is a Christian secularity, and no amount of probing will reveal a pagan core. As I felt in 1965, when I wrote the conclusion of what is now republished in book form, my study is not essential reading for scholars who write as if the typical Anglo-Saxon poet were working at a centre of learning which had, in a manner of speaking, the first hundred and fifty or hundred and seventy-five volumes of the *Patrologia Latina* (at least as well indexed as in Migne) on its shelves. There may, however, still be something in this monograph for those who want to understand the origins of modern Anglo-Saxon scholarship, not so much present errors as past misconceptions.

It is a pleasant duty to thank here Dr [now Professor] D.S. Brewer for his initiative in this republication: he was present when a very early stage of the study was read as a paper to a group of medievalists in the University of Birmingham; to Professor Geoffrey Shepherd, who suggested many improvements at that time; and to the Oxford University Press for allowing me to republish in book-form the series of articles first published in *Notes and Queries* ccix and ccx (vols xi and xii of the New Series), 1964–1965, with the same title as the book has now, *The Search for Anglo-Saxon Paganism*.

E.G. STANLEY

Queen Mary College,
University of London,
November 1973.

PART I

THE SEARCH FOR ANGLO-SAXON PAGANISM

1. The Romantic Background

A READING OF the past is at best a selective reading, at worst a reading into the past. For the earliest period of Germanic literature, sentiment makes the reader expect to find a noble and ennobling Heroic Age, rude but grand, a world not unlike that which Bishop Hurd associated with Chivalry and Romance:[1]

> I Look upon Chivalry, as on some mighty River, which the fablings of the poets have made immortal. It may have sprung up amidst rude rocks, and blind deserts. But the noise and rapidity of its course, the extent of country it adorns, and the towns and palaces it ennobles, may lead a traveller out of his way and invite him to take a view of those dark caverns,
>
> <div align="center">undè supernè
Plurimus Eridani per sylvam volvitur amnis.
[<i>Aeneid</i>, vi. 658–9]</div>

The aim of these chapters is to point to the continuity of a critical attitude which exalts whatever in the Germanic literature of the Dark Ages is primitive (that is, pagan), and belittles or even fails to understand whatever in it is civilized, learned, and cosmopolitan (that is, inspired by Christianity). If the rude rocks, the blind deserts, and those dark caverns of mythology are to be explored, the traveller's time will not be spent in surveying the land as a whole. He has selected his favourite haunts before he knows what the land has to offer, he will call that the richest part of the country which is richest in rocks, deserts, and caverns, while cultivated fields fail to win his praise, however luxuriant the harvest they bear.

A.R. Waller fits his Anglo-Saxon travellers into the heroic landscape:[2]

> Their love of nature is love of her wilder and more melancholy aspects. The rough woodland and the stormy sky, "the scream of the gannet" and "the moan of the seamew" find their mirror and echo in Old English literature. . . . The more placid aspects have their turn later,

---

[1] Richard Hurd, *Letters on Chivalry and Romance* (London and Cambridge, 1762), pp. 5–6.
[2] A.R. Waller, in *Cambridge History of English Literature*, I (Cambridge, 1907), pp. 2–3.

when the conquerors of the shore had penetrated inland and taken to more pastoral habits; when, also, the leaven of Christianity had worked.

Miss E.E. Wardale writes similarly on the nature element in *Beowulf*:[3] 'As in all genuine O.E. poetry, the aspects of nature described are stern or even gloomy and always in harmony with the action of the story.' Her use of the word *genuine* is precise; in her view, as in that of many, Old English verse that fails to obey this formula is spurious.

The Seafarer has an important place in this critical attitude. Like all seafarers, the Anglo-Saxon seafarer must have battled against the elements, but he loved the strife and the turmoil of the waves, for to him, as to Wordsworth,[4]

> whate'er
> I saw, or heard, or felt, was but a stream
> That flowed into a kindred stream; a gale,
> Confederate with the current of the soul,
> To speed my voyage.

That is how F. Kluge saw him:[5]

> The very changefulness of life at sea attracts the Young Seafarer. His mind leaves him no rest. He longs to be far away. A future, insecure, and unpredictable, awaits him at sea, as it awaits the mightiest, boldest adventure-seeking hero. His longing for the sea deprives him of all the pleasure of feasting; he knows nothing of woman's love.

É. Pons echoed Kluge's views on *The Seafarer*, though he by no means accepted them entirely:[6]

---

[3] E.E. Wardale, *Chapters on Old English Literature* (London, 1935), p. 101.

[4] Wm Wordsworth, *The Prelude, or Growth of a Poet's Mind: An autobiographical poem* (London, 1850), p. 166 (VI [742–6]).

[5] F. Kluge, 'Zu altenglischen dichtungen, I. Der Seefahrer', *Englische Studien* vi (1883), p. 323: 'gerade dieses wechselvolle leben auf dem meere hat für den jüngling reiz: sein inneres lässt ihm keine ruhe, er will hinaus in die ferne; eine unsichere, unberechenbare zukunft wartet auf der see seiner wie auch des mächtigsten, tapfersten recken. Die sehnsucht nach der see benimmt ihm jede freude an gelagen, frauenliebe ist ihm fremd.'

[6] É. Pons, *Le thème et le sentiment de la nature dans la poésie anglo-saxonne*, Publications de la Faculté des Lettres de l'Université de Strasbourg xxv (1925), p. 111: 'La solitude et les tristesses inhérentes à la mer sont l'apanage du poète, lui appartiennent comme le cri des mouettes ou le mugissement des flots; il ne permet pas que d'autres les profanent. A travers l'expression de ses souffrances en effet on devine par le simple jeu de l'oscillation entre des sentiments contraires et par la victoire finale de la joie, le secret amour du marin pour son âpre existence. Mais, par une délicatesse remarquable, qui provient de sa sincérité, le poète se garde de s'abandonner à des sentiments extrêmes et à un enthousiasme sans discernement: si l'horreur des tempêtes et du froid ne peuvent abolir en son cœur

> The loneliness and the miseries which are an intrinsic part of the sea are the endowment of the poet, and belong to him as much as the cry of the sea-gulls and the roar of the waves; he will not allow others to profane them. Indeed, the simple device of interplaying, contrary emotions, and the final victory of bliss enable us to sense, beyond the statements of what the seafarer suffers, his secret love of the harsh life he leads. With rare tact, which is rooted in his sincerity, the poet refrains, however, from abandoning himself to violent emotions and undiscerning enthusiasm; if fear of gales and of the cold cannot extinguish in his heart his love of the sea, that fear makes him esteem on the contrary the sweeter aspects of Nature, the gentle beauty of spring on the land, the woods in bud, the gardens in flower.

Miss Wardale, it seems from the following sentence, would not have allowed love of the sweeter of Nature a place in the genuine and early parts of *The Seafarer*:[7]

> The early delight in grand and wild aspects lasted on after the end of the O.E. period, but side by side with it the charm of sunshine and flowers made itself felt, first by translation as in the Phoenix, but also in due time it showed itself in native works as in the little poem on the Doomsday.

G.K. Anderson repeatedly praises Anglo-Saxon poets for their love and knowledge of Nature; thus, Cynewulf is described as 'the true sea-poet of the age';[8] the saint's death-scene in *Guthlac* lines 1276–82, sunset, darkness, mist, leads Anderson to aver enthusiastically 'that the author of a Cynewulfian poem must know the sky as well as the sea'.[9] All these are more refined expressions of the idea found at its crudest in C.C. Ferrell's Leipzig doctoral dissertation:[10]

> At the time when our poem was composed the Anglo-saxons were as a race still in their childhood, and lived still so near to the great heart of nature that they could hear its very throb.

Ferrell's Hegelian metaphor recalls Shelley's 'For the savage is to ages what the child is to years' (*A Defence of Poetry*, paragraph 2), though the idea goes back, by implication at least, to King Psammetichus' experiment in ontogenetic linguistics as recorded by Herodotus at the beginning of the second book of his *History*. The critical attitude is Romantic, and these critics, like many Romantic critics, think that the literature to

---

son amour pour la mer, elle lui fait apprécier, par contraste, les aspects plus doux de la nature, la beauté apaisante du printemps sur la terre, des bois bourgeonnants, des jardins en fleurs.'
[7] Wardale, *Chapters on Old English Literature*, p. 13.
[8] G.K. Anderson, *The Literature of the Anglo-Saxons* (Princeton, 1949), p. 125.
[9] Anderson, *Literature of the Anglo-Saxons*, p. 137.
[10] Ferrell, *Teutonic Antiquities in the Anglo-Saxon Genesis* (Halle, 1893), p. 26.

which they devote themselves is Romantic too. This is stated by É. Legouis:[11]

> The authors of these poems [*Widsith, Deor, Beowulf*] had kept the old passion for adventure, together with the memory of the wild life of their ancestors and the ancestral legends and verses. There is a certain analogy between their state of mind and that which the nineteenth century called romanticism.

G.K. Anderson expresses the same view with fewer qualifications, 'For Old English literature is essentially romantic.'[12]

Modern Anglo-Saxon scholarship was born of the Romantic Movement, and for the origin of the critical attitude exemplified in these quotations we must go to Germany at the beginning of the nineteenth century, to the defeat of Prussia at Jena in 1806 and the ensuing national resurgence which produced the victorious Wars of Liberation from Napoleon. G.G. Gervinus characterized the spirit of the age as 'that half-affecting, half-ridiculous fit of Germanity-mongering among our youth in the years of Liberation of the nation'.[13] According to Dr G.P.Gooch 'Historiography was' up to that time 'particularist or cosmopolitan, not yet national'.[14] By the end of the first half of the century German historiography and the literary criticism connected with it had gone as far towards extreme German nationalism as, in the field of Anglo-Saxon scholarship, it was ever to go.

---

[11] É. Legouis, trans. H.D. Irvine, in É. Legouis and L. Cazamian, *A History of English Literature*, I, *The Middle Ages and the Renascence (650–1660)* (London, 1926), p. 12. Originally published as *Histoire de la littérature anglaise*, I, *Le moyen âge et la renaissance (650–1660)* (Paris, 1924).

[12] Anderson, *Literature of the Anglo-Saxons*, p. 408.

[13] G.G. Gervinus, *Zur Geschichte der Deutschen Literatur* (Besonderer Abdruck aus den Heidelb[erger] Jahrbüchern d[er] Literatur) (Heidelberg, 1834), p. 2: 'jener halb rührende, halb lächerliche Anflug von Deutschthümelei unter unserer Jugend aus den Befreiungsjahren der Nation'.

[14] G.P. Gooch, *History and Historians in the Nineteenth Century* (London, 1913), p. 64.

2. The English Branch of the German Tree

FROM THE POINT of view of Germany, English is German except to the extent to which it has been corrupted by alien elements. Count Friedrich Leopold zu Stolberg, who in his youth, in order to forget an incomparable English lady, had been Goethe's fellow-traveller to Switzerland, wrote lovingly still of the English language in his old age:[15]

> The German language became the language of England, and remained fairly pure though from the ninth century on the Danes introduced some alloy, till it was totally corrupted in the eleventh century through the Normans and French with whom William the Conqueror subjugated the beautiful land of England. There came into being then the English language of today, a composite of German, Danish, Norman, and French ingredients. . . . English is a mixture of many languages, very imperfect in itself, but, as a result of the constitution of the country which favours and practises eloquence, as a result of liberty which illumines the mind and gives it life and lifts up the heart, and for that reason also through a great number of ingenious authors, it has gained a position of honour secured by resoluteness, a language that has been made noble through forceful use in speech, writing, and song.

H. Leo, less concerned than Stolberg with the restoration of glory lost to foreign influence, produced a reader to demonstrate[16]

---

[15] F.L. Graf zu Stolberg, *Leben Alfred des Grossen, Königes in England* (Münster 1815), pp. 72–3: 'Die deutsche Sprache ward Englands Sprache, und erhielt sich, obschon nicht ohne einigen Zusaz, welchen ihr vom neunten Jahrhundert an die Dänen brachten, ziemlich rein, bis sie im elften Jahrhundert ganz verfälschet ward, durch die Normannen und Franzosen, mit welchen Wilhelm der Eroberer das schöne England unterjochte. Da entstand aus deutschen, dänischen, normannischen, und französichen Bestandtheilen . . . die itzige englische Sprache. Sie ist ein Gemisch vieler Sprachen, an sich sehr unvollkommen, aber, durch Verfassung des Landes, welche die Beredsamkeit begünstiget und übt; durch Freiheit, welche den Geist erhellet, ihm Schwung gibt, und das Herz erhebt, daher auch durch grosse Zahl geistreicher Schriftsteller, zu einer Würde gelanget, welche durch Bestimmtheit, und, durch kräftigen Gebrauch, in Rede, Schrift und Gesang, edel geworden.'

[16] H. Leo, *Altsächsische und Angelsächsische Sprachproben* (Halle, 1838), pp. x–xi: 'wie für den, der die Gesetze des angelsächsischen Lautwechsels kennt, die altächsische und angelsächsische Mundart wirklich nur Zweiglein eines und

how, for anyone familiar with the laws of Anglo-Saxon sound-changes, the Old Saxon and the Anglo-Saxon dialects are truly nothing other than twigs of one single branch, and indeed perfect twin-sisters; how the Anglo-Saxon dialect was by no means alienated from us by transplantation to Britain; how it was then, and has remained ever since, a *German* dialect in the strictest sense of the word.

Naturally, all literature in the Anglo-Saxon dialect was, in the same sense of the word, German, that is Teutonic, literature, and was proudly recognized in England as such by Sir Francis Palgrave:[17]

> The obscurity attending the origin of the Cædmonian poems will perhaps increase the interest excited by them. Whoever may have been their author, their remote antiquity is unquestionable. In poetical imagery and feeling they excel all the other remains of the North. And I trust I may be allowed to congratulate our Society [of Antiquaries] in having determined to commence their series of Anglo-Saxon publications, by a work which belongs not only to Englishmen, but to every branch of the great Teutonic family.

In Germany the orientation and the emphasis were a little different. Anglo-Saxon literature was not merely, as Leo called it, 'this fair branch of our German literature',[18] it was a part of German literature which had been alienated. The poet Ludwig Uhland, whom W.W. Skeat hailed as 'so true a patriot',[19] wrote in a letter (dated 31 March 1842) to Ludwig Ettmüller:[20]

> I am glad to hear that we shall soon be able to thank you also for the *Beowulf* in Anglo-Saxon, which by your translation and scholarly investigation you have already won back for its homeland.

The Angles, Saxons and Jutes took with them to Britain their folk-poetry, a part of the common heritage of the Germanic nations, and at that time still unadultered by alien influences. The nature of the pristine

---

desselben Astes und in der That vollkommen Zwillingsschwestern sind; wie die angelsächsische Mundart nicht etwa durch die Ueberpflanzung nach Brittannien uns entfremdet, wie sie eine d e u t s c h e Mundart im engsten Sinne des Wortes war und geblieben ist'.

[17] Sir F. Palgrave, 'Observations on the History of Cædmon', *Archaeologia: or, Miscellaneous Tracts Relating to Antiquity* xxiv (1832), p. 343.

[18] H. Leo, *Beówulf, dasz älteste deutsche, in angelsächsischer mundart erhaltene, heldengedicht* (Halle, 1839), p. iii: 'dieser schöne zweig unsrer deutschen litteratur, die angelsächsische'.

[19] W.W. Skeat, *Uhland's Songs and Ballads* (London, 1864), p. ix.

[20] J. Hartmann (ed.), *Uhlands Briefwechsel*, III, Veröffentlichungen des Schwäbischen Schillervereins VI (Stuttgart and Berlin, 1914), letter 1897, p. 194: 'Es freut mich, zu hören, dass wir Ihnen den Beowulf bald auch angelsächsisch zu danken haben werden, den Sie bereits durch Uebersetzung und Forschung dem Stammlande zurückgewonnen haben.'

poetry of Germany, as it was conceived of by German scholars of the early nineteenth century, may be inferred from Lachmann's strictures on Otfrid's *Evangelienbuch*:[21]

> Otfrid very often . . . introduces reflections in his narrative; he was not the first to do so, for the Saxon Gospels [i.e. *Heliand*] and the Bavarian verses on the end of the world [i.e. *Muspilli*] contain them likewise, but less frequently and better. In introducing reflections the religious poets probably follow the example of homilies rather than that of folk-poetry; Otfrid's reflections are almost entirely devoid of poetry and form. They become attractive and graceful only when Otfrid succeeds in describing, in simple innocent truth, an emotional state.

---

[21] K. Lachmann, 'Otfried', first published in J.S. Ersch and J.G. Gruber, *Allgemeine Encyclopädie der Wissenschaften*, Abtheilung III, vol. VII (Leipzig, 1836), pp. 278–82; quoted from *Kleinere Schriften, Kleinere Schriften zur deutschen Philologie* (Berlin, 1876), ed. K. Müllenhoff, who was able to use Lachmann's personal copy for the reprint, pp. 453–4: 'Otfried hat neben der Erzählung sehr häufig . . . Betrachtungen; nicht er zuerst, denn in dem sächsischen Evangelium und in den bairischen Versen vom Weltende finden sie sich ebenfalls, aber seltener und besser. Die geistlichen Dichter haben dabei wol minder die Weise der Volkspoesie als die der Predigten befolgt, und bei Otfried sind sie auch fast durchaus ohne Poesie und Form. Sie werden nur anmuthing, wo es ihm gelingt, einen Zustand des Gemüths in einfacher unschuldiger Wahrheit darzustellen.'

3. Christianity Puts an End to Folk-Poetry

AS IN GERMANY so in England the national poetic heritage was withered at the blighting touch of Christianity. That is how Jacob Grimm saw it:[22]

> After the introduction of Christianity the art of poetry took a religious turn, to which we owe many remarkable poems. But the freedom of the poetry and its roots in the people had perished.

Scholars from the first half of the nineteenth century to the present day have followed, in varying degrees of ferocity, Grimm's relatively mild disparagement of the Christian element in the extant Germanic poetry. Throughout, the assumption is made, explicitly or implicitly, that whatever was not touched by Christianity, whatever remained purely Germanic, purely pagan, was more original and more glorious. The quotations that follow show that this fundamental attitude to the literature of the Germanic peoples after their conversion (for no literature survives from before the conversion) has had, and still has, an abiding place in Anglo-Saxon scholarship.

Thomas Wright (1846):[23]

> The Saxon bards seem to have possessed most of inspiration while their countrymen retained their paganism. We trace distinctly two periods of their poetry – a period when it was full of freedom, and originality, and genius, and a later time, when the poets were imitators, who made their verse by freely using the thoughts and expressions of those who had gone before them. The religious poetry of the Christian Saxons abounds in passages taken from Beowulf; and probably a large part of what is not imitated from that poem is taken from others of the early Saxon cycles.

Louis F. Klipstein (1849) on line 13 to the end of *The Husband's Message*:[24] 'As a composition, it probably belongs to the period ante-

---

[22] J. Grimm, *Deutsche Grammatik*, I, 1st edn (Göttingen, 1819), p. lxvii: 'Die Dichtkunst nahm seit der Einführung des Christenthums eine geistliche Richtung, der wir wohl manches merkwürdige Gedicht verdanken; aber um die Freiheit und Volksmäßigkeit der Poesie war es geschehn.'

[23] Thomas Wright, *Essays on Subjects Connected with the Literature, Popular Superstitions, and History of England in the Middle Ages* (London, 1846), I, p. 14.

[24] L.F. Klipstein (ed.), *Analecta Anglo-Saxonica: Selections, in Prose and Verse, from the Anglo-Saxon Literature* (New York, 1849), II, p. 437.

cedent to the introduction of Christianity and the Roman letters, a period to which some of the best poetry in the language can be referred.'

B. ten Brink (1877):[25] 'The introduction of Christianity was doubtless one of the causes that destroyed the productive power of epic poetry.'

Max Rau (1889) on *Exodus*:[26] 'The biblical material is treated here with complete poetic licence by a minstrel who must have led his life right in the middle of the people, to whom life in war and at sea was familiar, who did not look upon nature with the eye of a medieval monk, but who entertained the same ideas about nature as were the common property of his people.'

B. Symons (1900):[27] 'The development of heroic song and of the epic was interrupted by Christianity.'

Miss M. Bentinck Smith (1907) on *Judith*:[28] 'there seems to be ground for supposing that this beautiful fragment, worthy of the skill of a scop whose Christianity had not sufficed to quell his martial instincts, his pride in battle and his manly prowess, is of later date than has been thought by certain historians.'

A. Brandl (1908) on *Bede's Death Song*:[29] 'The five alliterative lines of which it consists are constructed like a Latin period rather than a singable song; their purpose is merely to inculcate readiness to die upon the soul; the freshness of the minstrel is foreign to them.'

Professor Bruce Dickins (1915):[30]

---

[25] B. ten Brink, *Early English Literature*, translated by H.M. Kennedy (London, 1887), p. 28. See the original version: B. ten Brink, *Geschichte der Englischen Litteratur*, I (Berlin, 1877), p. 35: 'Ohne Zweifel war die Einführung des Christenthums eine der Ursachen, welche die Triebkraft der epischen Dichtung zerstörten.'

[26] M. Rau, *Germanische Altertümer in der Angelsächsischen Exodus* (Leipzig doctoral dissertation, 1889), p. 4: 'Der bibelstoff ist hier mit voller dichterischer freiheit von einem sänger behandelt, welcher mitten unter dem volke gestanden haben muß, dem das leben im kriege und auf der see wohl bekannt war, welcher die natur nicht mit dem auge eines mittelalterlichen mönches schaute, sondern von ihr dieselben vorstellungen hegte, welche gemeingut seines volkes waren.'

[27] B. Symons, in H. Paul (ed.), *Grundriss der germanischen Philologie*, 2nd edn, III (Strassburg, 1900), p. 630: 'Die Entwicklung des Heldensanges und des Epos wurde unterbrochen durch das Christentum.'

[28] M. Bentinck Smith, in *Cambridge History of English Literature*, I (Cambridge, 1907), p. 64.

[29] A. Brandl, 'Geschichte der altenglischen Literatur', I, Angelsächsische Periode bis zur Mitte des zwölften Jahrhunderts', in H. Paul (ed.), *Grundriss der germanischen Philologie*, 2nd edn, II/1 (Strassburg, 1908), p. 1032 (= p. 92 of separate): 'die fünf stabreimenden Zeilen, aus denen letzterer [*scil. Bede's Death Song*] besteht, sind eher wie eine lateinische Periode gebaut als wie ein sangbares Lied; sie wollen nur Todesvorbereitung für die Seele einschärfen; der frische Zug, des Spielmanns liegt ihnen ferne.'

[30] B. Dickins (ed.), *Runic and Heroic Poems of the Old Teutonic Peoples* (Cambridge, 1915), p. vi. The reference is to Zachary Boyd (1585?–1653), a Presbyterian divine, whose poetic works, many of them in manuscript at Glasgow University and still largely unpublished, were mocked by his contemporaries for their ornate style, a

Finn, mutilated and corrupt, is yet the fine flower of Anglo-Saxon heroic poetry. Full of rapid transitions and real poetic glow, the fight in Finn's beleaguered hall, lighted by the flash of swords and echoing with the din of combat, is one of the most vivid battle-pieces in any language – a theme too often worn threadbare by dull mechanical prentice-work in later Anglo-Saxon poetry, when versifying the scriptures became a devastating industry and the school of Cynewulf anticipated by some eight centuries the school of Boyd.

H. Bütow (1935) on *The Dream of the Rood*:[31] 'But in the first place we may discern a high literary value in the fact that the poet's veneration of the Cross is never bogged down in Christian conventionalism, but rather has the appearance of expressing deep personal emotion.'

R.H. Hodgkin (1935):[32]

Cædmon's sudden 'gift of song' was thus only the beginning of *Christian* poetry in England. In a sense it was the end rather than the beginning of popular poetry, for the new model of versified Bible and Saints' stories dammed rather than set flowing the inspiration of the people.

Emily D. Grubl (1948):[33] 'It is generally known that in the later period of Anglo-Saxon literature the power of linguistic coining waned, while it manifested itself strongly during the early Anglo-Saxon period.'

G.K. Anderson (1949) on the Cædmonian school:[34] 'The homiletic tendency of the Germanic writer in general and of the Old English churchman in particular cannot be avoided; and passages of dreary moralizing and prolix didacticism follow hard upon the heels of passages of authentic poetry.' Anderson on *Deor*:[35] 'Fortunately there remains at least one separate piece which exists in a strictly lyric form before any Christian allusion comes in to mar the picture.'

Mrs Ida L. Gordon (1960) on *The Seafarer*:[36]

There is a remarkable freedom from clerical influence in its style and diction. Except in the direct Christian admonition at the end of the

style not in the least like that of Cynewulf or of those formerly considered to be of the School of Cynewulf.

[31] H. Bütow (ed.), *Das altenglische 'Traumgesicht vom Kreuz'*, Anglistische Forschungen LXXVIII (1935), pp. 91–2: 'Vor allem aber scheint sich uns ein hoher literarischer Wert darin erkennen zu lassen, daß des Dichters Kreuzverehrung nirgends in christlicher Konvention stecken bleibt, sondern als Ausdruck einer persönlichen Erschütterung wirkt.'

[32] R.H. Hodgkin, *A History of the Anglo-Saxons* (Oxford, 1935), II, p. 444.

[33] E.D. Grubl, *Studien zu den angelsächsischen Elegien* (Marburg doctoral dissertation, 1948), p. 29: 'Es ist allgemein bekannt, daß in der späteren Epoche der angelsächsischen Literatur die sprachschöpferische Kraft nachließ, während sie in der frühangelsächsischen Zeit stark an den Tag trat.'

[34] Anderson, *Literature of the Anglo-Saxons*, p. 123.

[35] Anderson, *Literature of the Anglo-Saxons*, p. 155.

[36] I.L. Gordon (ed.), *The Seafarer* (London, 1960), p. 26.

poem, the poet has transformed his homiletic material into terms and concepts which belong to a poetic milieu nearer to that of *Beowulf* than to the more stereotyped school of poetry such as we have in the Cynewulfian poems.

4. 'Half-veiled remains of pagan poetry'

In the early nineteenth century the critical attitude of Anglo-Saxon scholars determined the selection of texts which they thought worthy of attention; rude rocks, blind deserts, and dark caverns were what they loved most, and when a textbook provided them with extracts that seemed to them too far removed from their favourite haunts, they protested and attacked the compiler of the book. In 1838 Leo published his book of selections, including religious as well as secular texts. He was savagely attacked for it by Ettmüller, especially for including Ælfric's preface to Genesis, 'Surely such things could today only find acceptance and praise from brain-sick conventiclers.' Leo (after quoting Ettmüller's vituperation) defended himself:[37]

> As if it were right to select from the literature of a nation which we wish to get to know those things only which accord with the interests of the present day. What better means than by this extract could I have found for characterizing the manner of Old Testament exegesis which Sts Ambrose and Augustine made supreme, and which St Boniface and Alcuin caused to be the only one in Germany for a long time?

Perhaps Ettmüller's attack was a reaction against Leo's extreme championship of church history. G.P. Gooch quotes, as typical no doubt, Leo's utterance, 'Since Constantine the history of the Christian Church forms the kernel, the soul, the life of universal history.'[38] Leo may often have gone too far in his historical writings, but what he said of the Anglo-Saxons in answer to Ettmüller was sound enough, and seems to anticipate modern historians. We may compare W. Levison:[39]

---

[37] H. Leo, *Bëówulf* (1839), p. xi: 'Er [*scil.* Ludwig Ettmüller] sagt . . . : "Gewis solche dinge können heute höchstens noch bei hirnsiechen conventicularen anname und beifal finden" – als wenn man ausz der litteratur eines volkes, die man kennen lernen wil, blosz dasz auszhöbe, wasz den zeitinteressen gemäsz ist! – wie hätte ich beszer die vom heil. Ambrosius und Augustinus in der abendländischen christenheit zur herschaft gefürte typische auszlegung der schriften alten testamentes, welche der heil. Bonifacius und Alcuin auch in Deutschland lange zur ausszschlieszlichen machten, beszer characterisiren können, als durch diese probe?'

[38] G.P. Gooch, *History and Historians in the Nineteenth Century*, p. 104.

[39] W. Levison, *England and the Continent in the Eighth Century* (Oxford, 1946), pp. 3–4.

Gregory had set the course which not only in the end reached its goal in Britain but also had momentous consequences for the Continent. A new religious superstructure, rudimentary as it was, was built on the foundations of pagan England from materials brought over from the Mediterranean world; a vigorous civilization grew up on a receptive soil, in which the mingling of native and foreign elements yielded a rich harvest. . . . The names of Aldhelm and Bede, of Cædmon and Beowulf may be mentioned as illustrations of this fresh growth. . . . A new chapter was opened in the relations between Great Britain and the lands across the sea. England was, in the main, in the seventh century the recipient of extraneous influences; in the next century the new member of the medieval Western world was herself to become the donor.

But in the early nineteenth century Leo's was a voice in the wilderness. Ettmüller's at the other extreme was one voice among many.

In 1840 appeared Jacob Grimm's brilliant edition of *Andreas* and *Elene*. It is worth quoting at length from his Introduction, for his approach, emphasizing the essentially Germanic characteristics and customs of the figures in these Christian poems, remained the standard approach to Anglo-Saxon literature for a very long time:[40]

---

[40] J. Grimm (ed.), *Andreas und Elene* (Kassel, 1840), pp. iv–vi: 'Angelsächsische gedichte bedürfen für keinen, der sich mit geschichte und sprache unseres alterthums befasst, einer empfehlung, sie gehören dem ganzen Deutschland, wie England an, ja indem grade mehr als die altnordischen, nach welchem auch ihre mundart der unsrigen verwandter liegt. Von althochdeutscher poesie sind uns nur kümmerliche bruchstücke gefristet, gerade so viel noch, um sicher schliessen zu dürfen, dass besseres, reicheres untergegangen ist. Aber das vermögen der sprache, den nationalen stil der dichtkunst erkennen lassen uns nur die angelsächsischen und altnordischen lieder, jene weil sie dessen älteste, diese weil sie eine noch heidnische auffassung sind. Denn der annahme wird jetzt überhaupt wenig widerspruch bevorstehen, dass das deutsche heidenthum seine eigne poesie und sage, besessen, ausgebildet, nacher aber gegen das christenthum eingebüsst habe. Nicht alsogleich liess das volk von angestammten tiefwurzelnden ausdrucksweisen, und die christliche lehre gestattete oder trachtete selbst, ihren milden sinn, ihr innigeres gefühl der rauhen rinde des frischkräftigen holzes heidnischer anschauungen einzuimpfen, woraus zweige trieben und früchte entsprossen, deren künstlicher wachsthum etwas gestörtes verräth, noch nicht alle gesunde derbheit der alten säfte verleugnet. Die verwandlung geschah aber hier oder dort unter sehr verschiednen bedingungen und erfolgen. Kaum anflüge des neuen und fremden hat die nordische edda, in ihrem umfang lagert breit und ungezwängt das heidenthum; unter den früher bekehrten Hochdeutschen hatte die unmittelbar dringende gewalt der lateinischen kirche immer auf vernichtung der einheimischen überlieferung hingearbeitet, was zu Otfrieds zeit noch alte volksansicht bezeugen konnte, liess die subjektivität des dichters auf dem grunde seiner arbeit beinahe gar nicht mehr vorbrechen. Im altsächsischen Heliand streift die darstellung gerne noch an ehmalige form, aber der vorgesteckte heilige stof übte zu grossen einfluss. Offenbar waren die Angelsachsen, deren geistlichkeit der

Anglo-Saxon poems need no recommendation for anyone whose interest lies in the history and language of our antiquity; they belong to all Germany as much as to England; indeed, they belong to us more than Old Norse poems in so far as their language is closer to ours. Time has left us only poor fragments of Old High German poetry, just enough to allow us to infer with certainty that what has perished was better and richer. Only the Anglo-Saxon and Old Norse songs can give us an idea of the capacity of the language, of the national style of poetic art; the Anglo-Saxon songs because they are the oldest in the language, the Old Norse because their conception is still pagan. For there is now little likelihood that the supposition, that German paganism possessed and developed its own poetry and store of legends but later lost it to Christianity, will meet with any contradiction. The people did not so quickly abandon their customary, deep-rooted ways of expression; and Christian teaching permitted, nay, strove even, that it might graft its mildness, its more profoundly, more fervently affecting feeling on the rough bark of the strong healthy wood of pagan conceptions; branches grew and bore fruits whose artificial growth showed some signs of disturbance, without being entirely false to the rude health of the old sap. However, in different places change came about under varying conditions and with differing success. The Northern Edda bears hardly a trace of what was new and foreign; in its compass a pagan world lies spacious and unconstrained. Among the High Germans, converted earlier, the immediate pressing power of the Latin Church was always working towards the destruction of the native tradition. Otfrid's subjective approach hardly allowed to erupt, even deep down in his work, those things to which at his time old popular concepts would still have attested. The presentation of the Old Saxon *Heliand* still touches often the traditional form, but the superimposed sacred subject exerted too strong an influence. It seems that the Anglo-Saxons, whose clergy

muttersprache befreundet blieb, am nächsten daran, eine vereinigung beider elemente zu stande zu bringen. Die genesis verstattete schon grössere freiheit der behandlung als der inhalt des neuen testaments; in der paraphrase, die Cædmons namen trägt, aber jünger scheint, laufen weit mehr züge der volksmässigen dichtungsweise unter, als in jenem Heliand. Noch günstiger bot sich den dichtern die kirchliche legende zu geschickter auswahl dar, und in Judith, Andreas, Helena durfte ohne verletzung der sage der altgewohnte ton völlig festgehalten werden: unter der masse des ergossenen neuen stofs regen sich hergebrachte epische formeln und heidnische vorstellungen in menge fort. man brauchte zuweilen nur die namen und einzelne umstände abzuändern, um der erzählung das aussehen einer ursprünglich angelsächsischen zu verschaffen. Im Beóvulf ist freilich mehr als dieser schein, man spürt echte grundlage hindurch, wie sie keiner von aussen zugetragnen fabel kann verliehen werden: allein was die form selbst betrift, stehn ihm jene gedichte wenig nach und alles positiv heidnische ist in ihm unterdrückt, wie in jenen vermieden. Es ist an sich nicht ohne reiz und bringt der forschung gewinn, diese halbverschleierten überreste heidnischer poesie in den frühsten anfängen der christlichen unter den Angelsachsen aufzudecken und zu betrachten.'

retained their regard for the mother tongue, came nearest to achieving a unification of the two elements. The story of Genesis admitted of greater freedom of treatment than the contents of the New Testament. Far more characteristics of popular poetic technique than in *Heliand* occur in the paraphrase which bears Cædmon's name but seems to be later. Ecclesiastical legends offered themselves even more suitably for the poets' skilful selection; and in the figures of Judith, Andreas, and Helena it was possible, without detriment to the story, to retain unchanged the traditional tone; traditional epic formulas and pagan conceptions live on in great number under the effused mass of the new subject matter. At times it would only be necessary to alter the names and individual circumstances to give to the story the appearance of an original Anglo-Saxon narrative. In *Beowulf* it is more than just appearance; we can feel the genuine foundation, such as can be given to no story imported from outside; but as far as the form is concerned, the other poems hardly come short of *Beowulf*; in *Beowulf* all that is positively pagan is suppressed, just as it is avoided in the other poems. To discover and to consider these half-veiled remains of pagan poetry in the earliest beginnings of Christian poetry among the Anglo-Saxons is in itself not unattractive and is to the advantage of scholarship.

After a summary of *Andreas* and *Elene* Grimm goes on to the favourite topics of Germanic antiquity, warfare and paganism:[41]

> To hear of war and victory was the delight of the Germans.... Though there is no actual fighting in *Andreas*, a solemn *folk-thing* is held, and lots are drawn. The listeners may have had special pleasure in the description of the sea-voyage in which the Divine Pilot appears almost like the pagan Woden of whom many legends were current that he ferried people across and saved them in the disguise of a ferryman.

And a little later:[42]

> The way in which battles and war, the favourite occupations of antiquity, are described deserves our attention in the first place. There is something splendid in every battle-scene. Wolf, eagle and raven with joyous cry go forward in the van of the army, scenting their prey.

---

[41] J. Grimm, *Andreas und Elene*, pp. xxiv–xxv: 'Von kampf und sieg zu hören war des Deutschen lust.... Im Andreas wird zwar nicht gefochten, doch ein feierliches volksding gehalten und geloost; vor allem aber mag die schilderung der seefahrt den zuhörern gefallen haben, in welcher der göttliche steuermann beinahe wie ein heidnischer Vôden erscheint, von dem manche sagen umgiengen, dass er in verhüllung eines fergen die menschen überschifte und rettete.'

[42] J. Grimm, *Andreas und Elene*, p. xxv: 'Vor allem verdient die art und weise, wie kampf und krieg, das liebste geschäft des alterthums, geschildert werden, unsre aufmerksamkeit; alle schlachtschilderungen haben etwas prächtiges. w o l f, a d l e r und r a b e ziehen mit frohem geschrei dem heer voran, ihre beute witternd.'

Grimm gives a survey of the use in Anglo-Saxon poetry of the beasts of battle, which he ends with the words:[43]

> All this is pagan through and through, and breathes the oldest poetry of our antiquity. Let us remember that these three animals were considered noble, brave, a portent of good luck, sacred to the highest god. They resisted all the more strongly a Christian view which saw something devilish in the wolf and the raven. The Norse Oðin has two wolves and two ravens in his retinue.

Grimm proceeds to discuss the uses in Norse literature of the beasts of battle, as if the literatures of the various Germanic nations were one single Germanic literature written in several dialects. J.M. Kemble's treatment of the same material was far more cautious:[44] 'Wolves and ravens appear to have been Oþinn's sacred animals: the Saxon legends do not record anything on this subject.'

Grimm's Introduction deals with all those things which he thought the pagan poems had in common with the Christian poems, a wide range of ideas, descriptions and customs, and, especially, the poetic vocabulary, the use of formulas and single words. In everything, a pale reflection of original pagan poetry is to be seen in the Christian poems, of which he has edited two:[45]

> We gladly contemplate and ponder the past. In spring, the sun rising higher had drawn forth blades of grass, herbs, and blossoms from the cold, wintry earth; but when autumn comes, though the soil still harbours the warmth of summer, the tips and tree-tops begin to wither with the cold. It is then that the green foliage of a few trees, before it takes on its final, yellow hue, changes its colour to red. Anglo-Saxon poetry rooted in paganism seems thus autumnal to me; still its sap undergoes change just once more, not without a weak reflection, and proclaims that its death is near.

---

[43] J. Grimm, *Andreas und Elene*, p. xxvii: 'Alles das ist durch und durch heidnisch und athmet die älteste poesie unsrer vorzeit. Man erwäge, dass diese drei thiere für edle, mutige, glückbringende angesehn wurden und dem höchsten gott geheiligt waren; um so mehr widerstanden sie christlicher ansicht, die in wolf und rabe etwas teuflisches fand. Der nordische Oðinn hat zwei wölfe und zwei raben in seinem geleite.'

[44] J.M. Kemble, *The Saxons in England: A History of the English Commonwealth till the Norman Conquest* (London, 1849), I, p. 343 (footnote).

[45] J. Grimm, *Andreas und Elene*, p. lviii: 'Wir sinnen und trachten gern über die vergangenheit. Wenn im frühling die höher steigende sonne aus der winterkalten erde gräser, halme, blüten treibt, so hegt im herbst der boden zwar noch wärme des sommers, aber spitzen und wipfel beginnen erkaltend abzuwelken. Dann geschieht es, dass das grüne laub einiger baüme, vor dem letzten falben, seine farbe wechselt und in röthe übergeht. Solch ein herbstes aussehn hat mir die im heidenthum wurzelnde angelsächsische dichtung: nicht ohne matten widerschein setzt sie ihre säfte noch noch einmal um, und verkündet ihren nahen tod.'

Grimm's method and attitude must be clearly understood to understand the methods and attitudes of Anglo-Saxon scholars for the rest of the nineteenth century and after. As late as 1907 an English writer, Miss M. Bentinck Smith, uses Grimm's very manner:[46]

> it is hard not to regret much that was lost in the acquisition of the new. The reflection of the spirit of paganism, the development of epic and lyric as we see them in the fragments that remain, begin to fade and change; at first, Christianity is seen to be a thin veneer over the old heathen virtues, and the gradual assimilation of the Christian spirit was not accomplished without harm to the national poetry, or without resentment on the part of the people.

The use of the poetic vocabulary of the Anglo-Saxons to illustrate the continuity of pagan concepts even after the introduction of Christianity is a feature of much of Jacob Grimm's philological work; and following him it became a standard feature of Anglo-Saxon scholarship. Two examples from his writings must suffice, though many others as good could be quoted. Grimm asserts that phrases like *hilde woma* are redolent of paganism because *woma* is etymologically connected with *Omi*, one of the Norse names of Oþin, and means 'a noise' like that of an approaching god.[47] Grimm later repeated these ideas with further examples and with some heightening of the mythological interpretation:[48]

> The element of noise aroused a feeling of awe and the sense of a god's immediate presence; as Woden was also called Woma, and Oðin also Omi and Yggr, so the expressions *woma*, *sweg*, *broga*, and *egesa* are used by the Anglo-Saxon poets almost synonymously for spirits and divine manifestations.

Furthermore, *hild* (as also *guð*) is to Grimm the name of one of the Valkyries; 'Hild,' he says, 'was the pagan goddess of war, Bellona,' and in *Deutsche Mythologie* he interprets *gif mec Hild nime* (*Beowulf* lines 452, 1481), *Guð nimeð* (*Beowulf* line 2536), *Guð fornam* (*Beowulf* line 1123) as fully mythological.[49] *Hilde woma* is, therefore, the awe-inspiring

---

[46] *Cambridge History of English Literature*, I, p. 64.
[47] J. Grimm, *Andreas und Elene*, pp. xxx, xxxii.
[48] J. Grimm, *Deutsche Mythologie*, 2nd edn (Göttingen, 1844), p. 217: 'Das rauschende element erregte schauer und den gedanken an eines gottes unmittelbare nähe; wie Vôden auch Vôma hiess ..., Oðinn Omi und Yggr, so werden von ags. Dichtern die ausdrücke vôma, svêg, brôga und egesa beinahe gleichbedeutend für geisterhafte, göttliche erscheinungen verwendet.'
[49] J. Grimm, *Andreas und Elene*. p. xxxi: 'Die Hild war heidnische kriegsgöttin, Bellona'; Grimm wrote similarly in *Deutsche Mythologie*, 1st edn (Göttingen, 1835), p. 237, and more fully 2nd edn (1844). The full mythological theory underlying such personifications was set out by Grimm in the second edition of

noise of the Valkyrie's arrival. Grimm's explanation is beautifully plausible:[50]

> If we look carefully we shall find that traces of pagan gods adhere to the poetry which followed immediately upon the conversion of the Germanic tribes; and how could it be otherwise, seeing that all religion permeates also language, expression, and the processes of thought?

In a somewhat later work of Grimm's, his paper of 1849 on cremations, we find a good example of how Grimm demonstrated the survival of paganism:[51]

> In singing of Abraham and Isaac or of the three men in the fiery furnace Cædmon still uses everywhere the heathen expressions. He says *ad hladan* (*Genesis* 2902), *ad* and *bælfyr* (2856f.), *on bæl ahof* (2904), *on ad ahof* (2930), *adfyr onbran* (*Exodus* 398), *bælblyse* (*Exodus* 401, *Daniel* 231), *geboden to bæle* (*Daniel* 413).

What Grimm means when he talks of Cædmon's use of heathen expressions is quite unconnected with the Anglo-Saxon contexts. He is referring to the fact that in Scandinavian literature cognate words, like *bál*, are used in similar idioms, and that, moreover, these idioms sometimes occur in indisputably pagan contexts, some of which are quoted by Grimm in his paper.

Grimm's line of investigation was followed by A.F.C. Vilmar in his analysis of the German antiquities of the Old Saxon *Heliand*, issued in 1845 as a supplement to the programme of the Electoral *Gymnasium* at Marburg of which Vilmar was head master. Of the *Heliand* he says:[52]

Deutsche Mythologie (1844), ch. XXIX. It will be discussed later in connection with *wyrd*; see pp. 88–9 and nn. 271–2, below.

[50] J. Grimm, *Andreas und Elene*. pp. xxxii–xxxiii: 'Es haften also, wenn man fleissig beobachten will, in der zunächst auf die bekehrung der Deutschen gefolgten poesie noch spuren heidnischer götter, und wie könnte es anders sein, da alle religion auch sprache, ausdruck und gedankengang durchdringt?'

[51] J. Grimm, 'Über das Verbrennen der Leichen', *Abhandlungen der Königlichen Akademie der Wissenschaften zu Berlin*, Philosophisch-historische Klasse (1849), p. 232 (reprinted in J. Grimm, *Kleinere Schriften*, II Abhandlungen zur Mythologie und Sittenkunde, ed. K. Müllenhoff [Berlin, 1865], p. 264): 'Cædmon, da wo Abraham und Issac, oder die drei männer im feurigen ofen besungen werden, verwendet überall noch die heidnischen ausdrücke; er sagt . . . .'

[52] A.F.C. Vilmar, *Deutsche Altertümer im Héliand als Einkleidung der evangelischen Geschichte – Beiträge zur erklärung des altsächsischen Héliand und zur innern geschichte der einführung des Christentums in Deutschland*, issued with the *Schulprogramm* of the *Kurfürstliches Gymnasium* (Marburg, 1845), p. 1: 'es ist das Christentum im deutschen gewande, eingekleidet die poesie und sitte eines edlen deutschen stammes, welches uns hier entgegentritt, mit unverkennbarer liebe und treuer hingebung geschildert, mit allem grossen und schönen ausgestattet, was das deutsche volk, das deutsche herz und leben zu geben hatte. es ist ein deutscher

It is Christianity in German dress, clad in the poetry and manners of a noble German tribe who here stand before us described with unmistakable love and loyal devotion, endowed with all that is great and beautiful, with all that the German nation, its heart and life were able to provide. It is a German Christ, it is in its most proper sense *our* Christ, our dear Lord and our most mighty national King, presented to us in the poetry of a folk-minstrel.

The 'German dress' of the *Heliand* is, as Vilmar sees it, partly the way of life described in the poem, and partly the poetic language. Vilmar has this to say of the epic formulas:[53]

These formulas, which rest as much on ancient tradition as they characterize oral tradition, create the agreeable impression that we are here dealing with nothing invented, nothing artificial, nothing affected, and with no mere book-learning, but rather with a lively narrative which completely fills the narrator and is always at his call.

Time and again Vilmar underlines the Germanness of the biblical characters in the *Heliand*. Zachariah is 'an old German warrior grown incapable of battle'.[54] The Germanness of the *Heliand* makes it a better instrument for the propagation of Christianity:[55]

The pagan listener is at once won over to the child by means of a traditional description which became and remained dear to many generations: John is turned into a dear German child, almost into the listener's own child.

Vilmar never asks himself how other than in terms familiar to the poet he could have told his life of Christ. Vilmar's constant emphasis of the anachronistic Germanization makes what may well have been the only way for the poet seem a significantly exceptional procedure: 'It is as if the poet presupposes that everything he relates took place among the Germans, among his fellow tribesmen.'[56] Moreover, Vilmar

---

Christus, es ist im eigensten sinne *unser* Christus, unser lieber herr und mächtiger volkskönig, welchen die dichtung des volkssängers uns darstellt'.

[53] Vilmar, *Deutsche Altertümer im Hêliand*, p. 4: 'es gewähren diese formeln, welche eben so auf alter tradition beruhen, wie sie die mündliche tradition bezeichnen, den wolthuenden eindruck, dass hier nichts ersonnenes, künstliches und gemachtes, auch nicht blosses buchwissen vorliege, sondern eine lebendige erzählung, welche den erzähler ganz erfüllt und ihm jeden augenblick zu gebote steht'.

[54] Vilmar, *Deutsche Altertümer im Hêliand*, p. 22: 'so tritt hier Zacharias in der gestalt eines alten, zum kampfe unfähig gewordenen deutschen kriegers auf.'

[55] Vilmar, *Deutsche Altertümer im Hêliand*, p. 22: 'durch diese schilderung, die altgewohnte und vielen geschlechtern lieb gewordene und gebliebene, wurde der heidnische hörer sofort für das geschilderte kind gewonnen, Johannes zu einem lieben deutschen kinde, gleichsam zum eigenen, gemacht.'

[56] Vilmar, *Deutsche Altertümer im Hêliand*, p. 27: 'Der dichter setzt gleichsam

considers as typically German, traits that have a much wider currency:[57]

> Besides joy in one's home and in the possession of land which pervades the whole poem, the lively joy of the Germans in movable wealth, especially in gold and clothes, manifests itself [in the Old Saxon poem] quite as strongly as in Anglo-Saxon poetry, indeed, it perhaps manifests itself even more insistently, certainly more frequently.

This is especially true of the virtues, for Vilmar seems to have annexed them for the Germans as their special characteristics:[58]

> If it is true, as history and experience teach, that such simple decidedness of character as is found in a man of heroic disposition is best suited to receive the Gospel and to yield himself up to it whole and undivided, while cowardice, weakness, undecidedness and duplicity, calculating caution, and cunning can never inwardly and never wholly attain to the Gospel, then our poem provides a not inconsiderable proof of the ability to receive, preserve, and propagate the Gospel which must be adjudged to be a preeminent characteristic of the German attitude of mind. Our poet bestows on the Gospel the fullest force of his inclination; but on the enemies of Christ and of His Gospel he turns the fullest force of the hatred which a German heart could contain.

This is the spiritual basis of the ideas of kingship, comitatus, and of loyalty and honour in warfare which Vilmar lovingly analyses in the *Heliand*. He is never anti-Christian, but he distorts the evidence towards Germanness by selection rather than by direct twisting. His paper was almost as influential and formative as Grimm's Introduction to *Andreas*

---

voraus, dass alles, was er erzählt, sich bei den Deutschen, bei seinen stammesverwandten zugetragen habe.'

[57] Vilmar, *Deutsche Altertümer im Hêliand*, p. 32: 'Neben dieser freude an heimat und grundbesitz, welche durch unser ganzes gedicht ausgebreitet ist, zeigt sich auch die lebhafte freude des Deutschen an beweglichem vermögen, vor allem an gold und gewändern, ganz in derselben stärke wie in den angelsächsischen gedichten, ja sie äussert sich fast noch eindringlicher, wenigstens häufiger.'

[58] Vilmar, *Deutsche Altertümer im Hêliand*, p. 23: 'wenn überhaupt, wie die geschichte und erfahrung lehrt, eine solche einfache entschiedenheit, wenn ein heldencharakter am geeignetsten ist, das evangelium aufzunehmen und sich demselben ganz und ungetheilt hinzugeben, während die feigheit, die schwäche, die unentschiedenheit und doppelseitigkeit, die berechnende vorsicht und die schlauheit niemals innerlich und niemals ganz zu dem evangelium gelangen, so liefert unser gedicht einen nicht unerheblichen beleg für diese dem deutschen sinne vorzugsweise zuzusprechende befähigung für die aufnahme, bewahrung und verbreitung des evangeliums: die vollste stärke der neigung lässt unser dichter dem evangelium zu gute kommen, die vollste stärke des hasses, wie sie im deutschen herzen liegen konnte, wendet er gegen die feinde Christi und seines evangeliums.'

und Elene. In the work of Anglo-Saxon scholars of later generations we see again and again the scientific method of Grimm and hear the accents of Vilmar.

Vilmar's influence on one Anglo-Saxon scholar was of a more personal nature. His investigation of the *Heliand* was issued together with an invitation to the public examination of the pupils of his school, and school notices. From this programme we learn that Vilmar himself taught only one subject, German, and he only taught the senior form. Among those who left the school on 25 September, 1844, was Christian Wilhelm Michael Grein of Willingshausen in the district of Ziegenhain, aged 19. He had spent five years in the school, two of them in the senior form, and left to read mathematics and natural science at Marburg. Eleven pupils received certificates of maturity in 1844, ten of them bore the mark *good*; Grein's mark was *very good*.

5. English and German Views of the Conversion of the English

WE MUST NOW turn to England. English opinion in the early nineteenth century was not anti-Christian. Wordsworth's *Ecclesiastical Sonnet* 'Glad Tidings' (1821) on the conversion of the English is probably typical in recognizing the benefits of Christianity and in thinking that the Anglo-Saxons were barbarians:[59]

> By Augustin led
> They come – and onward travel without dread,
> Chaunting in barbarous ears a tuneful prayer,
> Sung for themselves, and those whom they would free!

Wordsworth based his *Ecclesiastical Sonnets* on wide reading, for which his editor, Professor de Selincourt, held fast in a critical attitude which Wordsworth had outgrown, takes him to task.[60] His principal modern authority for the Anglo-Saxon period was the third edition of Sharon Turner's *History of the Anglo-Saxons*, where we read, 'Till Gregory planted Christianity in England, there was no means or causes of intellectual improvement to our fierce and active ancestors.'[61]

An extreme view of pagan England and the conversion is expressed fully and forcibly by John Lingard in *The History and Antiquities of the Anglo-Saxon Church*, the third edition of which appeared in 1845, the year of Vilmar's paper on the *Heliand*. A writer in *The Edinburgh Review* describes the third edition as 'almost a new work',[62] but the passages quoted here are, with some changes as in the editions of 1806 and 1810, and presumably represent what Lingard thought abidingly true:[63]

---

[59] Wm Wordsworth, *Ecclesiastical Sketches* (London, 1822), p. 16, sonnet 'XIV. Glad Tidings'.
[60] E. de Selincourt and H. Darbishire (eds), *The Poetical Works of William Wordsworth*, III (Oxford, 1946), the sonnet p. 348, the criticism of the *Ecclesiastical Sonnets* at p. 558: 'No other work of W.'s was based on such wide reading definitely undertaken with a view to poetic composition, and it is not perhaps surprising that poems which so closely follow prose authorities, often even incorporating their phraseology, should lack imaginative colour, and be somewhat pedestrian in style.'
[61] Sharon Turner, *History of the Anglo-Saxons*, 3rd edn (London, 1820), III, p. 419.
[62] Review of J. Lingard, *The History and the Antiquities of the Anglo-Saxon Church*, 3rd edn (London, 1845), *Edinburgh Review* lxxxix (1849), p. 153.
[63] J. Lingard, *The History and the Antiquities of the Anglo-Saxon Church*, 3rd edn, I,

> The Anglo-Saxons, when they first landed on our shores, were hordes of ferocious pirates: by religion they were reclaimed from savage life, and taught to admire and practise the virtues of the Gospel.

Similarly:[64]

> By the ancient writers, the Saxons are unanimously classed with the most barbarous of the nations, which invaded and dismembered the Roman empire. Their valour was disgraced by its brutality.

And again:[65]

> the impartial observer will acknowledge the impossibility of eradicating at once the fiercer passions of a whole nation; nor be surprised if he behold several of them relapse into their former manners, and on some occasions unite the actions of savages with the professions of christians. To judge of the advantage which the Saxons derived from their conversion, he will fix his eyes on their virtues. *They* were the offspring of the gospel; their vices were the relics of paganism.

The reviewers of Lingard's book deny him the character of an impartial observer. Even so, they concede that some of the views expressed by him are right, in spite of the fact that he is a Roman Catholic and in spite of the warmth with which he expresses himself. *The Quarterly Review*, reviewing the first edition of Lingard's book, apologizes that 'We have been provoked by the petulance of the author to express a warmth to which we have not been accustomed.'[66] Nevertheless, the reviewer has to admit that in Lingard's account 'The beneficial effects of Christianity, however, upon the manners and temporal happiness of the Saxon Converts are pleasingly represented.'[67] The more temperate critic [John Allen] of Lingard's second edition[68] says in *The Edinburgh Review*:[69]

---

p. vi; see (with the original title) *The Antiquities of the Anglo-Saxon Church*, 1st edn (Newcastle, 1806), I, p. v: 'The Anglo-Saxons were originally hordes of ferocious pirates. By religion they were reclaimed from savage life, and raised to a degree of civilization, which, at one period, excited the wonder of the other nations of Europe.' Unchanged in the 2nd edn (Newcastle, 1910), pp. iv–v.

[64] Lingard, *The Antiquities* (1806), I, p. 43.
[65] Lingard, *The Antiquities* (1806), I, pp. 48–9.
[66] Review of J. Lingard, *The Antiquities*, *The Quarterly Review* vii (1812), p. 93.
[67] *Quarterly Review* vii, p. 96.
[68] The review is anonymous: the identification of the reviewer is taken from S.A. Allibone (ed.), *A Critical Dictionary of English Literature and British and American Authors*, I (Philadelphia, 1858), p. 1103, confirmed by W.A. Copinger, *On the Authorship of the First Hundred Numbers of the 'Edinburgh Review'* (*Bibliographiana*, II; Manchester, 1895), p. 26. The second edition (Newcastle, 1810) of Lingard's book has the same title as the first, of which it is merely a reprint in one volume.
[69] *Edinburgh Review* xxv (1815), p. 346.

It would be unreasonable, then, to expect that a Catholic clergyman, zealously attached to his communion, should be able to write, with impartiality, the history of a period obscured and perplexed by the controversies of Catholic and Protestant. Let us do justice, however, to Mr Lingard. . . . We cannot say we feel much interest or curiosity about the form of words, in which our barbarous ancestors chose to clothe their ignorance of the mystery of transubstantiation; but we can understand that Mr Lingard annexes importance to such inquiries. We can excuse his admiration of monks, and listen with patience to his eulogies of celibacy. We neither believe in the miracles, nor can give our implicit assent to the virtues and merits of his saints and confessors; but we agree with him in reprobating the rash and illiberal censures of modern historians, who stigmatize them in a body as a collection of knaves and hypocrites. To the clergy of the dark ages, Europe owes much of her civilization, her learning, and her liberty.

Though Lingard's book was the work of a violent partisan, his critics agree with him on a number of fundamental points in which he is at variance with his German contemporaries: the barbarism of the tribes which settled here and the improvement conferred on them by Christianity. From the time that the work of German scholars of Anglo-Saxon had made its influence felt far and wide, such a view became unthinkable, except after a conscious rejection of the German glorification of the Germanic tribes. É. Legouis was among those who resisted this influence, and was thus able to write in a manner not unlike that of scholars a hundred years earlier:[70] 'Everything derived from the barbaric past had been purified and ennobled, and also enervated in an atmosphere of Christianity which already was almost one of chivalry.' The parenthetical 'and also enervated' may show that even Legouis was not able to eradicate German influence entirely. Yet, surely, Lingard went too far. He failed to see how it was that England was good ground on which to sow the seed of the new teaching; we look in vain in his book for the kind of sensitive understanding which made Adolf Ebert write of the Anglo-Saxons:[71]

> The quick acceptance, the easy acquisition of Latin Christianity, an acquisition that so soon turned into a rich, productive, and learned

---

[70] Legouis, in Legouis and Cazamian, *A History of English Literature*, I, *The Middle Ages and the Renascence*, p. 4.

[71] A. Ebert, *Allgemeine Geschichte der Literatur des Mittelalters im Abendlande*, III (Leipzig, 1887), p. 3: 'Die schnelle Aufnahme, die leichte Aneignung der christlich-lateinischen Kultur, eine Aneignung, die so bald zu einer reichen productiven gelehrten Thätigkeit in lateinischer Sprache überging, war nicht bloss eine Folge der grossen Begabung dieses germanischen Volkes, sondern sie setzt auch einen höheren Grad nationaler Bildung voraus. Diese konnte freilich nicht wissenschaftlicher Natur sein, sondern es war eine Bildung des Charakters, des Herzens, der Phantasie.'

activity in the Latin language, was not simply a result of the great talents of this Germanic nation; it presupposes a higher degree of *national refinement of the mind*. Naturally, this refinement did not lie in the pursuit of learning; it was a refinement of character, of the heart, and of the imagination.

Though Lingard's and John Allen's inadequate knowledge of Old English made it impossible for them to have secure first-hand knowledge of the literature of the Anglo-Saxons, it is clear that they would have seen it as part of the literature of Western Christendom, and not, as the ascendant German scholarship was alleging, as part of the common Germanic literary heritage marred in preservation. There were, of course, even in England exceptional voices fiercely hostile to the civilizing influence of medieval Christianity. There is no statement in Ritson quite so violent as that which Isaac D'Israeli invents for him in his account of the miracle of Cædmon:[72]

> A lingering lover of the Mediæval genius can perceive nothing more in a *circumstantial legend*, than 'a little exaggeration.' I seem to hear the shrill attenuated tones of Ritson, in his usual idiomatic diction, screaming, 'It is a *Lie* and an *Imposture* of the stinking *Monks!*'

This scream of Ritson's is supposititious, though perhaps not untypical of him. For true parallels, however, we must turn to Germany, as English scholars did increasingly in the eighteen-thirties and 'forties, to their great gain in philological knowledge and great loss in literary good sense. There G.G. Gervinus described the Old High German *Hildebrandslied* as 'almost the only remain that allows us to glimpse the rich national poetry which must have existed in the eighth to tenth centuries, before the clergy succeeded in removing altogether from the nation these fragments of paganism.'[73] Over a hundred years later, in 1944, Georg Baesecke, in a facsimile edition of the *Hildebrandslied* offered to the University of Halle in celebration of the two-hundred-and-fiftieth anniversary of its foundation, still looked upon Christianity as an intrusion on the German spirit; he praised the poem as:[74]

[72] I. D'Israeli, *Amenities of Literature* (London, 1841), I, p. 62 footnote.
[73] G.G. Gervinus, *Historische Schriften*, II, *Geschichte der deutschen Dichtung*, 1ter Theil (title on the second title page), *Geschichte der poetischen National-Literatur der Deutschen*, 2nd edn (1840), p. 68: '. . . dem berühmten Hildebrandliede . . . , dem fast einzigen Reste, der uns auf die reiche Volksdichtung blicken läßt, die im 8–10. Jahrhundert geherrscht haben muß, ehe es den Geistlichen gelang, diese Trümmer des Heidenthums dem Volke ganz zu entziehen'.
[74] G. Baesecke, ed., *Das Hildebrandlied. Eine geschichtliche Einleitung für Laien* (Halle, 1945), p. 34: 'Zugleich eine herzweitende Erhebung zu dem Bilde des durch Ehre und Pflicht allein gebundenen Mannestums, wie es in unserm kriegerischen Volk quer durch alle Jahrhunderte und quer durch all ihre christlichen Erfahrungen hindurch hochgehalten und gepriesen ist und immer gepriesen bleibe.'

At once a heart-stirring uplift to that image of manhood, bound only by honour and duty, as it has been held in high esteem and praised in our warlike nation across all centuries, and across all our Christian experiences; may it be praised for ever.

When in 1945 the publishing house of Niemeyer, Halle, gave this work of Baesecke's to the world it was thought politic to paste over this sentence. G.K. Anderson provides a later parallel:[75]

> The prestige of the fighter never departed during the Old English period. But broaden the stage a trifle. Consider the Germanic world and its long, adventurous development. Can it be fairly maintained that the glory of the warrior has ever been lost there?

The reason why Gervinus and those who thought like him accused the clergy of wishing to extirpate Germanic national poetry was not merely because this poetry contained traces of paganism, but because their monkhood implied that they were rooted in the Church and not in the warlike nation among whom they lived. Charles Kingsley states very clearly what is involved:[76]

> The priest or monk, by becoming such, more or less renounced his nationality. It was the object of the Church to make him renounce it utterly; to make him regard himself no longer as Englishman, Frank, Lombard, or Goth: but as the representative, by an hereditary descent, considered all the more real because it was spiritual and not carnal, of the Roman Church.

There is, of course, much justification for the view that the clergy considered themselves as bound in obedience ultimately to Rome. But Gervinus was writing of the eighth to tenth centuries and Kingsley specifically of St Alphege and his martyrdom in 1012, and in that context there is little basis for the assumption that good patriots striving to preserve their national poetry were deliberately opposed by clerics out to destroy it. Men like Gervinus assumed a distaste for Christian literature in Germanic patriots, because they themselves were not interested in it. Gervinus says that there is no doubt that 'these days we no longer rate highly the Christian interest in Germanic literature, but all the more highly the linguistic interest.'[77]

---

[75] Anderson, *Literature of the Anglo-Saxons*, pp. 95–6.
[76] C. Kingsley, *The Roman and the Teuton: A Series of Lectures Delivered before the University of Cambridge* (Cambridge and London, 1864), p. 225.
[77] Gervinus, *Historische Schriften*, II, *Geschichte der poetischen National-Literatur der Deutschen*, p. 78: 'In unsern Tagen schlägt man das letztere [*scil.* das christliche Interesse] nicht mehr hoch an, das sprachliche hingegen um so höher.'

6. J.M. Kemble

IN THE NINETEENTH century Germany was the centre of the world of Germanic philology, including Anglo-Saxon philology. Wülker, writing the history of Anglo-Saxon scholarship, very properly divides Old English grammars up to that time into Old Grammars and New Grammars.[78] Effectively, the old grammars begin with Hickes in the late seventeenth century.[79] They end, pathetically, with J.L. Sisson's *The Elements of Anglo-Saxon Grammar*, 1819;[80] pathetically, because 1819 is the year when the first edition of the first volume of Grimm's *Deutsche Grammatik* was published.[81] Sisson's *Grammar* was the feeble last descendant of a line whose founders had not been ignoble; in his 'Advertisement' (i.e. preface) Sisson says:

> The following Pages have been compiled with a view of offering to the Public, in a compressed Form, the principal Parts of Dr. Hickes's Anglo-Saxon Grammar, a Book now seldom to be met with.

In Grimm's *Grammatik* linguistic learning was ranged in new, and seemingly perfect, panoply.

It is no great marvel that after the publication of Grimm's *Grammatik* anyone who aspired to be an Anglo-Saxon scholar had to go to

---

[78] R. Wülker, *Grundriss zur Geschichte der angelsächsischen Litteratur. Mit einer Übersicht der angelsächsischen Sprachwissenschaft* (Leipzig, 1885), pp. 95–9.
[79] G. Hickes, *Institutiones Grammaticæ Anglo-Saxonicæ, et Mæso-Gothicæ* (Oxford, 1689); and G. Hickes, *Linguarum Vett. Septentrionalium Thesaurus Grammatico-Criticus et Archæologicus* (Oxford, 1705, 1703).
[80] J.L. Sisson, *The Elements of Anglo-Saxon Grammar, to which are added a Praxis and Vocabulary* (Leeds, 1819).
[81] J. Grimm, *Deutsche Grammatik*, I; superseded by the 2nd edn (Göttingen, 1822), in which 'Grimm's Law' appears for the first time, though that had been anticipated to some extent by R.K. Rask, *Undersögelse om det gamle Nordiske eller Islandske Sprogs Oprindelse* (Copenhagen, 1818). Rask's *Angelsaksisk Sproglære tilligemed en kort Læsebog* (Stockholm, 1817), is, like his several elementary grammars of other languages, a serviceable work for learning the language, but contains nothing as fundamentally new as the *Undersögelse*. B. Thorpe provided a translation of the *Sproglære*: *A Grammar of the Anglo-Saxon Tongue, with a Praxis . . . A New Edition enlarged and improved by the author* (Copenhagen, 1830).

Germany. Among young Englishmen who went to Germany the foremost is John Mitchell Kemble. He acquired there a sound knowledge of philology, his political views, his literary views, and his wife, of which acquisitions all but the first were unfortunate in some respects. As a link between Germany and England he is of the greatest importance in the history of Anglo-Saxon studies in the nineteenth century. We have Professor Bruce Dickins as a guide to Kemble's biography,[82] and he leads us to one of his sources, Fanny Kemble.[83] The biographer of a scholar must look at the schooling of his subject for the first signs of the scholar's bent. We have seen that Grein was at school under Vilmar, and Fanny Kemble tells us that her brother John was at school under Charles Richardson, the compiler of *A New Dictionary of the English Language*, in which was introduced for the first time the principle of historical illustration; she relates[84] that, when her brother went to school, Mr Richardson

> was then compiling his excellent dictionary, in which labour he employed the assistance of such of his pupils as showed themselves intelligent enough for the occupation; and I have no doubt that to this beginning of philological study my brother owed his subsequent predilection for and addiction to the science of language.

Fanny Kemble tells us how the acting family into which John was born took a 'delight in the dry bones of language', though 'none of them spoke foreign languages with ease or fluency':[85]

> My brother John, who was a learned linguist, and familiar with the modern European languages, spoke none of them well, not even German, though he resided for many years at Hanover, where he was curator of the royal museum and had married a German wife, and had among his most intimate friends and correspondents both the Grimms, Gervinus, and many of the principal literary men of Germany.

His views on politics and religion are important because of his influence on Anglo-Saxon philology in England. He had intended to read for the bar, renounced his intention and determined to study for the

---

[82] B. Dickins, 'John Mitchell Kemble and Old English Scholarship (with a Bibliography of his Writings)', *Proceedings of the British Academy* XXV (1941), pp. 51–84.
[83] Frances Ann Kemble, *Record of a Girlhood* (London, 1878).
[84] *Record of a Girlhood*, I, p. 62. C. Richardson (ed.), *A New Dictionary of the English Language* (London, 1836–37), received high praise from W.A. Craigie and C.T. Onions, the editors of 'Introduction, Supplement, and Bibliography', *A New English Dictionary on Historical Principles* (Oxford, 1933), p. vii.
[85] *Record of a Girlhood*, I, pp. 82–3.

Church. At the same time we find, according to his sister, that he had a 'fanatical admiration for Jeremy Bentham and [James] Mill, who . . . are our near neighbours here, and whose houses we never pass without John being inclined to salute them, I think, as the shrines of some beneficent powers of renovation'.[86] She also tells us:[87]

> He left the University [Cambridge] without taking his degree, and went to Heidelberg, where he laid the foundation of his subsequent thorough knowledge of German, and developed a taste for the especial philological studies to which he eventually devoted himself.

He developed a taste for German metaphysics there, and a respect for German patriotism, as he found it with Jacob and Wilhelm Grimm, an attractive patriotism without the overtones which our hindsight connects with the expansion of Prussia and the history of Germany in the present century.

It was presumably Kemble who wrote in his periodical, *British and Foreign Review*, of Jacob Grimm:[88]

> He may be said to have given a right direction to the sentiment of nationality, which broke forth with such energy in the beginning of the present century. He it was who directed the ardour of research to the relics of poetry and wisdom, preserved in the traditions and customs handed down from olden times. He entwined the naked ruin and the dried-up moat with the undying wreath of native poetry, and, by example as well as by precept, encouraged his countrymen to cultivate the flowers indigenous to their soil, in preference to hunting for exotic importations of foreign tastes and feelings.

When the ardour of research burnt within Kemble it turned him, who had thought himself destined for the Church, 'a latter Luther and a soldier-priest' in the words of Tennyson's sonnet,[89] into a naïve admirer of paganism: in a paper on heathen interment he writes about the grave of the typical Anglo-Saxon:[90]

> Accustomed to a free life among the beautiful features of nature, he would not be separated from them in death. It was his wish that his

---

[86] *Record of a Girlhood*, I, p. 293.
[87] *Record of a Girlhood*, I, p. 298.
[88] *British and Foreign Review*, 1840, p. 42. The article is unsigned, but, though not referred to by B. Dickins in his bibliography (see n. 82, above), Kemble's authorship seems certain.
[89] Alfred Tennyson, *Poems, Chiefly Lyrical* (London, 1830), p. 152, 'Sonnet to J.M.K.'
[90] J.M. Kemble, 'Notices of Heathen Interment in the Codex Diplomaticus, *Archæological Journal* xiv (1857), p. 122; reprinted in J.M. Kemble (ed. R.G. Latham and A.W. Franks), *Horæ Ferales; or, Studies in the Archæology of the Northern Nations* (London, 1863), p. 109.

bones should lie by the side of the stream, or on the summit of the rocks that overlooked the ocean which he had traversed; or he loved to lie in the shade of deep forests, or on the glorious uplands that commanded the level country; nor was it till long after Christianity had made him acquainted with other motives and higher hopes, till the exigencies of increasing population made new modes of disposing of the dead necessary, and till the clergy discovered a source of power and profit in taking possession of the ceremonies of interment, that regular churchyards attached to the consecrated building became possible.

7. The Views of the Founders Seen through the Writings of their Lesser Contemporaries

THE GERMANIC SCHOLARSHIP which has been considered so far was the work of scholars, in the case of Grimm, Gervinus and Kemble, of very great scholars. Before leaving the formative period of modern Germanic scholarship it may be worth looking at the writings of men of less standing. Often they put more bluntly what seems to be implied in the works of men of greater sensitivity or more profound learning. The few quotations given here, and far more could have been relevantly quoted, are extreme statements.

J.P.E.Greverus, head master of the Gymnasium at Oldenburg, recommends in the Supplement to the school programme for 1848 the study of the Anglo-Saxon language at school and in the home:[91]

> For who does not long for better knowledge of the earlier language of his people! Yet this literature has, in addition to its age and linguistic interest, an inestimable *factual value* in relation to our oldest folk-characteristics; and it contains, moreover, a treasure of poetry and of poetic linguistic elements which in our day refreshes and strengthens the heart, all the more since the form in which it is presented is rough indeed, yet full of primitive strength, even though it has here and there been muddied and weakened by the influence of Christian clerics, and has been deprived of its pagan magnificence and soundness to the core.

Greverus tells us how it was that the Anglo-Saxons kept themselves free from the influence of both the Romans and the Celts:[92]

---

[91] J.P.E. Greverus, *Empfehlung des Studium der angelsächsischen Sprache für Schule und Haus* (Oldenburg, 1848), p. 4: 'Denn wer sehnt sich nicht nach einer näheren Kenntnis der früheren Sprache seines Volks! Aber diese Literatur hat, abgesehen von ihrem Alter und dem Sprachlichen, auch einen unschätzbaren Real-Werth in Beziehung auf unsere älteste Volksthümlichkeit, und daneben einen Schatz von Poesie und poetischen Sprachelementen der in unserer Zeit um so mehr das Herz erquickt und stärkt, als die Form, in der sie geboten wird, zwar roh, aber urkräftig, wenn auch hie und da durch christlicher Pfaffen Einwirkung getrübt und abgeschwächt, und um ihre heidnische Kerngesundheit und Grossartigkeit gebracht ist.'

[92] Greverus, *Empfehlung*, pp. 5–6: 'Der grund liegt einmal und vorzüglich in dem angelsächsischen, deutschen und besonders norddeutschen Volkscharakter, der

The reason lies on the one hand, and pre-eminently, in the Anglo-Saxon, nay, German and particularly North German, national character, which held fast tenaciously to the old and the traditional, to the folk-characteristics and which, through a predominant inclination typical of all Germans to this day to lead their family life apart, has preserved them from the influence of foreigners on their language and customs. That was why the Anglo-Saxons did not mix with the British inhabitants; rather we see them from the first shutting themselves off from the alien Celts as regards land and soil, and forming their own realms. On the other hand, when the Anglo-Saxons settled in the country, the Romans had already moved out, and the British, softened by Roman Culture and vice, had nothing that could inspire the mighty sons of nature with respect. British slackness, disloyalty and cowardice had taken the place of Roman might; and the rough children of the North had no feeling for the more refined Culture, for luxury, or for the arts and sciences of which remnants might have been left behind.

Greverus lists some of the Old English words which he thinks (often wrongly) are borrowed from Latin or Greek. He regards the language as relatively pure Germanic, and sees in the nature of the English language of today a terrible example to those who pronounce German mumblingly.[93] The study of Anglo-Saxon civilization is instructive also because the English constitution is the direct development of Germanic institutions; in the laws of the Anglo-Saxons 'we can see most unmistakably the outline of English government and communal constitution of today, and we rejoice that the pure Germanic character developed at least in this one country, and rejected what was alien to it.'[94]

Of the beginnings of English literature Greverus has this to say:[95]

> zähe am Alten und Gewohnten, an seiner Volksthümlichkeit festhielt, und durch seine vorwaltende Neigung zum abgesonderten Familienleben, die allen Deutschen bis auf den heutigen Tag eigenthümlich ist, sie vor dem Einflusse der Fremden auf Sprache und Sitte bewahrte. Aus diesem Grunde vermischten die Angelsachsen sich nicht mit den britischen Einwohnern, sondern wir sehen sie von vornherein, auch dem Lande und dem Boden nach, sich von den Wälschen abschließen und ihre eigenen Reiche bilden. Von der andern Seite waren die Römer, als die Angelsachsen sich im Lande festsetzten, schon aus demselben abgezogen, und die durch römische Cultur und Laster verweichlichten Briten hatten nichts, wodurch sie den kräftigen Natursöhnen Achtung einflößen konnten. An die Stelle der römischen Kraft war britische Schlaffheit, Treulosigkeit und Feigheit getreten, und für die feinere etwa zurückgebliebene Cultur, für Luxus, Kunst und Wissenschaft, von denen Reste vorhanden sein mochten, hatten die rauhen Kinder des Nordens keinen Sinn.'

[93] Greverus, *Empfehlung*, p. 8.
[94] Greverus, *Empfehlung*, p. 19: 'Daneben sehen wir schon die jetzige englische Staats- und Gemeine-Verfassung in den unverkennbarsten Grundzügen, und freuen uns, daß die germanische Natur doch wenigstens in einem Lande sich rein entwickelte und das Fremdartige von sich stieß.'
[95] Greverus, *Empfehlung*, pp. 20–1: 'Es gewährt ein unendliches Vergnügen, eine

It gives us infinite pleasure to observe a language on its first entry into literature, to see a nation's original, primitive genius, as it were, stirring and using its strength. We feel as in a virgin forest; everything is great, full of primitive might and youthful purity, breathing the refreshing odour of life. We draw the word at the very fountain-head, we see in the clear depth of the spring the spirit of the whole nation, and recognize in the source the direction and the power of the entire mighty river that flows from it. Behold Hercules in his cradle, how he moves and stretches his limbs, how his bed is soon too small for him!

Coming to *Beowulf* he says:[96]

In *Beowulf* . . . the ancient Germanic national character stands rough, but pure, in its colossal Nordic pagan magnificence, perhaps superficially tainted here and there with Christian dogma, but fundamentally the ancient manful pagan world sound to the core.

Greverus is not to be regarded as an isolated phenomenon, though he may well have been alone in thinking that the lesson provided by the struggle of the Germanic ideal – national virtues, language, institutions, and literature – against alien influences cannot be learnt soon enough. An unexpected, later expression of this idea is to be found in Charles Kingsley's professorial lectures at Cambridge:[97]

Happy for us Englishmen, that we were forced to seek our adventures here, in this lonely isle; to turn aside from the great stream of Teutonic immigration; and settle here, each man on his forest-clearing, to till the ground in comparative peace, keeping unbroken the old Teutonic laws, unstained the old Teutonic faith and virtue.

The whole conception of Kingsley's lectures seems to be, but need not have been since their outlook was not uncommon, based on a lecture given by H.F. Massmann, the gymnast philologist, to celebrate the millennium since the Treaty of Verdun in 843. The subject of the lecture was 'German and Gallic, or the world-struggle of the Teutons and the Romans'; it contains sentiments not unlike those expressed in connection

---

Sprache zu beobachten bei ihrem ersten Eintritt in die Literatur, den Urgeist eines Volks gleichsam sich regen und walten sehen: Da ist uns, wie in einem Urwalde: Alles ist groß, urkräftig, jugendlich rein, und erquickenden Lebensduft hauchend! Frisch am Born schöpft man da das Wort, und sieht in seiner klaren Tiefe das geistige Wesen des ganzen Volks, erkennt am Quell die Richtung und die Kraft des ganzen großen Stroms, der aus ihm hervorgeht; schaut den Hercules in der Wiege, wie er die Glieder regt und reckt, und sein Bett ihm zu eng wird!'

[96] Greverus, *Empfehlung*, p. 23: 'In Beowulf . . . steht das altgermanische Volksthum in seiner colossalen nordischen Heiden-Größe roh, aber rein, da, nur an der Oberfläche theilweise von dogmatisch-christlichen Ideen angeflogen, im Grunde das alte kerngesunde, mannkräftige Heidenthum.'

[97] C. Kingsley, *The Roman and the Teuton*, p. 17.

with England by Greverus, and in connection with modern Germany by Baesecke in 1944:[98]

> And so I am immeasurably of the opinion that we *Germans, the nation of the future as of the past*, have reason to be sincerely grateful to God for the glorious and variegated circle and encirclement which *Gaulish or Roman* peoples form around us, as for a school, somewhat long-lasting indeed, and vigorous, in which we have grown to greatness and come of age, to achieve ever truer unity and ever truer consciousness of what we are called upon to do in the world, and of those duties towards ourselves which are the consequence of that call.

The state of Anglo-Saxon learning in England in the eighteen-forties is delineated by two anonymous reviews in *The Edinburgh Review*; the one, of 1845, is well-informed on Germanic literature and, therefore, directly or indirectly influenced by the views current in Germany; the other, of 1848, combines sound critical sense, which enabled its author to recognize a Christian poem when he saw one, with ignorance of Old English and Old English scholarship (though not of Old French and Provençal philology, the principal subject matter of the review).

The critic of 1845 writes of *Beowulf*:[99]

> It is certain that in its original structure it must have been composed in times of Paganism, if not even at a date anterior to the Saxon settlement of England. But all traces of the higher Pagan mythology have been carefully effaced, and adventitious allusions to Christianity introduced.

He says of the Cædmonian poems:[100]

> If these fragments had related to a Pagan theme, they would have been more admired; but we cannot allow their merit to be depreciated because they are founded on the book of Genesis.

The same idea is repeated in connection with *Andreas* and *Elene*:[101] 'If the subjects had been of native origin, they would have been of higher interest.' And there is praise of Grimm's edition:[102]

---

[98] H.F. Massmann, *Deutsch und Welsch oder der Weltkampf der Germanen und Romanen. Ein Rückblick auf unsere Urgeschichte zur tausendjährigen Erinnerung an den Vertrag von Verdun* (Munich, 1843), p. 33: 'Und so bin ich denn unmaßgeblich gemeint, daß wir D e u t s c h e, d a s V o l k d e r Z u k u n f t w i e d e r V e r g a n g e n h e i t, Gott auch aufrichtig für den reichen Ring der Umgebung und Umgarnung danken dürfen, den die w e l s c h e n oder r o m a n i s c h e n Völker um uns her bilden, als für eine freilich etwas lange und lebhafte Schule, in der wir groß wuchsen und mündig werden zu immer wahrerer Einheit, zu immer klarerem Bewußtseyn unsers Weltberufes, so wie der daraus entspringenden Pflichten gegen uns selbst.' For Baesecke's utterance, see p. 28, above.

[99] *Edinburgh Review* lxxxii (1845), p. 310; review of S. Laing (trans.), *The Heimskringla, Chronicle of the Kings of Norway by Snorro Sturleson* (London, 1845).

[100] *Edinburgh Review* lxxxii (1845), p. 311.

[101] *Edinburgh Review* lxxxii (1845), p. 312.

[102] *Edinburgh Review* lxxxii (1845), p. 312.

an excellent edition of both the poems by Grimm, with valuable notes and an admirable introduction, – presenting, as we think, a just and impartial view of the character and merits of Anglo-Saxon poetry.

The critic of 1848 (who thinks *Beowulf* is of the twelfth century, which he takes to be the date of the *Beowulf* manuscript also) says:[103]

> The Anglo-Saxon poem Beowulf is considered by some of our zealous antiquaries to be a poem of the pagan times of the Anglo-Saxons, composed before their arrival in our island, or when the traditionary legends of their native seats were not yet extinct. . . . The pagan origin of this poem, which would place its date about the end of the sixth century, or first half of the seventh, if it be an Anglo-Saxon composition, is a conjecture for which the poem itself furnishes no grounds. It is not composed in the spirit of paganism. . . . The poem of Beowulf bears strong internal evidence of being the production of a Christian doctrine and Bible history.

---

[103] *Edinburgh Review* lxxxviii (1848), p. 20; review of five works: C.-C. Fauriel, *Histoire de la Poésie Provençale* (Paris, 1846), G. de la Rue, *Essais Historiques sur les Bardes, Les Jongleurs et les Trouvères Normands et Anglo-Normands* (Caen, 1834), A.-M. Dinaux, *Les Trouvères Cambresiens* (Paris, 1837), A.W. von Schlegel, *Observations sur la Littérature Provençale: Essais Littéraires et Historiques* (Bonn, 1842), F. Diez, *Leben und Werke der Troubadours. Ein Beytrag zur näheren Kenntnisse des Mittelalters* (Zwickau, 1829).
[104] *Edinburgh Review* lxxxviii (1848), p. 19.

8. English Views of the Late Nineteenth Century and After

WE MUST TURN now to the last quarter of the nineteenth century and the beginning of the twentieth. It was a time when many of the ideas on Anglo-Saxon literature initiated in the first half of the nineteenth century were more fully exploited and coarsened in a vast number of doctoral theses and programme supplements which poured forth from the German universities and schools. The study of the Old English language was served in the same way, as is shown clearly by Henry Sweet's complaint:[105]

> it became too evident that the historical study of English was being rapidly annexed by the Germans, and that English editors would have to abandon all hopes of working up their materials themselves, and resign themselves to the more humble rôle of purveyors to the swarms of young program-mongers turned out every year by the German universities, so thoroughly trained in all the mechanical details of what may be called 'parasite philology' that no English dilettante can hope to compete with them – except by Germanizing himself and losing all his nationality.

Sweet seems to have resented only the amount of German activity, and that young scholarly leeches sucked themselves full of the scholarship provided by those with hard-got, first-hand knowledge of the material. He himself was imbued with the outlook on Anglo-Saxon literature prevalent in Germany:[106]

> A marked feature of Anglo-Saxon poetry is a tendency to melancholy and pathos, which tinges the whole literature: even the song of victory shows it, and joined to the heathen fatalism of the oldest poems, it produces a deep gloom, which would be painful were it not relieved by the high moral idealism which is never wanting in Anglo-Saxon poetry. . . . such passages as the descriptions of Grendel's abode in Beowulf . . . have a vividness and individuality which make them not inferior to the

---

[105] H. Sweet (ed.), *The Oldest English Texts*, EETS, o.s. 83 (1885), p. v.
[106] H. Sweet, 'Sketch of the History of Anglo-Saxon Poetry', in W. Carew Hazlitt (ed.), *History of English Poetry by Thomas Warton* (London, 1871), II, pp. 6–7.

most perfect examples of descriptive poetry in modern English literature, – perhaps the highest praise that can be given. This characteristic forms a strong bond of union between the two literatures, so different in many other respects, and it is not impossible that some of the higher qualities of modern English poetry are to be assigned to traditions of the old Anglo-Saxon literature, obscured for a time by those didactic, political, and allegorical tendencies which almost extinguished genuine poetry in the Early English period.

Some idea of late nineteenth-century literary sensibility, by no means confined to Sweet among scholars of Anglo-Saxon literature, is given by his comment on *The Later Genesis*:[107]

> The best portions of his [Cædmon's] poetry are those which narrate the creation and fall of the rebellious angels. These passages have all the grandeur of Milton, without his bombastic pedantry.

No one would go to J.R. Green's *Short History of the English People* for an authoritative opinion on Old English literature; but Green had the ability to express in vivid terms the accepted opinion of the day, and he writes thus of Old English verse:[108]

> It was not that any revolution had been wrought by Cædmon [*scil.* when inspired to 'this sudden burst of song'] in the outer form of English song, as it had grown out of the stormy life of the pirates of the sea. The war-song still remained the true type of English verse, a verse without art or conscious development or the delight that springs from reflection, powerful without beauty, obscured by harsh metaphors and involved construction, but eminently the verse of warriors, the brief passionate expression of brief passionate emotions. Image after image, phrase after phrase, in these early poems, starts out vivid, harsh and emphatic. The very metre is rough with a sort of self-violence and repression; the verses fall like sword-strokes in the thick of battle. Harsh toilers, fierce fighters, with huge appetites whether for meat or the ale-bowl, the one breath of poetry that quickened the animal life of the first Englishman was the poetry of war. [Later versions of Green's book add a reference to 'The love of natural description, the background of melancholy which gives its pathos to English verse, the poet only shared with earlier singers. But the faith of Christ brought in . . . new realms of fancy.']

---

[107] Sweet, 'Sketch of the History of Anglo-Saxon Poetry', p. 16.
[108] J.R. Green, *A Short History of the English People* (London, 1874), pp. 26–7; the wording in later editions is somewhat changed, significantly so by the addition of the sentence quoted above [in brackets] from the 'Illustrated Edition' (London, 1902), I, p. 53.

9. Stock Views Disintegrating Old English Poems and Finding Germanic Antiquities in them

THE VIEWS on Old English poetry held by Sweet, who had a full and first-hand knowledge of the material, and also by J.R. Green, who did not, correspond to the preconceptions underlying the two principal activities on which the writers of dissertations and school programmes trained in the universities of Germany spent their immense energies. The first of these two activities was disintegration: poems held to be pagan (among them *Beowulf*, the Old English elegies, and the Gnomic Poems) were freed from what were thought Christian accretions, the genuine was freed from the spurious. The second activity was the reading of the Anglo-Saxon 'Christian epics' for Germanic and even pagan antiquities. The guiding method here was that employed by Grimm for *Andreas* and *Elene* and by Vilmar for the Old Saxon *Heliand*.

A. *Disintegration*

The excision of Christian elements is based on the wishful thought that such Old English literature as is not obviously Christian in subject-matter is pre-Christian and therefore early. It is part of a wider view, well described by Gösta Langenfelt in connection with *Widsith*:[109]

> The principal reason why Widsith is considered to be an ancient piece of OE poetry is, however, that it began to be analysed, examined, investigated, dug into, at a date in the 19th cent. when philologists were enthusiastic about the discovery of the kinship of I[ndo-]Eur[opean] languages, when they compared roots of words of different languages in the light of sound-laws, and when, hence, Germanic linguistic antiquity was lifted out of its misty regions and assumed a regular shape. Then Widsith was numbered among the early specimens (the first specimen) of Germanic literary activities. In the case of Widsith there lingers over the views, and the results, of 19th cent. research a

---

[109] G. Langenfelt, 'Studies on *Widsith*', *Namn och Bygd* xlvii (1959), p. 109.

Germanic 'nationalism', so to speak, – which would have been quite improbable if the Widsith matter had been handled by scholars of the Mediterranean countries. The results of folkloristic research: tales, stories, poems, 'Merkverse', traditions, etc., were also mobilized, and behind every name there always hung a (popular; tribal; Germanic folk-)tale the existence of which could not be proved, but was persistently assumed.

(i) *Beowulf*

There was also, as we have seen, the identification of the primitive with all that is, at a rather naïve level, romantically poetic, and the corresponding identification of all that is Christian and didactic with prolixity and platitudinarianism. G.K. Anderson, a fairly recent exponent of this view, puts it characteristically in the case of *Beowulf*, 'There is more than enough of platitude and of Christian admonition in the poem.'[110] The method adopted in pruning often involves the circular argument, that, once the Christian elements have been excised, the poem will be seen to contain no Christian influence. Miss Edith Wardale, writing on *Waldere*, illustrates the method:[111] 'There is no Christian influence to be traced in the sentiments, for the few Christian lines have clearly been added later.' The history of the disintegration of *Beowulf* is well told by John Earle, twice Professor of Anglo-Saxon in the University of Oxford, and by R.W. Chambers. Earle was writing at a time when, all around him, scholars were hacking the poem about, and he was one of a very small number of competent scholars who resisted the process; Chambers was writing in 1921, by which time most scholars had accepted Klaeber's argument that the Christian elements in *Beowulf* are integrally part of the poem.[112] Chambers's views are familiar to every student of *Beowulf*, but Earle's seem to be forgotten. In 1884 he wrote:[113]

---

[110] Anderson, *Literature of the Anglo-Saxons*, p. 67.
[111] Wardale, *Chapters on Old English Literature*, p. 71.
[112] R.W. Chambers's account of the disintegrating theories comes in the third chapter, 'Theories as to the Origin, Date and Structure of the Poem', of his *Beowulf: An Introduction to the Study of the Poem with a Discussion of the Stories of Offa and Finn* (Cambridge, 1921). F. Klaeber's 'Die christlichen Elemente im Beowulf' came out in four articles in *Anglia* xxxv (1911–12), pp. 111–36, 249–70, 453–82, xxxvi (1912), pp. 169–99; Chambers, *Beowulf: An Introduction*, p. 406, 3rd edn (Cambridge, 1959), p. 576, describes this set of articles as 'Most important: demonstrates the fundamentally Christian character of the poem.'
[113] J. Earle, *Anglo-Saxon Literature*, The Dawn of European Literature (London, 1884), p. 134. Both L. Ettmüller's translation (in which Christian verses are set apart, as the result of reworking discussed by him at p. 63), *Beowulf. Heldengedicht des achten Jahrhunderts. Zum ersten Male aus dem Angelsächsischen in das Neuhochdeutsche stabreimend übersetzt* (Zürich, 1840), and his edition (in a

About the structure of this poem the same sort of questions are debated as those which Wolff raised about Homer – whether it is the work of a single poet, or a patchwork of older poems. Ludwig Ettmüller, of Zürich, who first gave the study of the 'Beowulf' a German basis, regarded the poem as originally a purely heathen work, or a compilation of smaller heathen poems, upon which the editorial hands of later and Christian poets had left their manifest traces. In his translation, one of the most vigorous efforts in the whole of Beowulf literature, he has distinguished, by a typographical arrangement, the later additions from what he regards as the original poetry. He is guided, however, by considerations different from those that affect the Homeric debate. He is chiefly guided by the relative shades of the heathen and Christian elements. Wherever the touch of the Christian hand is manifest, he arranges such parts as additions and interpolations.

Not every aspect of Earle's sensitive interpretation of the heathen myths in the poem will be accepted by modern readers, but his conclusion will meet with more respect now than will the views of those whose 'scientific' approach gave them for long the ascendancy over Earle:[114]

> I conceive that Beowulf was a genuine growth of that junction in time (define it where we may) when the heathen tales still kept their traditional interest, and yet the spirit of Christianity had taken full possession of the Saxon mind – at least, so much of it as was represented by this poetical literature.

In 1892 Earle ventured a prophecy:[115]

> My own impression is that in Müllenhoff's criticism of the Beowulf we have a *reductio ad absurdum* of the Wolffian hypothesis, and that by and bye less will be heard of it than heretofore.

He goes on to speak of Müllenhoff's close reading of the poem:[116]

---

rectoral *Programmschrift*), *Carmen de Beóvulfi Gautarum regis rebus praeclare gestis atque interitu, quale fuerit ante quam in manus interpolatoris, monachi Vestsaxonici, inciderat* (Zürich, 1875), discriminate against Christian verses – monkish interpolations – with the result that the poem as edited by him is only 2896 lines long. Earle (p. 134) has a footnote referring to K. Müllenhoff's paper, 'Die innere Geschichte des Beovulfs', originally published in *Zeitschrift für deutsches Alterthum* xiv (1869), pp. 193–244.

[114] Earle, *Anglo-Saxon Literature*, p. 136.
[115] J. Earle, *The Deeds of Beowulf: An English Epic of the Eighth Century Done into Modern Prose* (Oxford, 1892), p. xliii. Earle's reference in this and the next quotation is to K. Müllenhoff, *Beovulf Untersuchungen über das angelsächsische Epos und die älteste Geschichte der germanischen Seevölker* (Berlin, 1889), 'Die innere Geschichte des Beovulfs', pp. 110–60.
[116] Earle, *The Deeds of Beowulf*, p. xliii.

The minute examination of the text has been stimulated by the passionate desire of demonstrating that the poem is not what it seems, a poetical unit, the work of an author, but that it is a cluster of older and later material fortuitously aggregated, in short, that it is not that highly organized thing which is called a Poem, the life of which is found in unity of purpose and harmony of parts, but that, on the contrary, it is a thing of low organism, which is nowise injured by being torn asunder, inasmuch as the life of it resides in the parts and not in the whole – a thing without a core or any organic centre.

Earle, like W.P. Ker after him, though of course indebted to German linguistic scholarship, did not allow German literary theories to weigh so strongly with him that they overbalanced common sense. But their scholarship was exceptional; Henry Bradley's utterances on Old English literature were more in line with current opinion, thus, admittedly under the sub-heading 'Historical Value', he says of *Beowulf*:[117]

> though there are some distinctly Christian passages, they are so incongruous in tone with the rest of the poem that they must be regarded as interpolations. . . . If the mass of traditions which it purports to contain be genuine, the poem is of unique importance as a source of knowledge respecting the early history of the peoples of northern Germany and Scandinavia. But the value to be assigned to *Beowulf* in this respect can be determined only by ascertaining its probable date, origin and manner of composition. The criticism of the Old English epic has therefore for nearly a century been justly regarded as indispensable to the investigation of Germanic antiquities.

Miss M.G. Clarke, writing at about the same time, has views no different from Bradley's on *Beowulf*:[118] 'The value of the poem for us lies in the reference made by the poet to well-known characters of the Heroic Age.' In Bodley's copy of the book (shelfmark 2791 e.9) a post-Tolkienian reader has underlined the word *value* and pencilled this protest in the margin, 'No. Its value is the brooding elegiac quality which perfades [sic] it.' The final sentence of Miss Clarke's 'Conclusions' reads:[119]

> the primary interest of these poems [*scil.* the Old English heroic poems, *Beowulf, Widsith, The Finnesburh Fragment, Waldere, Deor*], which were originally designed for the amusement and entertainment of our warlike ancestors, now lies in their relation to the history of the far-away times which gave them birth.

---

[117] H. Bradley, '*Beowulf*', originally published in *Encyclopædia Britannica*, 11th edn (London, 1910), III, p. 759; here quoted from *The Collected Papers of Henry Bradley With a Memoir by Robert Bridges* (Oxford, 1928), pp. 200–201.

[118] M.G. Clarke, *Sidelights on Teutonic History during the Migration Period: Being Studies from 'Beowulf' and other Old English Poems*, Girton College Studies III (Cambridge, 1911), p. 7.

[119] Clarke, *Sidelights*, p. 259.

One passage in *Beowulf*, lines 181–8, seems especially to obtrude a Christian condemnation upon a context that has been found difficult to reconcile with it. Readers do not find it easy to dismiss the passage as merely one of the occasional inconsistencies of the poem; it involves too central an aspect of the poem for that.[120] Henry Bradley has this to say of it:[121]

> The Christian passages, which are poetically of no value, are evidently of literary origin, and may be of any date down to that of the extant MS. The curious passage which says that the subjects of Hrothgar sought deliverance from Grendel in prayer at the temple of the Devil, 'because they knew not the true God', must surely have been substituted for a passage referring sympathetically to the worship of the ancient gods.

Even J.R.R. Tolkien rejects these lines:[122]

> Not of course because of the apparent discrepancy – though it is a matter vital to the whole poem: we cannot dismiss lines simply because they offer difficulty of such a kind. But because, unless my ear and judgement are wholly at fault, they have a ring and measure unlike their context, and indeed unlike that of the poem as a whole.

C.L. Wrenn recognizes the danger of this subjective excision:[123]

> In the absence of knowledge of the exact level of Christian culture to be assumed in poet and audience, this homiletic tone is not in itself enough cause to reject this passage, unless we are to reject also the whole of Hrothgar's great sermon in ll. 1724 ff. for the same reason. How homiletic are the moralizing comments of the author and the patriarchal discourses of Hrothgar allowed to become in such contexts? We do not know the answer, and therefore had best not assume one. The real objection is probably metrical. There is something less *right*, less contextually fitting in *sound*, in the metre of these lines, though it would be difficult to define what seems wrong in technical language. But this is a somewhat subjective judgement; and it is perhaps wiser to assume some weakening in the poet's art at this point rather than that a later writer has sought to emphasize the specifically Christian attitude by an interpolation.

---

[120] Cf. E.G. Stanley, 'Hæthenra Hyht in *Beowulf*', in S.B. Greenfield (ed.), *Studies in Old English Literature in Honor of Arthur G. Brodeur* (Eugene, Oregon, 1963), pp. 136–51, where I have made an attempt to show how the acceptance of these lines is central to an understanding of the poem.

[121] Bradley, '*Beowulf*', *Encyclopædia Britannica*, III (1910), p. 760; *Collected Papers*, p. 207.

[122] J.R.R. Tolkien, '*Beowulf*: The Monsters and the Critics', *Proceedings of the British Academy* XXII (1936), p. 288.

[123] C.L. Wrenn (ed.), *Beowulf with the Finnesburg Fragment* (London, 1953), p. 68.

Our suspicion of the subjective rejection of these lines is strengthened when we remember Tolkien's note on his treatment of Hrothgar's so-called 'sermon':[124]

> Similarly it is the very marked character already by the poet given to Hrothgar which has induced and made possible without serious damage the probable revision and expansion of his sermon. Well done as the passage in itself is, the poem would be better with the excision of approximately lines 1740–60; and these lines are on quite independent grounds under the strongest suspicion of being due to later revision and addition.

Whenever we consider the rejection of a passage in *Beowulf* we should recall Earle's criticism of the usual method:[125]

> The German method of studying what they call the Inner History (*die innere Geschichte*) of this poem is to begin by forming an imaginary idea of the original Epic, and then to employ this ideal for a standard of criticism. Professor Ten Brink, the latest author who has worked upon these lines, has avowed this method in the most frank and unreserved manner, pleading that every attempt at *à priori* reasoning in this field *must* move in a circle. Of course it must; the remark is incontestable; – but is it not the natural inference that the *à priori* method is therefore essentially hollow and unfit to carry any superstructure?

Tolkien's views on *Beowulf* are of course not those current in Germany in 1892; but a suspicion, at least, remains that he has not avoided reasoning in a circle. Unless the subjective judgement which condemns these lines because of 'a ring and measure unlike their context' can be substantiated by some analysis of the difference between these lines and their context it will be best to give up this last vestige of disintegration, and to assume that the poem stands in the manuscript as its Christian author wrote it, except for such changes of detail as may have been introduced by a succession of scribes through carelessness, incomprehension, and the desire to modernize the language, especially the spellings.

Earle was not the only one in the late nineteenth century to look upon *Beowulf* as the work of a Christian poet. A. Ebert, who brought to the study of Anglo-Saxon literature the wider vision of a man steeped in the Latin literature of the Middle Ages, wrote of the poem in 1887:[126]

---

[124] Tolkien, 'The Monsters and the Critics', p. 295.
[125] Earle, *The Deeds of Beowulf*, pp. xlvii–xlviii. For *die innere Geschichte*, see nn. 113, 115, above.
[126] Ebert, *Allgemeine Geschichte der Literatur des Mittelalters im Abendlande*, III, p. 37: 'Der Autor zeigt ritterliche Gesinnung, höfische Erziehung und klerikale Bildung: das vereinte sich bei den Angelsachsen sehr wohl . . . namentlich in den höchsten Kreisen; legten doch öfters die tapfersten ihrer Könige Schwert und Scepter ab, um ganz einem asketischen Leben sich zu weihen. Der Dichter wusste

The poet manifests a chivalric disposition, courtly upbringing, and clerical learning: . . . these were very happily united among the Anglo-Saxons, especially of the highest circles; for very frequently the bravest of their kings laid down sword and sceptre to dedicate themselves entirely to the ascetic life. The poet knew how to assimilate the foreign material of the heroic legend belonging to another people, admittedly related to his, and to treat it, in spite of its pagan and mythical basis, so much in the spirit of his own people that his work has even been pronounced to be an Anglo-Saxon folk-epic! – in spite of the fact that its subject-matter is not Anglo-Saxon nor its execution popular.

In 1897 W.P. Ker fully endorsed Earle's views on the poem as we now have it:[127]

It is an extant book, whatever the history of its composition may have been; the book of the adventures of Beowulf, written out fair by two scribes in the tenth century; an epic poem, with a prologue at the beginning, and a judgement pronounced on the life of the hero at the end; a single book, considered as such by its transcribers, and making a claim to be so considered.

In the present century voices affirming that *Beowulf* is a unity have become increasingly common. A. Brandl in 1908, somewhat half-heartedly perhaps, defended the Christian elements:[128] 'Whoever wishes to remove the unpagan elements completely from the *Beowulf* epic will have to rewrite it.' In 1911 W.W. Lawrence put the same view more positively:[129] 'The futility of attempting to separate Christian and heathen conceptions in that poem is now well recognized.' 1911 saw the first three of F. Klaeber's four fundamental articles on the Christian elements in *Beowulf*. They contained the evidence in sufficient profusion for the correctness of the view that the poem as we have it is Christian in every part. It may be worth quoting here, not the many long passages all relevant to the theme of the present book, but just three sentences, because they are essentially modern; all three are taken from the last of the four articles by Klaeber:[130]

> den fremden Stoff der Heldensage eines andern, wenn auch verwandten Volkes trotz seiner heidnischen mythischen Grundlage sich so vollkommen anzueignen und im Geiste seiner Nationalität zu behandeln, dass man sein Werk sogar für ein angelsächsisches Volksepos erklären konnte! – obgleich es weder dem Stoff nach angelsächsisch, noch der Ausführung nach volksmässig ist.'

[127] W.P. Ker, *Epic and Romance* (London, 1897), pp. 182–3.
[128] Brandl, 'Geschichte der altenglischen Literatur', I, Angelsächsische Periode, in Paul (ed.), *Grundriss der germanischen Philologie*, II, 2nd edn, VI/6 § 30, p. 1003 (= p. 63 of separate): 'Wer die unheidnischen Elemente aus dem Beowulfepos vollständig entfernen will, muss es umdichten.' The emphasis here seems to be on *vollständig* 'completely'.
[129] W.W. Lawrence, 'The Song of Deor', *Modern Philology* ix (1911), p. 27, with reference to *Beowulf*.
[130] Klaeber, 'Die christlichen Elemente im Beowulf, p. 195: 'Der dichter würde eine

The poet would never have selected so singular a fable if it had not been exceptionally well suited to Christianization. . . . The poet, who shows himself to be fully conversant with the teaching and the spirit of Christianity, was of course no longer a Christian of the time of transition. . . . But one thing is sure: the poet of *Beowulf* was an unusually outstanding personality, amenable to the most varied influences, a 'Widsith' or Saxo in his knowledge of legends, an educated man who has received an ecclesiastical training, a sensitive person, an artist who among the Anglo-Saxons has not his equal in shaping poetic form to perfection.

There is no great distance from Earle, Ebert, Ker, and Klaeber to recent views. Morton W. Bloomfield's statement (published in 1951) provides a summary of the present position, and at the same time shows awareness of earlier points of view:[131]

Nineteenth-century romantic and nationalistic scholarship, often German, to which we owe much of both good and evil, over-emphasized the pagan aspects of the oldest known Germanic epic. It has been difficult to shed this point of view and to see the essential Christianity of *Beowulf*. It belongs to the Christian tradition, not only in mood and ideals, and in occasional Biblical references, but, at least partially and tentatively, in literary technique. An old Scandinavian tale has been changed into a Christian poem.

Perhaps Bloomfield's extension of the essential Christianity of the poem to the poet's mode of discourse is still in need of demonstration in detail before it will be as generally assented to as to the following statement of A.G. Brodeur's:[132]

In the figure of Beowulf the heroic ideals of Germanic paganism and of Anglo-Saxon Christendom have been reconciled and fused, so that the hero exemplifies the best of both. . . . The pagan and the Christian elements that combine in the person of Beowulf complement, rather than oppose, one another.

Klaeber's demonstration that the Christian elements were of a piece with the rest of *Beowulf* as we have it did not at once find acceptance with

---

solche einzigartige fabel überhaupt nicht gewählt haben, wäre dieselbe einer Christianisierung nicht so außerordentlich günstig gewesen'; p. 196: 'der dichter, der sich so völlig vertraut mit der lehre und dem geiste des christentums zeigt, war selbstverständlich kein übergangschrist mehr'; p. 199: 'Das eine aber steht: der Beowulfdichter war eine ungewöhnlich hervorragende persönlichkeit, die den verschiedenartigsten einflüssen zugänglich war, ein "Widsið" oder Saxo an sagenkenntnis, ein kirchlich geschulter, gebildeter mann, ein feinfühliger charakter, ein künstler, der in der vollendung der form unter den Angelsachsen seines gleichen nicht hat.'

[131] M.W. Bloomfield, '*Beowulf* and Christian Allegory: An Interpretation of Unferth', *Traditio* vii (1951), p. 415.

[132] A.G. Brodeur, *The Art of Beowulf* (Berkeley and Los Angeles, 1959), pp. 183–4.

all scholars; they had followed the scent of paganism for too long to be willing to recognize that they had been on a false trail. H.M. Chadwick's words, published in 1912, the year that saw the last one of Klaeber's articles, mark the passing of an epoch in *Beowulf* studies, and Chadwick regrets its passing:[133]

> Half a century ago, when the study of Teutonic antiquity was still young, there was a general eagerness to refer every institution and belief to a native origin. To-day we see the inevitable reaction – a hypercritical attitude towards every explanation of this character, coupled with a readiness to accept theories of biblical or classical influence on the slightest possible evidence. It is this intellectual atmosphere which, naturally enough, has given birth to the chimaera of a literary Beowulf – a creature which, if I am not mistaken, belongs to the same genus as certain well-known theories in Northern mythology.

His use of the word *literary* is characteristic. We have seen it so used by Henry Bradley, 'The Christian passages, which are poetically of no value, are evidently of literary origin.'[134]

After Klaeber the essential unity of the poem could no longer be denied. But it was still possible to question whether the poet's heart was in all that he was writing, or whether the Church approved of what he was writing. As early as 1840 Gervinus had suggested that Cædmon need not have had the support of the Church in his activities as a poet:[135]

> There never seems to have been any doubt among the Goths that the vernacular was the only means of propagating Christian writings; yet we may very justly doubt . . . how far Cædmon's, Otfrid's, and similar works were in fact composed with or against the wishes of the Church.

Gervinus' doubts are, we now think, obviously unwarranted. Perhaps they were merely the result of the Romantic image of the poet who feels compelled to utter his song regardless of the hostility of the world. W.W. Lawrence, writing in 1928, turns the *Beowulf* poet into an *entre-guerre* development of the Romantic poet, the man who toes the party-line opportunistically, though his heart is not in the business:[136]

> What, in a Christian era, were the court-poets, the *scops*, to do, except to fall in with the new ways? Probably many of them became minor

---

[133] H.M. Chadwick, *The Heroic Age* (Cambridge, 1912), p. 76.
[134] Bradley, '*Beowulf*'; see p. 44 and n. 121, above.
[135] Gervinus, *Historische Schriften*, II, *Geschichte der deutschen Dichtung*, pp. 76–7: 'Unter den Gothen scheint man gar nicht gezweifelt zu haben, daß die Vulgarsprache das einzige Mittel zu Verbreitung der christlichen Schriften sei: allein ob Cädmons und Otfrieds und ähnliche Werke mit oder gegen Willen der Kirche verfaßt seien, darüber kann man schon mit Recht . . . zweifelhaft sein.'
[136] W.W. Lawrence, *'Beowulf' and Epic Tradition* (Cambridge, Massachusetts, 1928), pp. 281–2.

clerics. Pious kings could not welcome unmodified heathendom, but they could enjoy good old stories with the curse removed. Such was the situation, apparently, that confronted the poet of *Beowulf*. Everything shows him to have been trained in the full technique of the professional poet. His heart was really in the pagan tales and traditions that had been celebrated for generations among his people by singers like himself. But, in the changed conditions of his time, he had to suppress all reference to the old gods, save for reprobation, and make over his pagans into good Christians or else show the hollowness of their heathen faith. How deep and sincere his own religious convictions were we cannot fathom, but he fell into line, as he had of necessity to do.

This is the thin veneer of Christianity which Miss M. Bentinck Smith was talking about:[137]

> at first, Christianity is seen to be but a thin veneer over the old heathen virtues, and the gradual assimilation of the Christian spirit was not accomplished without harm to the national poetry, or without resentment on the part of the people.

Views like those expressed by Miss Bentinck Smith and W.W. Lawrence were held also by H.M. and N.K. Chadwick in 1932, and for confirmation they seized on the lines of *Beowulf* which were to be excised even by Tolkien:[138]

> In England too, as elsewhere, when the courts had been converted, minstrels had to adapt their poems to the new conditions, if they were not to scrap their entire repertoire. Here also it was evidently regarded as improper for Christians to listen to purely heathen poems; but heroic poetry still retained its attractions, even for the slacker and less learned ecclesiastics. The minstrel then had two alternatives before him: he had either to represent the heroes as Christians or to denounce them as heathens. Naturally he chose the former course, and accordingly introduced Christian expressions in their speeches, as well as in the narratives. This expedient apparently succeeded in preserving the poems, though the more learned ecclesiastics knew what the heroes really were and repudiated them. But it is to be remembered that in one passage in *Beowulf* the alternative course has been followed, viz. in 175 ff., where the Danes are definitely represented as heathens, praying at heathen shrines, and denounced accordingly in a rather long homiletic adjunct. No satisfactory explanation of this passage is to be obtained from the hypothesis that the poem is the work of a learned Christian writer; one can only conclude that he must have been a very stupid fellow. But if it has come down from heathen times and acquired its Christian character gradually and piecemeal from a

---

[137] Bentinck Smith, *Cambridge History of English Literature*, I, p. 64.
[138] H.M. and N.K. Chadwick, *The Growth of Literature*, I, *The Ancient Literatures of Europe* (Cambridge, 1932), pp. 560–1.

succession of minstrels, such inconsistencies are natural, perhaps inevitable. Heathenism of a less flagrant kind peeps out often enough both in ideas and in practices.

One would have thought that a reading of the poem would reveal that what the poet has written hardly sounds as if it were the result merely of falling into line, of using the veneer of Christianity only as an expedient. What B. ten Brink said of *Genesis A* applies to a large extent to *Beowulf* also:[139]

> The paraphrase of the fourteenth chapter of the Bible, a stirring battle-picture with many accessories, shows our poet possessed by that glow of warlike enthusiasm which pervades all Teutonic antiquity. [Here follow lines 1982–93 in translation.] Nevertheless our poet does not appear in the character of a *scop* or *gleóman* who has donned the cowl and turned to religious poetising. He would have betrayed in other passages as well his preference for the customary epic armour, for weapons and the like, and would have brought out and utilised more prominently the martial element in the bearing and character of his heroes. The passion which fills the poet is essentially religious.

(ii) *The elegies*

The history of the disintegration of the Old English elegies has never been written; it is not such a fruitful subject as the disintegration of *Beowulf*; for some of the elegies obviously, if superficially, lack unity, so that disintegration consists simply in recognizing the parts. At a time when one of the major preoccupations of Germanic studies was the search for heathenisms, the recognition of disunity of tone in these poems was tantamount to a recognition of pagan and Christian portions.

The discussion whether the elegiac note of much Old English poetry was Germanic or Christian, that is, genuine or spurious, occupies an important place in the discussion of which parts of the poems are genuine or spurious.

---

[139] Ten Brink, *Early English Literature*, pp. 43–4. Cf. the original version: *Geschichte der Englischen Litteratur*, I, pp. 54–5: 'Die Paraphrase des vierzehnten biblischen Capitels zeigt in einem lebendigen, mit zahlreichen Zuthaten ausgestatteten Schlachtgemälde auch unsern Dichter ergriffen von jenem Hauch kriegerischer Begeisterung, der das ganze deutsche Alterthum durchweht. [He quotes *Genesis*, lines 1982–93, in the German translation by C.W.M. Grein, *Dichtungen der Angelsachsen stabreimend übersetzt*, I (Göttingen, 1857), pp. 55–6.] Gleichwohl erscheint unser Dichter nicht etwa im Licht eines *scop* oder *gleóman*, der die Kutte angezogen und der geistlichen Dichtung sich zugewandt hätte. Ein Solcher würde auch an andern Stellen seine Vorliebe für das gewöhnliche epische Rüstzeug, für Waffen und dergleichen verrathen, das kriegerische Element in Haltung und Wesen seiner Helden entschiedener durchgeführt und zur Geltung gebracht haben. Das Pathos, das unsern Dichter erfüllt, ist doch vorzugsweise ein religiöses.'

Some circular argument was almost inevitable; since the elegiac portions are often very good, and since what is good is Germanic in contrast with the spurious, it follows that the elegiac portions must be genuine.

In 1875 R. Heinzel, surprisingly in view of this prevailing prejudice, thought it likely enough that:[140]

> The Anglo-Saxon epic of the seventh century [*Beowulf*] differs from the oldest poetry of all other Germanic peoples because of its tender feelings and the idealization of what is presented; in no other Germanic nation did Christianity take root so early or so deeply. Should we not assume, then, that there is a connection between the two, and since the conversion took place before the *Beowulf*-lays came into being – all of them contain evidence, not merely of acquaintance with, but of acceptance of the new teaching – may we not derive their most prominent poetic characteristics from Christianity?

A little later he answers these rhetorical questions:[141] 'The idealizing poetry is intimately related to the essence of Christianity.'

To F.B. Gummere this seemed an intolerable attack on a central characteristic of the Anglo-Saxons, and he criticizes Heinzel sharply for it:[142]

> The elegiac mood has been attributed by a German critic, not to a tendency in the race itself, but rather to the softening influence of Christianity. This seems to be a surface-criticism; melancholy of some sort is inherent in the Germanic temperament, and a sheer ferocity of the Viking or even Berserker type is not enough to offset the countless examples of the elegiac and pathetic in our oldest literature.

E. Sieper's book on the Anglo-Saxon elegy was written in amplification of the thesis that elegies formed part of primitive Germanic ritual, though the surviving elegies contain Christian additions and show signs of superficial accommodation to Christianity even in the genuine parts.[143]

---

[140] R. Heinzel, *Über den Stil der altgermanischen Poesie*, Quellen und Forschungen zur Sprach- und Culturgeschichte der germanischen Völker x (1875), p. 38: 'das angelsächsische Epos des siebenten Jahrhunderts unterscheidet sich durch Gefühlsweichheit und idealisirende Darstellung von den ältesten Poesien aller übrigen Germanen, und bei keinem germanischen Volke hatte das Christenthum so früh und so tief Wurzel geschlagen. Sollen wir da nicht einen Zusammenhang beider Erscheinungen vermuthen, und da die Bekehrung vor die Entstehung der Beowulflieder fällt – alle zeugen nicht nur von Kenntniß, sondern von Annahme der neuen Lehre – dürfen wir nicht deren hervorstechende poetische Eigenschaften vom Christianthume ableiten?'

[141] Heinzel, *Über den Stil*, p. 39: 'Die idealisirende Poesie hat zu dem Wesen des Christenthums eine innere Verwandtschaft.'

[142] F.B. Gummere, *Germanic Origins: A Study in Primitive Culture* (New York, 1892), p. 331. Gummere refers to Heinzel in a footnote.

[143] E. Sieper, *Die altenglische Elegie* (Strassburg, 1915).

He attached importance to the views of Eugen Mogk and Gustav Neckel that the figure of Wayland was traditionally gentle, deserving of pity, elegiac;[144] and he uses the Wayland stanza in *Deor* as proof that tenderness of spirit is characteristically Germanic:[145]

> The song of Wayland supplies the proof that tender emotions, unconnected with tribal feeling, were by no means foreign to Germanic paganism. It is obvious that emotions of this kind were more richly developed through the influence of a progressing civilization and of Christianity which later gained ascendancy. However, we are not concerned here with a foreign graft, but rather with the development of native seed-buds.

Miss Wardale was more modest in her claim:[146]

> In England, the warlike tone, the aristocratic colouring, natural to lays glorifying the victories or lamenting the overthrow of kings and heroes, lasted on, and with the power of vigorous description may be looked upon as part of the Germanic heritage. But side by side with them appears a note of seriousness, amounting sometimes to melancholy. Indeed almost all the lyrical poems are elegies. This may be due to the religious outlook of the Anglo-Saxons in pre-Christian days.

The supposed additions are characterized, in Brandl's phrase, by 'monkish pusillanimity'[147] which reveals itself in moralizing, pious talk. The clerical author of these additions may, like Aldhelm at the bridge in William of Malmesbury's account, assume the rôle of a true poet for a while to ingratiate himself the better with his audience,[148] 'until,' Brandl says, 'right at the end, where the homiletic tone sets in and the redactor drops his mask'.[149]

Louis F. Klipstein, writing in 1849 on *The Wanderer*, illustrates both

---

[144] Sieper, *Die altenglische Elegie*, p. 114.
[145] Sieper, *Die altenglische Elegie*, p. 122: 'Das Wielandslied liefert den Beweis, daß dem heidnischen Germanentum weiche Regungen, die mit Stammesgefühl nichts zu tun haben, durchaus nicht fremd waren. Daß Regungen dieser Art unter dem Einfluß einer fortschreitenden Kultur und des späterhin zur Herrschaft gelangenden Christentums zur reichern Entfaltung kamen, liegt auf der Hand. Doch handelt es sich dabei nicht um fremdes Pfropfreis sondern um die Entwicklung bodenständiger Keime.'
[146] Wardale, *Chapters in Old English Literature*, p. 8.
[147] Brandl, 'Geschichte der altenglischen Literatur', I, Angelsächsische Periode, in Paul (ed.), *Grundriss der germanischen Philologie*, II, 2nd edn, VI/6 § 46, p. 1039 (= p. 99 of separate): 'mönchische Engherzigkeit'.
[148] William of Malmesbury, *De Gestis Pontificum Anglorum*, ed. N.E.S.A. Hamilton, Rolls Series, 52 (1870), p. 336.
[149] Brandl, 'Geschichte der altenglischen Literatur', I Angelsächsische Periode, in Paul (ed.), *Grundriss der germanischen Philologie*, II, 2nd edn, VI/6 § 11, p. 960 (= p. 20 of separate), writing of the Cotton *Gnomes*: 'bis ganz am Ende (55 ff.), wo der Predigtton einsetzt und der Bearbeiter jede Maske ablegt'.

the assurance with which scholars separated the late from the early, and also the value attached by them to each of the two parts:[150]

> This piece consists of two parts, the Lament of an Ancient Scóp, whom war and destruction had driven from the 'mead-hall' of his chieftain, and from his country, and lines by a later hand, in which what remains of the poem itself is enchased as a precious stone, or preserved as a relic.

M. Rieger's analysis of *The Wanderer* is far more subtle. He distinguished the pagan outlook of the Wanderer himself from the Christian outlook of the poet:[151]

> The poem is, as it were, framed by two interrelated religious ideas. It begins with the sentence: 'Often a man pursued by misfortune experiences help, God's mercy.' The end reverts to this beginning: 'Well is it with him who seeks help and consolation with the Father in heaven, from whom all comfort comes to us.' Thus the poet, when he speaks in his own name, confesses himself to the belief that God is the hope and the comfort of the unhappy. It is different with the speaker whom he introduces in his poem. He does not speak of God at all; on the other hand he speaks of Fate.... The *eardstapa* lacks altogether any religious conception of his lot. He never thinks of the sin for which God is punishing him, of the penance to which God is calling him, of the eternal bliss which God has promised to those who repent. He understands only that proud manliness with which the pagan knows how to suffer in silence, and the comfortless contemplation of the vanity of

---

[150] Klipstein, *Analecta Anglo-Saxonica*, II, p. 431.
[151] M. Rieger, 'Über Cynewulf. III', *Zeitschrift für deutsche Philologie* i (1869), p. 329: 'Das gedicht ist zwischen zwei einander verwante religiöse gedanken gewissermassen eingerahmt. Es hebt an mit dem satze: oft erlebt der vom unglück verfolgte hilfe, gottes erbarmung; und zu diesem anfang kehrt der schluss zurück: wol dem, der hilfe und trost bei dem vater im himmel sucht, von dem uns alle stärkung kommt. So bekennt sich also der dichter, wo er im eignen namen spricht, zu dem glauben, dass gott die hoffnung und der trost der unglücklichen sei. Anders die person, die er redend einführt. Sie spricht überhaupt nicht von gott, wol aber vom schicksal. . . . dem *eardstapa* fehlt überhaupt jede religiöse auffassung seines looses, jeder gedanke an die sünde, um die ihn gott heimsucht, an die busse zu der ihn ruft, an die ewige freude, die er dem bussfertigen verheisst. Er kennt nur den stolzen mannessinn, mit dem der heide lautlos zu dulden weiss, und die trostlose betrachtung der eitelkeit alles irdischen sowie der allgemeinen vernichtung, der die welt zueilt. Nicht einmal diese letztere ist ein besonderer gedanke des christentums, auch der heide glaubte einen weltwinter und eine götterdämmerung. Dieser gewiss bemerkenswerte umstand also, dass nur die epische einkleidung, nicht der lyrische kern des gedichtes christlich-religiöse wendungen enthält, lässt sich auf zweierlei weise erklären. Entweder sind diese wendungen nur ein tribut an das herkommen, an die christliche sitte, die auch der volksmässigen dichtung mächtig geworden war; oder der dichter hat einem früher gedichteten liede die epische einkleidung erst nach der zeit seiner religiösen erweckung zugefügt.'

everything on earth, the contemplation also of the universal destruction to which the world hastens. Not even this last idea is peculiar to Christianity; pagans likewise believed in a world-winter and a twilight of the gods. This, surely remarkable fact, that only the epic outer dress, not the lyric core of the poem, contains Christian religious expressions, may be explained in two ways. Either these expressions are merely a tribute to what is customary, to Christian etiquette that came to have a hold on folk-poetry; or, after the time of his own religious awakening, the poet added this epic dress to a song he had composed earlier.

The variety of style in *The Seafarer* is even more marked than in *The Wanderer*. F. Kluge analysed the poem thus:[152]

> The dialogue between the Old Seafarer and the Youth ends, I think, at line 64a. The rest of the poem likewise contains several heterogeneous elements. At all events, lines 80b–93 are the work of an elegiast who is not merely competent technically as a poet, but also reveals his forceful idealism in a comparison of the mighty past with the petty present. He draws an impressive contrast between the generation, now dead, which aspired to lofty aims and practised deeds worthy of fame, and the living generation of weaklings toiling till weary. We may suppose that the poet of these lines had more to say about ideal and reality, for he introduces us to a situation, of whose exposition the homilist has robbed us. Lines 91–3 contain the beginning of a situation the treatment of which Anglo-Saxon poets often attempted. . . . I can find no connection between lines 80–93 and what follows; yet it is obvious that the mention of death (*eorðan forgiefene* line 93) offered to the homilist a convenient peg for his edifying unbosomings. This short passage is such a pleasant contrast to the homilist's hackneyed theological subject-matter and prose formulas that it must have been composed by a different man.

[152] F. Kluge, 'Zu altenglischen dichtungen. I. Der Seefahrer', *Englische Studien* vi (1883), pp. 325–6: 'Den dialog zwischen dem alten seefahrer und dem jüngling schliesse ich also mit v. 64 resp. 65. Der rest des damit in zusammenhang gebrachten stückes enthält auch mehrere heterogene elemente. Jedenfalls gehören v. 80a [*sic*]–93 einem elegiker an, der nicht bloss die poetische technik beherrscht, sondern auch einen idealen schwung in der vergleichung einer grossen vergangenheit mit einer kleinlichen gegenwart verräth. Der gegensatz einer ausgestorbenen generation, die hohen zielen nachstrebte und ruhmeswerthe thaten übte, und dem lebenden geschlecht von schwächlingen, das sich abarbeitet, wird eindringlich zur darstellung gebracht, und es lässt sich vermuthen dass der dichter dieser zeilen mehr über das thema von ideal und wirklichkeit zu sagen hatte; denn er führt uns in eine situation hinein, deren ausführung der homilet uns entrissen hat: V. 91–93 enthalten den anfang einer situation in deren behandlung angelsächsische dichter sich gern versuchten. . . . Beziehung der v. 80–93 zum folgenden kann ich nirgends finden; doch ist es augenfällig, dass die erwähnung des todes (eorðan forgiefene v. 93) dem homileten eine bequeme anknüpfung für seine erbauliche expectoration ergab. Aber gegen seine theologischen alltagsthemata und prosaformeln sticht jene kleine partie so vortheilhaft ab, dass sie einen eigenen verfasser haben muss.'

E. Sieper divided *The Seafarer* at line 58:[153]

> It is quite impossible to suppose that the poet, who in the first half shows his mastery of the ancient art of versification, should later on in the poem have composed such ponderous lines; and that a poet, who writes of his subject with such lively sensitiveness and complete concentration, should now suddenly degenerate into the unbounded diffuseness of edifying garrulity. In the first half of the poem we have true poetry which will at once move every perceptive reader. In the second half we have pious talk which is not the product of artistic necessity but the result of a desire to instruct and convert.

Even in Sieper's 'genuine' first half he detected impurities:[154]

> [Lines 39–43] are, for reasons of metre and subject-matter, to be regarded as interpolated. The general reflection does not fit into a personal poem. The double mention of *dryhten* is particularly suspicious. I regard as interpolations all those passages in the older elegies in which *dryhten* refers to the Christian God.

Miss Wardale echoes Sieper in a remark on the Charm *For a Sudden Stitch* (line 28), 'Obviously the term "Lord" is an addition of the scribes.'[155] In the context of the Charm, however, there may perhaps be greater justification for the view that the last three words, which include the word *dryhten*, are not part of the original. Miss Wardale's own views on *The Wanderer* and *The Seafarer* provide an exceptionally clear example of circular argument:[156]

> If the view is accepted that the Prologue and Epilogue of the Wanderer are later additions and that the real Seafarer consists of the first sixty-four lines only, it is clear that the outlook on life in both is purely pagan. Any Christian touches which appear in either are quite

---

[153] Sieper, *Die altenglische Elegie*, p. 191: 'Es ist schlechthin unmöglich, anzunehmen, daß der Autor, der sich in der ersten Hälfte als ein Meister der alten Verstechnik verrät, im weiteren Fortgange seines Gedichtes solch ungefüge Verse verfaßt habe und daß ein Dichter, der mit solch reger Einfühlungsfähigkeit und vollkommener Konzentration seinen Gegenstand behandelt, nun plötzlich in die uferlose Breite erbaulicher Geschwätzigkeit verfällt. Im ersten Teile des Gedichtes haben wir wahre Poesie, die jeden empfänglichen Menschen unmittelbar ergreift. Im zweiten Teile haben wir frommes Gerede, das nicht aus künstlerischer Nötigung, sondern aus dem Verlangen zu belehren und zu bekehren hervorgegangen ist.'

[154] Sieper, *Die altenglische Elegie*, pp. 193–4: '. . . v. 39–43 und 55b bis 57. Die erste Stelle ist aus metrischen und inhaltlichen Gründen als interpoliert zu betrachten. Die allgemeine Reflexion fällt aus dem Rahmen des Individualgedichtes heraus. Die zweimalige Erwähnung von *dryhten* ist besonders verdächtig. Alle Stellen der ältern Elegien, in denen *dryhten* auf dem Christengott bezüglich erscheint, halte ich für interpoliert.'

[155] Wardale, *Chapters on Old English Literature*, p. 25.

[156] Wardale, *Chapters on Old English Literature*, p. 61.

out of character and must be looked upon as later insertions, probably due to the scribe who added the continuation of the Seafarer.

What she means by 'out of character' is shown by her remarks on *The Wanderer*:[157] 'Five lines end the poem, lines of little poetic value and of a marked didactic and Christian character.'

G.K. Anderson's remarks on the two poems show that such views may not be dead:[158]

> *The Seafarer*, with its celebration of the sea, is an indestructable tribute to the mariners of England. . . . Still, it is reasonably clear that *The Seafarer*, for all its pagan vitality, did not escape the almost inevitable Christian adulteration.

And similarly:[159]

> *The Wanderer* and *The Seafarer* obtrude their moralizing most unscrupulously upon the lyric mood; and what is true of these poems is true in greater or less degree of the other important pieces of Old English elegiac verse.

The other elegies are not quite so easily dissected, though lines 28–34 of *Deor* (which, among other elements that aroused suspicion, contain *dryhten*) were denied a place in the poem by most of the early commentators. Karl Müllenhoff's views on the poem were widely accepted:[160]

> The last stanza . . . has been provided with an introduction of at least seven lines (28–34); their author, probably a cleric, wished to remind his audience of the providential alternation of good fortune and bad fortune as a consolation for the unfortunate; but he expressed himself so awkwardly that according to his wording the consolation would have to consist in other people's good fortune. . . . If we delete these pitiful lines with their wretched repetition of the same expressions . . . there still remains a stanza of seven lines.

Half a century later Brandl rejected the same lines:[161]

---

[157] Wardale, *Chapters on Old English Literature*, p. 43.
[158] Anderson, *Literature of the Anglo-Saxons*, p. 161.
[159] Anderson, *Literature of the Anglo-Saxons*, p. 168.
[160] K. Müllenhoff, 'Zur kritik des angelsächsischen volksepos. I. Deors klage', *Zeitschrift für deutsches Alterthum* xi (1859), pp. 274–5: 'die letzte strophe . . . hat eine einleitung von mindestens sieben zeilen v. 28–34 erhalten, worin wahrscheinlich ein geistlicher zum trost für unglückliche an den providentiellen wechsel von glück und unglück erinnern wollte, aber so ungeschickt sich ausdrückte daß nach seinen worten der trost in dem glück das andern zu theil wird bestehen müste. . . . streichen wir diese kümmerlichen zeilen mit ihren armseligen wiederholungen derselben ausdrücke . . . so bleibt noch eine strophe von sieben zeilen übrig'.
[161] Brandl, 'Geschichte der altenglischen Literatur', I, Angelsächsische Periode, in Paul (ed.), *Grundriss der germanischen Philologie*, II, 2nd edn, VI/6 § 18, p. 975 (= p. 35 of separate): 'sie passen durchaus nicht in die Komposition herein,

They do not at all fit into the composition and are among the most certainly interpolated passages that can be discovered in Anglo-Saxon poetry; but they may have been the immediate cause why so personal an occasional poem should have been written down and preserved.

Émile Legouis, in spite of his conscious resistance to German scholarship, was sufficiently influenced by it to generalize the kind of remark made by Brandl specifically of *Deor*:[162]

> The Anglo-Saxon literature which has reached us is, on the whole, the work of clerks who lived from the seventh to the eleventh century. If they did not create all of it, they preserved it all. It is therefore an essentially Christian literature. The editors allowed nothing to survive which seemed to them to conflict formally with their religion. Hence came a vast elimination of which we cannot even conjecture the importance. Hence also arose modifications and amplifications of such of the old legends as were not sacrificed, changes which gave them an edifying turn certainly not theirs originally.

Those elegies in which critics failed to find any interpolations provided them with an opportunity of reminding their readers that such textual purity is exceptional. Thus Sieper, in whose book this is a particularly common method of praise, wrote of *The Wife's Lament*:[163] 'The poem has been spared the interpolations and additions with which a Christian scribe sinned against his exemplar in *Deor*, *The Wanderer*, and *The Seafarer*.'

Bearing in mind statements such as that, it seems surprising and perhaps even generous that Sieper was willing to concede that Christianity need not have been entirely disastrous to the elegy. It is his general, underlying thesis that the Old English elegy 'had its roots in pagan burial ritual'.[164] He had this to say of the influence of Christianity on this genre:[165]

---

gehören zu den sichersten Interpolationen, die man in ags. Poesie aufdecken kann, waren aber vielleicht der Anlass, dass ein so privates Gelegenheitsgedicht aufgezeichnet und gerettet wurde.'

[162] Legouis, in Legouis and Cazamian, *A History of English Literature*, I, *The Middle Ages and the Renascence*, p. 3.

[163] E. Sieper, *Die altenglische Elegie* (1915), p. 223: 'Das Gedicht ist von den Interpolationen und Zutaten verschont geblieben, mit denen sich in Dêors Klage, in Wanderer und Seefahrer ein christlicher Schreiber an seiner Vorlage versündigt hat.'

[164] Sieper, *Die altenglische Elegie*, p. xiii: 'Im heidnischen Ritual der Bestattung wurzelnd'.

[165] Sieper, *Die altenglische Elegie*, pp. 15–16: 'An einer Dichtungsart, die mit dem heidnischen Rituale in so enger Verknüpfung stand und aus den heidnischen Vorstellungen vom Walten des Schicksals gewissermaßen herausgeboren wurde, konnte die Einführung des Christentums nicht spurlos vorübergehen. Wir brauchen nicht ohne weiteres anzunehmen, dass der Einfluß des Christentums ein verderblicher gewesen sein müsse. Die Epik bietet uns ja ein Beispiel, wie eine Dichtungsart, ursprünglich altheidnischen Lebensverhältnissen entwachsend,

The introduction of Christianity could not completely ignore a poetic genre which was so closely connected with pagan ritual and which is, as it were, born of pagan notions of the governance of Fate. Yet we need not immediately assume that the influence of Christianity was of necessity disastrous. After all, epic poetry provides us with an example of a genre which outgrew the original, ancient, pagan conditions of life, and yet was capable of further development at a time when Christianity had radically changed former conceptions. The ideals of the ancient Germanic *comitatus*: loyalty even unto death, deeds in which might holds sway, battle, victory, glory, these indeed were not unknown in Christian salvation-history.

Sieper was willing to concede that, but no more:[166]

> the Christian scribe who thought himself called upon to alter or enlarge the old texts was neither a poet nor even a man gifted with poetic sensibility. . . . His interpolations are in every case not so much transformations as disfigurations of the original poems.

There were, however, critics who accepted that Christianity was part of some of the elegies that have come down to us. As early as 1877 Bernhard ten Brink had accepted the Christian elements of *The Wanderer* and *The Seafarer*. In *The Wanderer* ten Brink commended 'the manly resignation with which the hero locks his grief in his own breast',[167] and, pointing to the very end of the poem, he added that 'Christianity supplemented this resignation with the solace which springs from faith in God's providence.'[168] According to ten Brink:[169]

---

auch unter den gänzlich veränderten Anschauungen des Christentums sich weiter entfalten konnte. Die Ideale des altgermanischen Gefolgschaftswesens: – Treue bis an den Tod, kraftgewaltiges Wirken, Kampf, Überwindung, Triumph – waren ja auch der christlichen Heilsgeschichte nicht fremd.'

[166] Sieper, *Die altenglische Elegie*, p. 17: '. . . daß der christliche Schreiber, der sich berufen glaubte, die alten Texte zu verändern, bzw. zu erweitern, weder ein Poet war, noch auch die Gabe der poetischen Nachempfindung besaß . . . seine Interpolationen, die in jedem Falle nicht sowohl eine Umwandlung als vielmehr eine Verunzierung der ursprünglichen Gedichte bedeuten . . .'.

[167] Ten Brink, *Early English Literature*, p. 62. Cf. the original version: *Geschichte der Englischen Litteratur*, I, p. 79: 'die männliche Resignation, das Verschließen des Grames in der eignen Brust'.

[168] Ten Brink, *Early English Literature*, p. 63. Cf. ten Brink, *Geschichte der Englischen Litteratur*, I, p. 80: 'Das Christenthum fügte diesem Gedanken den Trost hinzu, der aus dem Vertrauen auf die Fügung Gottes entspringt.'

[169] Ten Brink, *Early English Literature*, p. 63. Cf. ten Brink, *Geschichte der Englischen Litteratur*, I, p. 80: 'Im Seefahrer, der von christlichen Anschauungen ganz durchzogen erscheint, wird der Gegensatz zwischen den Leiden und Schrecken der einsamen Seereise und der Sehnsucht, die trotzdem im Frühling das Herz zur See hintreibt, in Beziehung gesetzt zu dem Gegensatz zwischen der Vergänglichkeit des Erdenlebens und dem ewigen Jubel des Himmels, den man sich durch kühnes Streben erringen soll.'

The *Seafarer* is quite permeated by Christian views: the contrast of the pains and terrors of the lonely sea-voyage with the longing which yet impels the heart to the sea in spring, is opposed to the contrast of this perishable earthly life with the eternal jubilee of heaven to be won by bold endeavour.

Sieper was troubled by ten Brink's analysis of the poem.[170] He acknowledged that the author of the second half of the poem must have thought it somehow connected with the first half; but Sieper refused to see the poem as a unity. His reasons are fundamentally subjective:[171]

> the author of the first half does at all events reveal himself as a true poet. If he himself had had the idea of applying to the Christian life the contrast of which he had written [in the first he half], his poetic power would have enabled him to bestow on this idea a truly poetic, tangible form. However, the subject-matter of the second half is so inconsistent, and it is poetically so inferior that we cannot possibly ascribe it to the poet of the first half. The same considerations apply also in part to EHRISMANN, who has again, in a recent, very remarkable essay, attempted to explain the poem as a work resulting from a single artistic conception.

Gustav Ehrismann's article was not, however, to be dismissed quite so readily.[172] Unlike Sieper's work, Ehrismann's is short, but it contains the beginnings of much that has been written in the last few years about *The Seafarer*, so that it almost seems as if recent writers on the poem have fetched their cart-loads of examples to underpin Ehrismann's royal edifice. He wrote of the poet of *The Seafarer*:[173]

---

[170] Sieper, *Die altenglische Elegie*, pp. 187–8.

[171] Sieper, *Die altenglische Elegie*, pp. 188–9: '. . . daß sich der Verfasser des ersten Teiles jedenfalls als ein wahrer Dichter verrät. Wäre ihm selbst der Gedanke gekommen, dem von ihm behandelten Gegensatz eine Anwendung auf das christliche Leben zu geben, so hätte ihn seine Dichterkraft befähigt, diesem Gedanken anschauliche, wirklich poetische Form zu geben. Die Verse des zweiten Teiles sind aber inhaltlich so wenig konsistent und poetisch so minderwertig, daß wir sie unmöglich dem Dichter des ersten Teiles zutrauen dürfen. Dieselben Erwägungen richten sich zum Teil auch gegen Ehrismann, der in einem recht bemerkenswerten Aufsatz das Gedicht unlängst noch einmal als das Werk einer einheitlichen künstlerischen Konzeption zu erklären versucht hat.'

[172] G. Ehrismann, 'Religionsgeschichtliche beiträge zum germanischen frühchristentum. II. Das gedicht vom Seefahrer', *Beiträge zur Geschichte der deutschen Sprache und Literatur* xxxv (1909), pp. 213–18.

[173] Ehrismann, 'Religionsgeschichtliche beiträge', p. 216: 'Er arbeitet, wie jeder germanische durchschnitts-scop, durchaus gebunden. Aus überlieferten anschauungen und mit überlieferten formalen mitteln setzt er sein lied zusammen. In seinem vortragsrepertoire besitzt er das motiv von der gefahrvollen seefahrt als bild für die menschlichen mühsale, das motiv von der ausfahrt im frühjahr mit der seelenstimmung der sehnsucht, er findet dort vorgebildet das leben des edelings als höchsten ausdruck für die freude am dasein, und findet ebenso die vergänglichkeit

Like that of every Germanic *scop* of average competence his work is bound in tradition. He has put his poem together by drawing on traditional conceptions and by using formal means which were traditional. In his repertoire there exists the topos of the perilous sea-voyage as a figure for human hardships, the topos of departure in spring connected with the longing of the soul; there is available for his use the topos of the nobleman's life as the highest expression of the joy in existence, and he finds there also the themes of mutability of things on earth and the arrogance of the rich. Out of all this he constructs lines 1–102 of his poem, and he does so in epic language, which is likewise traditional, and which he has learnt. The folk-epic, however, provides no model for the religious teaching of the end of the poem; for the phrases of the end he is indebted to gnomic and homiletic writings, which he follows perhaps even more slavishly.

The work of Ehrismann, like that of Klaeber a few years later, made the hackneyed questions, spurious or genuine?, Christian or pagan?, seem irrelevant to a true understanding of the literature to which it was applied. Andreas Heusler strove to direct scholarly inquiry into a more fruitful line of approach:[174]

> We should not ask the question, 'Pagan or Christian?' These songs [*Deor, The Wanderer, The Seafarer, The Wife's Lament, The Husband's Message, Wulf and Eadwacer*] are entirely Christian. . . . We can only distinguish 'secular and ecclesiastical'.

Yet Heusler, because he felt the disunity of tone, went on to speak of additions:[175]

> If we recognize the edifying passages in *Deor*, and especially in *The Wanderer* and *The Seafarer*, as additions, then all six poems are secular in subject-matter and mood. . . . The songs themselves reveal no

---

des irdischen wie den übermut der reichen vor. Daraus setzt er die verse 1–102 seines gedichtes zusammen und zwar in der ihm ebenfalls überlieferten, angelernten epischen sprache. Für den schluss aber, für die geistlichen lehren, hat er keinen anhalt in der volksepik, hierfür nimmt er die ausdrücke, womöglich noch sclavischer, aus der gnomik . . . und aus der predigt.'

[174] A. Heusler, *Die altgermanische Dichtung*, in O. Walzel (ed.), *Handbuch der Literaturwissenschaft*, XI (Berlin–Neubabelsberg, 1923), p. 140, 2nd edn (Potsdam, 1943 [copyright given as 1941]), p. 146: 'Die Frage "heidnisch oder christlich?" sollte man nicht stellen: diese Lieder sind ganz und gar christlich . . . Nur "weltlich und kirchlich" kann man sondern.'

[175] Heusler, *Die altgermanische Dichtung* (1923), p. 140, (1943), p. 146: 'Erkennt man die erbaulichen Teile in Sängers Trost und namentlich in Wandrer und Seefahrer als Zutaten an, dann sind die Lieder alle sechs weltlich nach Stoff und Stimmung. . . . Die Lieder selbst kennen keinen Weltschmerz, ihre Klage gilt nicht dem Leben als Jammertal, sondern ganz bestimmten Schicksalen.

'Dies schließt geistliche Urheberschaft nicht aus. Mit weltlicher würde sich bei Sängers Trost und der Wulfklage der Stil vertragen.'

weltschmerz; their lament is not directed to life as in this vale of tears, but to quite specific fates.

This does not exclude the assumption of clerical authorship. The style of *Deor* and of *Wulf and Eadwacer* would agree well with the assumption of secular authorship.

Heusler's discussion of these poems shows that the emphasis was changing, and Christianity was being accepted as a part of that aspect of Germanic civilization known to us through Anglo-Saxon literature. Even so, as late as 1927, E.V. Gordon was able to say:[176] 'The fashion of distinguishing heathen and Christian elements in Old English poetry now seems to be well established.' And Miss Wardale's account of the seven elegies in the Exeter Book demonstrates that Gordon was right:[177]

> All must be early, for all are essentially heathen in character. This is seen in the kind of fatalistic acquiescence which runs through Deor's Lament, in the belief in the irresistible power of Fate which pervades the Wanderer, and in the absence of any Christian thought in the others. A later scribe has occasionally substituted a Christian for a heathen term, and probably it is such a scribe who has added a long passage of didactic nature at the end of the Seafarer, but such words or passages betray their later date by being out of harmony with the rest of the matter.

(iii) *Gnomic Poems*

Scholarly treatment of the Old English *Gnomic Poems* ran along parallel lines. The certainty of being in contact with something very primitive made scholars equally certain that all Christian elements in them must be spurious, so that they wielded the pruning-hook, if anything, with even greater assurance than in the case of the elegies. Brandl provides a good example in his criticism of the Cotton *Gnomes*:[178]

---

[176] E.V. Gordon, *The Year's Work in English Studies* for 1925 (reviewing É. Pons, *Le théme et le sentiment de la nature dans la poésie anglo-saxonne*), p. 70.

[177] Wardale, *Chapters on Old English Literature*, pp. 29–30.

[178] Brandl, 'Geschichte der altenglischen Literatur', I, Angelsächsische Periode, in Paul (ed.), *Grundriss der germanischen Philologie*, II, 2nd edn, VI/6 § 11, p. 960 (= p. 20 of separate): 'Er hebt an mit einer Lehre von den übermenschlichen Mächten, wobei neben dem Christentum noch deutlich die Mythe durchklingt. Da steht voran der König, den sich ja der Angelsachse nach dem Zeugnis Bedas stets als Nachkommen Wodans, also göttlicher Herkunft, dachte; neben ihm erscheinen die Riesen, der Wind, der Donner und das Schicksal; die vier Jahreszeiten reihen sich an, samt Wahrheit, Goldschatz, Altersweisheit und Schmerz: "die Wolken schreiten" (v. 1–13). Mitten in diesem heidnischen Natursystem erstaunt uns der Satz "die Machttaten Christi sind gross"; wir hören den Missionar seinen Gott als den gewaltigsten verkünden, während er Wodan und Donar zu Himmelserscheinungen zurückschraubt; bald wird er sich auch an den König wagen und

The poet begins by teaching of superhuman powers, and here, next to Christianity, the ancient myths clearly chime on. First comes the king, and, according to Bede's testimony, the Anglo-Saxons at all times thought of kings as the descendants of Woden, and thus of divine lineage; beside the king, giants, wind, thunder, and fate appear, followed in turn by the seasons, together with truth, gold-treasure, the wisdom of old age, and woe: 'the clouds go their way' (lines 1–13). In the middle of this pagan natural order the sentence, 'Christ's mighty deeds are great,' astounds us; we hear the missionary proclaiming his god as the mightiest, at the same time depressing Woden and Thunor into meteorological phenomena: it will not be long before he has the audacity to assail the king himself and force him from his position as the first, nay, force him out from the superhuman sphere to which he belongs. . . . Throughout the poem two elements have been visibly fused: a pagan and courtly core, and some redactor's piously Christian additions.

Blanche C. Williams in her edition of the Old English Gnomic Poems put forward similar views.[179] Her Introduction includes an analysis of the gnomic passages in the Elegies. She has a note on *The Wanderer* line 112a (*Til bið se þe his treowe gehealdeð*) in which she says that the half-line 'is a kind usually found in passages suspiciously Christian'.[180] Her criticism of *The Gifts of Men* is characteristic of her book:[181]

> Lines 1–29 are obviously the composition of a monk, as are also 103–113, the homiletic close, besides 86–95 in the heart of the poem. The remainder have a heathen ring; they have at best no reference to tokens and symbols of Christianity, but celebrate harp-playing, seamanship, smithcraft, and the like. . . . A dilemma arises, therefore: did a monkish redactor prefix his beginning and add his conclusion to a gnomic poem of heathen origin? Or did he compose the whole poem, extending the *sum* type which he knew from Christian sources?

She subjects the Cotton *Gnomes* to the same treatment, though her conclusions are different:[182]

> It is not, I believe, an old heathen poem redacted, but one written entire by a learned monk, who was not so lost in his bookish Christianity that he had not sufficient appreciation of secular gifts to include them with the spiritual.

ihn von der ersten Stelle, überhaupt aus der übermenschlichen Sphäre wegschieben. . . . Im ganzen Gedicht sind ersichtlich zweierlei Elemente zusammengeflossen: ein heidnisch-höfischer Kern und christlich-fromme Zutaten eines Überarbeiters.'

[179] B.C. Williams (ed.), *Gnomic Poetry in Anglo-Saxon*, Columbia University Studies in English and Comparative Literature (New York, 1914).
[180] Williams, *Gnomic Poetry*, p. 46.
[181] Williams, *Gnomic Poetry*, p. 53.
[182] Williams, *Gnomic Poetry*, p. 57.

The phrase 'not so lost in his bookish Christianity' shows her attitude, as does her use of adjectives in her remarks on the Vercelli *Homiletic Fragment* and the Exeter poem *Vainglory* (which she calls *Monitory Poem*):[183]

> [*The Homiletic Fragment*] is . . . merely a fragment of a homily based on the twenty-eighth Psalm, and it has scarcely a vestige of gnomic expression left in its desultory didacticism. In this, and in the *Monitory Poem*, crisp heathen teaching, definite precepts of morality, brief bits of philosophy, – all have lengthened into a homiletic dullness. The ancient current leaped and dashed in sudden vigorous bursts; the later stream dissipates its energy in the shallow flats of homily, level and monotonous.

The tone of her comments on *Solomon and Saturn* is no different:[184]

> Germanic wisdom . . . has been 'touched up' by the Christian artist, but the original picture is clear under the Christian varnish.

B. *The Search for Germanic Antiquities*

So far we have dealt with only the first of the two major activities on which the *Anglisten* of the late nineteenth and the early twentieth century spent their energies: the freeing of what were thought the genuine remains of Germanic poetry from Christian accretions and excrescences. The second major activity in which the programme and thesis-mongers trained in the German universities were engaged, especially at Leipzig under Richard Paul Wülker, was to search for Teutonic antiquities and pagan remains both in poetry like *Beowulf* and the Old English elegies (regarded by them as pagan in origin) and also in poetry the subject matter of which was indisputably Christian. Their work followed the example of Grimm's investigation of *Andreas* and *Elene* and Vilmar's of *Heliand*. Typical investigations of this kind include those of Köhler (1868) on *Beowulf*, Kent (1887) on *Andreas* and *Elene*, Rau (1889) on *Exodus*, Ferrell (1893) on *Genesis* and (1894) on *The Wanderer* and *The Seafarer*, Price (1896) on the Cynewulfian poetry, and Brincker (1898) on *Judith*.[185] Later work, similar in direction but wider in scope and

---

[183] Williams, *Gnomic Poetry*, pp. 58–9.
[184] Williams, *Gnomic Poetry*, p. 65
[185] A. Köhler, 'Germanische Alterthümer im Beóvulf', *Germania* xiii = new series i (1868), pp. 129–58; C.W. Kent, *Teutonic Antiquities in Andreas and Elene* (Halle, 1887), a doctoral dissertation of the University of Leipzig; M. Rau, *Germanische Altertümer in der Angelsächsischen Exodus*, a doctoral dissertation of the University of Leipzig (Leipzig–Reudnitz, 1889); Ferrell, *Teutonic Antiquities in the Anglo-Saxon Genesis*, a doctoral dissertation of the University of Leipzig, and C.C. Ferrell, 'Old Germanic Life in the Anglo-Saxon "Wanderer"

therefore more fruitful, includes Bartels's investigation (1913) of the legal antiquities in the whole of Old English poetry, and Müller's investigation (1914) of *Beowulf*.[186]

Germanic society as described by Tacitus was central in these studies. The 'ethnographical romanticism' of Tacitus corresponded to the sentiments of these late nineteenth- and early twentieth-century investigators, so that they failed to see the weakness of the *Germania* as historical evidence for this specific purpose, a weakness brought out by G. Ekholm in his discussion of the *Germania*:[187]

> A further weakness in the work, though a very explicable one, is that the Roman author, who had himself seen the dark sides of civilization at close quarters – the reign of terror under Domitian – sometimes unconsciously idealizes in his description of the unspoiled children of nature. As has been shown, this 'ethnographical romanticism,' despite its Rousseauist character, is also old and ultimately has its roots in the Stoic conception of the baleful influence of culture on mankind.

Especially those chapters of the *Germania* dealing with the limitations of royal power and with the Germanic king and his comitatus proved fruitful for comparison with accounts in Old English poetry. Thus Ferrell, whose exceptionally naïve statements not infrequently lay bare critical attitudes which are present, though less clearly exposed, in the critical writings of his contemporaries, had this to say of the position of the king as he appears in *Genesis*:[188]

> As the king is the friend *wine* (v. 1194, 2817) of his people, so he is the joy of the young men, *hægstealdra wyn* (v. 1862). We can imagine what joy the youthful warriors must have experienced in associating with and emulating the worthy example of a chieftain who, as Tacitus (*Germania*, Cap. xiv) informs us, could not at the risk of incurring ignominy, allow himself to be surpassed in valor by any of his followers.

---

and "Seafarer"', *Modern Language Notes* ix (1894), pp. 201–4 (= cols 402–7); M.B. Price, *Teutonic Antiquities in the Generally Acknowledged Cynewulfian Poetry* (Leipzig, 1896), a doctoral dissertation of the University of Leipzig; F. Brincker, *Germanische Altertümer in dem angelsächsischen Gedichte 'Judith'*, Wissenschaftliche Beilage zum Bericht über das Schuljahr 1897–1898, Realschule vor dem Lübeckerthore zu Hamburg (Hamburg, 1898).

[186] A. Bartels, *Rechtsaltertümer in der angelsächsischen Dichtung* (Kiel, 1913), a doctoral dissertation of Kiel University; J. Müller, *Das Kulturbild des Beowulfepos*, Studien zur englischen Philologie LIII, originally a doctoral dissertation of the University of Göttingen.

[187] G. Ekholm, 'The *Germania* and the Civilization of the Germani', in *Cambridge Ancient History*, XI (Cambridge, 1936), II, v, p. 68.

[188] Ferrell, *Teutonic Antiquities in the Anglo-Saxon Genesis*, p. 35. Cf. M. Hutton (ed.), revised E.H. Warmington, *Tacitus*, I, The Loeb Classical Library (London and Cambridge, Massachusetts, 1970), 152–3, *Germania*, 14.1.

Ferrell assumed without discussion that Tacitus' description of the structure of Germanic society applies to Anglo-Saxon times. Johannes Müller used *Beowulf* line 73 – that the king distributes everything *buton folcscare ond feorum gumena* (with which he compares *Germania*, ch. vii) – as proof of the 'astonishingly tenacious constancy of Germanic conditions'.[189]

Theodor Schauffler devoted two school-programmes entirely to the connection between the *Germania* and Old Norse and Old English poetry;[190] but he cautiously warned his readers that they must not expect to find in Old Norse and Old English poetry instances of 'the development or continuation of customs reported by Tacitus, but . . . we are dealing rather with analogous conditions or with old customs that have come to life again in changed times'.[191] Even so, the view that Tacitus had described Germanic society as it existed in his day and as it was to exist unchanged for centuries to come was sufficiently prevalent for scholars to protest against it as late as 1935 and 1948. In 1935 Ritchie Girvan wrote:[192]

> I am protesting against the view that *Beowulf* carries us directly to the Germanic pagan past, and I shall endeavour to show that little or no trustworthy evidence of life and manners in the migration period, as distinct from later times, can be derived from the poem.

And with clear reference to the mistaken view that Germanic customs remained unchanged from the time of Tacitus, G.O. Sayles wrote in 1948:[193]

> It is beyond all dispute that the Anglo-Saxons introduced into their new home the principles of Germanic society simply because they were the only ones they knew. This does not, however, imply either that such principles tallied with those described by Tacitus three hundred years earlier or even with those which prevailed among them before they left the Continent.

As regards Old English literature, the view that the Germanic foundations were permanent was not simply a convenience. It was a

---

[189] Müller, *Das Kulturbild*, p. 2: '. . . eine erstaunliche Beharrlichkeit der germanischen Verhältnisse'. Cf. Tacitus, *Germania*, 7.1, ed. Hutton, revised Warmington (1970), pp. 141–2: *nec regibus infinita aut libera potestas*, 'the authority of their kings is not unlimited or arbitrary'.

[190] T. Schauffler, *Zeugnisse zur Germania des Tacitus aus der altnordischen und angelsächsischen Dichtung*, Beilage zum Schulprogramm des Kgl. Realgymnasiums und der Kgl. Realschule Ulm, I (Ulm, 1898), II (Ulm, 1900).

[191] Schauffler, *Zeugnisse zur Germania*, I (1898), p. 3: 'Man wird kaum sagen dürfen, daß es sich um eine Weiterentwicklung und ein Fortleben der von Tacitus berichteten Sitten handelt, sondern vielmehr . . . um analoge Verhältnisse, oder um ein Wiederaufleben unter veränderten Zeitumständen.'

[192] R. Girvan, *Beowulf and the Seventh Century* (London, 1935), p. 32.

[193] G.O. Sayles, *The Medieval Foundations of England* (London, 1948), p. 123.

necessary counterpart to the view that Christianity was an alien intrusion.

Andreas Heusler, in an admirable section devoted to 'the Christian epic', discussed both the nature of Germanic Christian poetry, in which the Christian subject-matter is dressed in the mask and the outward trappings of the noble vocabulary of warriors, and also the nature of the investigations by scholars of the nineteenth century and after, who, mistaking the mask and the trappings for the substance of the poems, thought that the poets are in earnest, not about their Christian subjects, but about their Germanic habiliments:[194]

> The dry *Genesis* is at its juiciest where it swells the account of Lot's deliverance by deploying the 'Germanic battle-style'. The *Exodus*, moreover, transforms the passive flight of the Israelites into a highly warlike action – though, of necessity, they do not actually come to blows: Moses is turned into a shield-bearing leader of troops who sounds the call to battle. Cynewulf contributes a mighty pitched battle against Huns, Goths and Franks to the introduction of the Legend of the Invention of the Cross. . . . The Old Saxon poet of the *Heliand* likewise hangs a vigorous little battle-scene on the only peg offered to him by his source, Peter's sword stroke.

---

[194] A. Heusler, *Die Altgermanische Dichtung* (1923), p. 184, (1943), p. 194: 'Die trockene Genesis wird am saftigsten, wo sie Loths Befreiung mit dem Aufwand des "germanischen Schlachtenstils" anschwellt. . . . Vollends die Exodus verwandelt die tatenlose Judenflucht in eine hochkriegerische Aktion – nur eben das Losschlagen fehlt notgedrungen!; aus Moses macht sie den beschildeten Scharenführer und Streitrufer. Cynewulf steuert zu dem Eingang der Kreuzfindungslegende eine große Feldschlacht bei gegen Hunnen, Goten und Franken. . . . Noch der sächsische Heliand hängt an den einzigen Pflock, den die Vorlage bietet, Petri Schwerthieb, ein eifriges Kampfbildchen.

'Aber auch wo der Schlachtstil ruht, hat man wenigstens die *Worte* ins Kriegeradliche umgesetzt. Nicht immer so grad heraus wie im Eingang des Andreas, der uns die Zwölfboten in aller Form vorstellt als "wackere und kampfeifrige Heerführer, tüchtige Krieger, da wo Schild und Faust auf dem Schlachtfelde den Helm schirmten . . ." Auch nicht vor der Gottheit hält diese Umkleidung: "Es rüstete sich der junge Held, stark und kraftgemut: kühn bestieg er den hohen Galgen" heißt es von Jesus.

'Hätte man Ernst gemacht mit dem Sinn solcher Ausdrücke, so wären Bibel und Legende in Stücke gegangen. Aber unsre Mönche machten nicht Ernst damit. Die Tatsachen in ihren Quellen ließen sie ja gehorsam stehn. Der Heerführer, die Faust und der Helm waren zwar keine Gleichnisrede – dies wäre ein schmerzliches Mißverständnis! – aber eine dünne, durchsichtige Maske. Mehr vor den Lesern des 19. Jahrh. als vor den Hörern des neunten hat der Heliand durch diese hofmännische Nomenklatur einen Schimmer von deutschem Königtum erhalten.'

Footnote: 'Seit Vilmar ist hier das Nachsprechen eine Macht geworden – die Brüder Grimm dachten noch kühler darüber. Bei einem Herausgeber aus der Kriegszeit lesen wir, der Heliand sei ein "kernhaftes Lied deutcher Männlichkeit". Auch ein Sieg des Wortes über den Geist!'

But even where this battle-style is not used, the *words* at least have been transposed into those for noble warriors. Not always so openly as at the beginning of *Andreas* where the Apostles are introduced to us in formal style as 'bold leaders of armies active in the fight, doughty warriors wherever in the field of battle shield and hand protected the helmet. . . .' This transposition does not stop short of God himself, and we learn of Christ, 'The young Hero put on his armour, strong and resolute: boldly he mounted the high gallows' [*Dream of the Rood* lines 39–40].

If the poets had been in earnest about the meaning of such expressions, the bible story and the legends would have gone to pieces. But our monks were not in earnest about it. After all, they dutifully allowed the facts of their sources to stand. Indeed, the army leaders, hand and helmet, were no allegories – that would be a painful misunderstanding! – but they form a thin, diaphanous mask. The *Heliand*, as a result of this courtly vocabulary, has received a sheen of German regality in the view of its nineteenth-century readers rather than in that of its ninth-century listeners.

And Heusler added a footnote:

Since Vilmar the repetition of what he said has been a powerful influence – before him, the brothers Grimm thought less passionately about it. In a war-time [1914–18] editor we read that the *Heliand* is a 'pithy song of German manhood'. What a victory of the word over the spirit!

However, those who pursued their investigations into the Teutonic antiquities supposedly contained in Old English poetry had neither Heusler's range nor his insight into Germanic poetry. They lacked also the qualities which made Grimm's Introduction to *Andreas und Elene* and Vilmar's programme on *Heliand* great: they followed Grimm and Vilmar, often with dutiful simple-mindedness.

C.W. Kent, whose subject is the same as Grimm's, outlined the method:[195]

I desire to follow the path which Grimm opened in his preface to Andreas and Elene . . . , in order to gather some additional facts to group with those noted by him and thus to form a picture, however incomplete, of the customs and manners of the Teutonic inhabitants of England. . . .

First of all, it is the religious conceptions that are of special interest. . . . The poems that are to be discussed treat of themes drawn from a new religion which had gained easy access and found almost universal acceptance, but had not been able to eradicate the mythological conceptions that had intertwined their roots with the very fibres of the Teutonic nature, and was even the less powerful to erase from the

---

[195] Kent, *Teutonic Antiquities in Andreas and Elene*, pp. 1–2.

current language words and expressions born of other beliefs nurtured by constant use and which prevail to some extent today.

After this it is hardly surprising to find Kent following Grimm's most Romantic theories, asserting [like Grimm, see pp. 19–20, above] that the expressions *hildewoma* and *wiges woma* 'resolve themselves into simple descriptions of the noise attending the movements of Bellona and Mars'.[196] He believed (in a somewhat weakened form) Grimm's mythological explanation of *woma* as 'in all probability a name of Woden, which has lost all of its power except the quality of noise'.[197] The first sign of weakening in the fully mythological interpretations of the pagan vocabulary of Old English verse, as Grimm regarded it, came in Kemble's preface to his edition of *Andreas*:[198]

> For, from internal evidence, it seems to me that the Vercelli poems are not referable to the old and purely epic period. There occurs from time to time something of the poet's own personality, and there is also a more lavish use of ornaments than was required in the truly national epos. To this, probably, similes were originally unknown, being replaced by metaphors: Beówulf has but two, and the much later Nibelunge Nót but two or three: in the Vercelli poems there are several, and one or two which have a smack of abstraction about them strongly indicative of an advanced (and corrupt) state of civilization. A fresh and lively nature, which does not analyse the processes of thought, but trusts itself and its own feeling, can venture, for example, to call a ship a 'sea-bird' without checking itself, and saying that 'it goes along *like* a sea-bird.' Grimm's opinion respecting the antiquity of our poems rests apparently upon the old epic words and phrases which abound in them beyond the common measure, and render them so extremely valuable to the Teutonic scholar. But this seems an insufficient ground for the assumption; since it is probable that these peculiarities belong to the poetical language of the Anglosaxons in contradistinction to their prose, and were kept up by tradition among their scôpas or poets. To this is owing the retention, even in Christian works, of modes of expression which must have had their origin in the heathen feeling, and which, in order to fit them for their new application, are gradually softened down and gain less personal and more abstract significations. The language of poetry is as distinct from that of prose among the Anglosaxons as any two different dialects. . . . It is in fact in their poems that the stubborn nationality of our forefathers shows itself most thoroughly: their prose works are almost always literal translations, and even if original, are deeply imbued with tramontane feelings, derived from the models

---

[196] Kent, *Teutonic Antiquities in Andreas and Elene*, p. 5.
[197] Kent, *Teutonic Antiquities in Andreas and Elene*, p. 5.
[198] J.M. Kemble, *The Poetry of the Codex Vercellensis with an English Translation*, I (London, 1843; Ælfric Society, No. 5, dated 1844), pp. ix–x.

most in vogue. But the epic forms maintained themselves despite of the book-learning which was so overprized; and even translations became originals, from the all-pervading Teutonic spirit which was unconsciously preserved in the forms and phrases of heathen poetry. In the use of these, far more than in the alliterative measure, consists the poetical element, and, without these, the alliteration cannot save a saint's legend from assuming the guise of a dull homily, and being read as such in the churches.

It will well repay the pains to read Grimm's excellent remarks upon this class of words in the introduction to 'Andreas und Elene;' he has collected together from all the Anglosaxon poems the principal expressions for the occurrences of warfare and seafaring, and the superstitious veneration for certain natural phænomena, such as day and night, sunrise, sunset, storms, dreams and death. He has himself shown the heathen character of these expressions, and the epic nature of others which continually occur in some of the poems.

The difference between Grimm and those who followed his example late in the nineteenth century has its beginning in Kemble's statement that 'the all-pervading Teutonic spirit . . . was *unconsciously* preserved in the forms and phrases' found in Old English verse. Doubt in the etymologies themselves came late: by the end of the first quarter of the twentieth century doubt in Grimm's mythological etymologies had, however, become the rule even among those who, like Richard Jente,[199] show themselves ready to look for and find concealed heathenisms in the vocabulary of the Anglo-Saxons. A clear instance of belief in Grimm's etymologies coupled with doubt that the poets who used the words were conscious of their heathen origins comes in Ferrell's discussion of the phrase *hlud hildesweg* (*Genesis* line 1991) and Grimm's explanation of it in *Andreas und Elene*:[200]

> Grimm thinks that this expression contains an allusion to the noise made by the movement of Hild (Bellona), the heathen goddess of war, which must be the correct interpretation; but it is impossible for us to determine whether our poet used it with a consciousness of this origin, or merely as a crystallized phrase to designate the clash of arms and din of battle.

M. Rau similarly investigated the vocabulary of *Exodus*, and his conclusions on *hreopon mearcweardas middum nihtum* (*Exodus* line 168) are as remarkable:[201]

---

[199] R. Jente, *Die mythologischen Ausdrücke im altenglischen Wortschatz*, Anglistische Forschungen LVI (1921). See, for example, Jente's rejection of Grimm's mythological explanation of *woma*, pp. 97–8.

[200] Ferrell, *Teutonic Antiquities in the Anglo-Saxon Genesis*, p. 6. See J. Grimm, *Andreas und Elene* (1840), p. xxxi.

[201] M. Rau, *Germanische Altertümer in der Angelsächsischen Exodus*, p. 8: 'mearcweard

mearcweardas I take to be one of those terms which have their roots in paganism. The borderland, the common land of the marches, did not merely serve to separate neighbouring tribes, but was regarded as 'the unifying principle the hallowing and consecration of which was of the highest importance in our antiquity' (cf. J. Grimm, *Kleinere Schriften*, vol. II, p. 31). The marches stood under the protection of the gods, especially under that of Woden (cf. Kemble, *Saxons in England*, I, 43 and 52). No literary monument survives which mentions the wolves under Woden's special orders as guardians of the marches; but if we consider how firmly Anglo-Saxon popular imagination must have adhered to the idea of the wolves as beasts sacred to the highest god, and further, if we remember the meaning of the march the protection of which was in the hands of this god, we will readily regard the name *mearcweard* as an emanation of pagan religion in that the wolves protect the march under Woden's direction. Thus we find in this word one of those reminiscences of paganism which we owe to the conservatism of language, recalling for us manners and customs that have long disappeared.

In the opinion of these investigators it was not merely linguistic conservatism that allowed the pagan past to gain some place in these Christian poems. As Miss Bentinck Smith said in discussing the groups of poems associated with Cædmon and Cynewulf:[202]

> It is safe to say that, in both groups, there is hardly a single poem of any length and importance in which whole passages are not permeated with the spirit of the untouched *Beowulf*, in which turns of speech,

---

fasse ich als eine jener bezeichnungen auf, deren entstehung im heidentume seine wurzeln hat. Das grenzgebiet, die allen gemeinsam gehörige mark, trennte nicht nur die nachbarstämme, sondern wurde auch als "einigendes princip" betrachtet, "dessen heiligung und weihe unserm altertum aufs höchste angelegen war" [footnote: vgl. J. Grimm, Kleinere Schriften, B. II, 31]. Die mark stand daher unter dem schutze von göttern, und vor allem unter dem Wodens [footnote: vgl. Kemble, Saxons in England, I 43 u. 52]. Es ist uns keine dichtung überliefert, welche die wölfe als hüter der mark im besonderen auftrage Wodens erwähnt. Wenn wir jedoch erwägen, wie fest im angelsächsischen volksgeiste die vorstellung der wölfe als heiliger tiere des höchsten gottes gehaftet haben muss, und ferner der bedeutung der mark eingedenk sind, deren beschützung in der hand dieses gottes lag, so werden wir gern den namen mearcweardas als ausfluss des heidnischen glaubens betrachten, dass die wölfe im auftrage Wodens die mark schützen. So finden wir in diesem worte einen jener nachklänge des heidentums, welche wir dem konservativen geiste der sprache verdanken, die uns an längst verschwundene sitten und gebräuche erinnern kann.' The references are to J. Grimm, 'Deutsche Grenzalterthümer', *Philologische und historische Abhandlungen der Königlichen Akademie der Wissenschaften zu Berlin. Aus dem Jahre 1843* (Berlin, 1845), p. 110, a lecture on Germanic border antiquities, reprinted in *Kleinere Schriften*, II (1865), p. 31, and to J.M. Kemble, *The Saxons in England*, ch. II, 'The Mark', I, pp. 43 and 52.

[202] Bentinck Smith, *Cambridge History of English Literature*, I, p. 63.

ideas, points of view, do not recall an earlier, a fiercer, a more self-reliant and fatalistic age. God the All-Ruler is fate metamorphosed; the powers of evil are identical with those once called giants and elves; the Paradise and Hell of the Christian are as realistic as the Walhalla and the Niflheim of the heathen ancestors.

Miss Bentinck Smith's criticism of *Andreas* gives us a good idea of how she applied her generalities to a specific Christian poem:[203]

> *Andreas* is a romance of the sea. Nowhere else are to be found such superb descriptions of the raging storm, of the successful struggle of man with the powers of the deep. It illustrates, moreover, in an unusual degree, the blending of the old spirit with the new. St Andrew, though professedly a Christian saint, is, in reality, a viking, though crusader in name he is more truly a seafarer on adventure bent. The Christ he serves is an aetheling, the apostles are folctogan – captains of the people – and temporal victory, not merely spiritual triumph, is the goal.

In a context systematically disparaging Christianity the overtones of *merely*, in 'merely spiritual', must be taken to be the intended expression of a characteristic attitude to a saint's life, here desacralized as 'a romance of the sea'.

Such out and out disparagement of the fundamental Christianity of Cynewulf and his 'School' is less common than hostile criticism of the diffuseness and repetitiousness of the poems, combined with praise of the Anglo-Saxon colouring. Adolf Ebert's criticism of the third part of *Christ* is a good example of the kind of thing of which we have had a taste above (pp. 10–13):[204]

> In his description of a subject like the Last Judgement, which is the common property of all Christendom and has been treated of so frequently, our poet, as a result of the strong national consciousness that governs him, nevertheless knows how to achieve originality, at the same time enhancing the liveliness of his effects. Though his description is, in all essentials, in the outlines of the delineation, founded on

---

[203] Bentinck Smith, *Cambridge History of English Literature*, I, p. 54.
[204] Ebert, *Allgemeine Geschichte der Literatur des Mittelalters im Abendlande*, III, p. 51: 'in der Schilderung eines so oft behandelten Gegenstandes, der christliches Gemeingut ist, wie das jüngste Gericht, weiss doch unser Dichter durch die Stärke des ihn beherrschenden Nationalbewusstseins Originalität zu erreichen und zugleich die Lebhaftigkeit der Wirkung zu erhöhen. Ruht auch die Schilderung in allen wesentlichen Momenten, in den Umrissen, der Zeichnung, auf der christlichen Ueberlieferung, so ist doch das Kolorit ein angelsächsisch-nationales. So erscheint Christus wie ein angelsächsiser König, der zu Gericht sitzt, die Engel als seine Degen. . . . Aber auch die Schwächen der Nationaldichtung seines Volks, Weitschweifigkeit und Wiederholungen, zu denen der Stabreim so leicht den Anlass gab sind seiner Darstellung keineswegs fremd geblieben.'

Christian tradition, the colouring is none the less nationally Anglo-Saxon. Thus Christ appears as an Anglo-Saxon king sitting in judgement, with the angels as his thegns. . . . But the weaknesses of the national poetry of his people, diffuseness and repetitions which were so easily occasioned by the alliterative metre, are by no means absent from his presentation.

Ebert's criticism is of course based on a comparison of the Anglo-Saxon poem with Latin treatments of the same subject. This is shown more clearly where an Anglo-Saxon poem is compared by him directly with its source, as is Cynewulf's *Juliana*:[205]

> If we compare Cynewulf's account with that of his source we find that what is characteristically his in the treatment of the material rests on two factors. In the first place he has provided it with an Anglo-Saxon national colouring. Even though he keeps the setting in Nicodemia . . . and the action still takes place at the time of the Emperor Maximian, the prefect appears nevertheless as an Anglo-Saxon reeve, and as such he sits in judgement before the people (line 184): when he meets Juliana's father to confer with him, the two 'battle-strong warriors' lean their spears to rest against each other (lines 63–4); they worship the gods with treasure (*welum weorþian*, line 76); the warlike character of the Germanic peoples which ruled entirely their public life and their imagination presents also the combat with the devil as a fight conducted with shield and helmet against arrows (lines 384–7, 395); the devil incites to battle men drunk with beer at the banquet (lines 486–90). On the other hand, the poet leaves out some of the things that might weaken the national colouring.
>
> In the second place he stresses the saintliness of Juliana more than the Latin account; he presents her from the very beginning as Christ's bride (lines 30–1, 106–7), which is by no means so in the source.

---

[205] Ebert, *Allgemeine Geschichte der Literatur des Mittelalters im Abendlande*, III, p. 54: 'Vergleichen wir die Darstellung Cynewulfs mit der seiner Vorlage, so finden wir, dass die ihm eigenthümliche Behandlung des Stoffes vornehmlich auf zwei Momenten beruht. Einmal hat er demselben ein national-angelsächsisches Kolorit gegeben. Wenn auch die Scene Nicomedien . . . bleibt, und die Handlung zur Zeit Kaiser Maximians spielt, so erscheint doch der Präfect als angelsächsischer Graf, der wie ein solcher vor dem Volke Gericht hält (v. 184); als er mit dem Vater zur Berathung zusammentrifft, lehnen die beiden "kampfstarken" die Speere zusammen (v. 63); sie verehren mit Schätzen (welum weorðian) die Götter (v. 76); die kriegerische Natur der Germanen, die ihr ganzes öffentliches Leben und die Phantasie beherrschte, schildert auch den Kampf mit dem Teufel als einen mit Schild und Helm gegen Pfeile geführten (v. 384 ff., 395); der Teufel reizt die vom Biere Trunkenen zum Streit beim Gelage (v. 486 ff.). Andrerseits lässt der dichter auch weg, was das nationale Kolorit beeinträchtigen könnte.

'Zweitens hebt er die Heiligkeit der Juliana mehr als der Lateinische Bericht hervor, er stellt sie von Anfang an als eine Braut Christi hin (v. 305, 106f.), was in der Vorlage keinswegs geschieht.'

William Strunk, unlike Ebert, found little to praise in the poem:[206]

> the dialogue is undramatic and tedious, especially in the long scene between Juliana and the tempter; the verse frequently lacks vigour; and the entire treatment of the story is bookish, and lacking in those touches of observation or imagination which might have redeemed it from tediousness. . . . Nowhere in the *Juliana* is there any real evidence that the author knew more of the acts and speech of men and women than what he had read in books. Little worse could be said of any poem introducing human figures.

The tone of one of Miss Rosemary Woolf's comments in her recent (and, of course, not anti-Christian) edition of *Juliana* is still the same. She singles out lines 93 ff. and 166 ff. as passages 'which echo a Latin warmth. . . . But these, whilst pleasant in themselves, fit somewhat incongruously into the bleaker atmosphere of the northern poem, and the true native vigour, found occasionally, as at ll. 216 ff, is preferable.'[207]

No doubt, the high praise given to *Judith* owes more than a little to the way in which the poet by the use of the traditional vocabulary gives the impression that he was introducing his heroine into a Germanic ambience. From Henry Sweet's appraisal onwards superlatives are common:[208]

> Mutilated as it is, this poem is one of the finest in the whole range of Anglo-Saxon literature. . . . the whole poem breathes only of triumph and warlike enthusiasm. In constructive skill and perfect command of his foreign subject, the unknown author of *Judith* surpasses both Cædmon and Cynewulf, while he is certainly not inferior to either of them in command of language and metre.

B. ten Brink's praise includes this comment:[209]

> This fragment . . . produces an impression more like that of the national epos, than is the case with any other religious poetry of that epoch. To a lucid, well-constructed narrative are joined epic profusion, vigour, and animation.

A. Ebert thought that *Judith* is 'without doubt the most successful of the poems of this period [Ebert assigned *Judith* to the date of the

---

[206] W. Strunk (ed.), *The Juliana of Cynewulf*, The Belles Lettres Series, Section I English Literature from its Beginnings to the Year 1100 (Boston, Massachusetts, and London, 1904), pp. xxxix–xl.

[207] R. Woolf (ed.), *Juliana* (London, 1955), pp. 17–18.

[208] H. Sweet, 'Sketch of the History of Anglo-Saxon Poetry', p. 16.

[209] Ten Brink, *Early English Literature*, p. 47. Cf. ten Brink, *Geschichte der Englischen Litteratur*, I p. 59: 'dieses Bruchstück . . . übt eine Wirkung, welche der des Volksepos näher kommt als der Eindruck irgend einer andern geistlichen Dichtung jener Epoche. Mit einer klaren, wohl gegliederten Erzählung verbindet sich epische Fülle, Kraft und Lebendigkeit der Diction.'

Cædmonian poems] dealing with Old Testament subjects, which have been preserved'; and a footnote extends the application of this superlative even further.[210] F. Brincker has a good summary of critical opinion current at the turn of the century:[211]

> What the critics praise specially is the poet's skill in adapting his source, and the art with which he clothes biblical material in a genuine Germanic garb. As is well known, the Anglo-Saxon epic poems sing only of foreign heroes and their deeds, so that it is impossible to speak of a national epic *sensu stricto.* Nevertheless we may, with some degree of justice, call *Judith* a national epic since the poem is so strongly stamped with a Germanic impress. Only the story is Hebraic, and even that is often altered to suit Germanic taste; everything else is purely Germanic. The city of Bethulia is represented to us as an Anglo-Saxon stronghold, the Assyrians like the Israelites are Germanic warriors, Judith and her maid are Germanic women and Christians. Germanic life, Germanic views, Germanic customs appear before us in every part of the poem, so that Cook in the Introduction of his edition remarks truly, 'It is Hebraic in incident and outline, Germanic in execution, sentiment, coloring, and all that constitutes the life of a poem.' If Jacob Grimm, in his edition of *Andreas und Elene*, and especially Vilmar, in his famous examination of the Germanic antiquities in *Heliand . . .*, have taught us to look upon the songs of our forefathers as mines for the history of Germanic culture, we may truly call *Judith* such a mine.

---

[210] Ebert, *Allgemeine Geschichte der Literatur des Mittelalters im Abendlande*, III, p. 26: 'Dies ist ohne Zweifel das gelungenste der uns aus dieser Periode erhaltenen Gedichte, welche alttestamentalische Stoffe behandeln.' Footnote, 'Wie überhaupt.'

[211] F. Brincker, *Germanische Altertümer in... 'Judith'* (1898), p. 5: 'Besonders gerühmt wird die Geschicklichkeit des Dichters, die Quelle zu behandeln, und seine Kunst, den biblischen Stoff in ein echt germanisches Gewand zu kleiden. Bekanntlich besingt die angelsächsische Epik nur fremde Helden und Heldenthaten, so daß man von einem Nationalepos im eigentlichen Sinne nicht reden kann. Judith aber darf man mit gewissem Rechte ein Nationalepos nennen, so stark tritt das germanische Gepräge der Dichtung hervor. Nur die Fabel ist hebräisch, und auch sie ist nach germanischem Geschmack vielfach umgestaltet; alles andere ist rein germanisch. Die Stadt Bethulia erscheint uns als eine angelsächsische Burg, die Assyrer sowohl wie die Hebräer sind germanische Krieger, Judith und ihre Dienerin sind germanische Frauen und Christinnen. Germanisches Leben, germanische Anschauungen, germanische Sitten treten uns in allen Teilen des Gedichts entgegen, so daß Cook in der Einleitung zu seiner Ausgabe (S. X) mit Recht sagt: "It is Hebraic in incident and outline, Germanic in execution, sentiment, coloring, and all that constitutes the life of a poem." Wenn Jacob Grimm in seiner Ausgabe von Andreas und Elene, besonders aber Vilmar in seiner berühmten Untersuchung über die deutschen Altertümer im Heliand . . . uns gelehrt hat, in den Liedern unserer Altvordern Fundgruben für die deutsche Kulturgeschichte zu sehen, so dürfen wir mit Recht die angelsächsische Judith als eine solche Fundstätte bezeichnen.' Brincker quotes from the introduction of A.S. Cook (ed.), *Judith an Old English Epic Fragment* (Boston, Massachusetts, 1888), p. x.

Much of what Brincker says in his school-programme can be seen as an expansion of Cook's section 'Art' in the Introduction to his edition. Under the heading 'Amplification' Cook said:[212]

> The poet dwells with especial fondness on feasting and war. This is a national trait, and should be considered without prejudice to the controlling art visible in every part of his production. Amplification rises to the dignity of invention in the lines which describe the wolf, the raven, and the eagle, haunters of the battle-field (205^b–212^a).

Benno J. Timmer in his recent edition of the poem confined himself to limited aspects of the praise given to the poem by earlier scholars, though he agreed with them that 'The poet has given Judith the features of an Anglo-Saxon woman, with everything the Anglo-Saxons admired in their women.'[213] Unlike earlier critics, Timmer distinguished the traditional vocabulary in which the poem is written from the traditional Germanic way of life which earlier scholars inferred from the vocabulary:[214]

> There is . . . no indication of the *comitatus*-idea: when the warriors find Holofernes dead, they take to their heels. On the whole the distance between Judith and her Hebrew followers, or between Holofernes and his followers, is much greater than between a Germanic lord and his retainers, even though the terminology is retained: the men are called ðegnas and Holofernes is *sinces brytta*.

In Adolf Ebert's discussion of paganism and Christianity in these Christian poems there is often, perhaps as a result of Ebert's profound and wide-ranging knowledge of the Latin literature of the Middle Ages, an attitude far removed from the thesis-mongers who were his contemporaries, and nearer to that of some recent views. His idea that the demons which assail the saint in *Guthlac* (lines 191–9) are reminiscent of Germanic sylvan deities will be regarded as extravagant today, but it is remarkable that, writing in 1887, he should have seen the joys and obligations of Germanic society as part of a Satanic system of temptations, a view which has particular application to *The Wanderer* (though Ebert did not apply it to any poem other than *Guthlac A*):[215]

---

[212] A.S. Cook (ed.), *Judith an Old English Epic Fragment*, 2nd edn (Boston, Massachusetts, 1889; rpt 1904), p. xli.

[213] B.J. Timmer (ed.), *Judith* (London, 1952), p. 13.

[214] Timmer, *Judith*, p. 12.

[215] Ebert, *Allgemeine Geschichte der Literatur des Mittelalters im Abendlande*, III, p. 61: 'Der Dichter schildert dann die Heimsuchung Guthlacs durch die Dämonen als einen Kampf um den Besitz des "Berges", d. h. des Hügels im Walde der Insel, auf welchem der Heilige seine Wohnung aufgeschlagen. Es war ihr Rastplatz, wenn sie müde von ihren Fahrten dorthin kamen (v. 180 [= 209] ff.). Sie mahnen Guthlac an seine Verwandtschaftspflichten; er soll der Männer Jubel wieder aufsuchen. So vertreten die Teufel in ihren Forderungen gewissermassen das alte Germanenthum, der Askese des Christenthums gegenüber, wie sie selbst auch

The poet then describes the visitation of Guthlac by demons as a battle for the possession of the 'mountain, i.e. the mound in the forest on the island on which the saint has established his dwelling. It used to be their place of rest when they arrived there weary from their travels (lines 209–14). They remind Guthlac of the obligations he has to his kin, and urge him to return to the rejoicings of men. The devils in their demands represent, as it were, the ancient Teutonism, as opposed to the asceticism of Christianity, and are in themselves at the same time reminiscent of the Germanic sylvan deities.

The recognition that the Germanic moral values could run counter to Christian values and that the Anglo-Saxon poets could in such cases fully embrace the foreign and reject the indigenous values must have seemed perverse to the majority of Anglo-Saxon scholars of the late nineteenth and early twentieth century. That it would have seemed so to G. Baesecke at an even later date is shown by what he wrote in 1933:[216]

> We shall have to trace back, by way of the Anglo-Saxons, the growth of a new *morality*, and here we can be surer that we are dealing with something indigenous than we were when we dealt with questions of the divine. Here the sources, especially those of heroic song, flow more plentifully, and since the strict Germanic ethos was not by nature tied to religion in the narrower sense, it was able to permeate more strongly the alien domination of Christianity, and moreover it did not allow the ancient concepts of honour and loyalty to be bowed down and reduced as the pagan deities had been, who had become mere names. The stock-example of battle and reconciliation is the *Heliand* with its Germanic liege lord, and in that particular case the Liege Lord's tragic battle was His servile Passion.

---

an die germanischen Waldgottheiten erinnern.' (Cf. E.G. Stanley, 'Hæthenra Hyht in *Beowulf*, p. 139.)

[216] G. Baesecke, *Der Vocabularius Sti. Galli in der angelsächsischen Mission* (Halle, 1933), p. 158: 'Auch das Werden einer neuen christlichen Sittlichkeit müssen wir über die Ags. zurückführen, und hier sind wir des Eignen sicherer als in Fragen des Göttlichen. Hier fließen die Quellen, zumal der Heldendichtung, reichlicher, und das strenge germanische Ethos hat, als nicht von Haus aus an Religion in engerem Sinne gebunden, kräftiger durch die christliche Überfremdung hindurchwachsen können und besonders die alten Ehr- und Treubegriffe nicht wie die zu Namen gewordenen heidnischen Götter hinunterbeugen lassen. Das Schulbeispiel für Kampf und Ausgleich ist der Heliand mit dem germanischen Gefolgsherrn, dessen tragischer Kampf in diesem Falle sein knechtisches Leiden ist.'

10. The Gods Themselves

A. *Appearances Veiled by Christianity*

THOSE WHO SEARCH Old English literature for evidence of the Germanic past can have no greater reward for their labours than to find references to the pagan deities themselves. We have seen how Grimm and his followers were often led to pagan deities by fanciful etymologies.[217] An example, similar in effect though even less controlled in method, is M.B. Price's comment on *sigorcynn on swegle* (*Elene* line 754) and on *engla þreatas sigeleoð sungon* (*Guthlac* lines 1314–15):[218]

> May not this conception of the angels as a victorious host, a triumphant race, which has overcome the machinations of evil and enjoys the compensation of victory have been suggested by the blissful condition of the heroes who receive their reward amid the joys of Walhalla?

The search may be conducted with greater pretentiousness. George Stephens, writing in 1866, provides a good example:[219]

> The excessive value of our oldest verse is not confined to its intrinsic merits, its frequent sublimity and beauty. It also reaches to the many reminiscences we there find of those older religious ideas which gradually gave way before a purer and nobler faith. And these reminiscences are not confined to the mere language.

Stephens found what he was looking for:[220]

---

[217] See pp. 19–20 and footnotes 48–50, above.
[218] Price, *Teutonic Antiquities in the Generally Acknowledged Cynewulfian Poetry*, p. 25.
[219] G. Stephens (ed.), *The Old-Northern Runic Monuments of Scandinavia and England*, I (London and Copenhagen, 1866[–1867]), p. 431; also separately, G. Stephens (ed.), *The Ruthwell Cross, Northumbria, from about A. D. 680, with its runic verses by Cædmon, and Cædmon's complete cross-lay 'The Holy Rood, a dream'* (London and Copenhagen, 1866), p. 29.
[220] Stephens, *The Old-Northern Runic Monuments*, p. 431; *The Ruthwell Cross*, p. 29.

But when BALDOR had fallen, the Death-goddess (HEL) said that he should be restored to the grieving deities *if all Creation wept*. So they sent out erranders; and stones, rocks, trees, metals, animals, men, all things shed tears for the beloved son of FRIGG. But one old witch (LOKI in the disguise of THÖKT) *refused*, and BALDOR came back no more!

Now in the light of all this let us read a poem, composed in an age when heathendom had but lately been laid aside, its mighty traditions still strong and fresh and impregnating everything, its spirit bound up in the language itself and reflected in a thousand native details.

I will not insist on a general coincidence, the remarkable expression at line 77 [= *The Dream of the Rood* line 39] On-gyrede hine þa GEONG HÆLEÐ / For the grapple then girded Him the YOUTHFUL HERO.

young helt, youthful hero, being most strange as applied to the Crucified, but perfectly in its place as a reminiscence of BALDOR.

Stephens was not the first to notice that Baldr and Christ have some similarity. It was sufficiently well known for Thomas Carlyle to refer to it:[221] 'Baldor again, the White God, the beautiful, the just and benignant (whom the early Christian Missionaries found to resemble Christ), is the Sun, – beautifullest of visible things.'

Jacob Grimm connected Christ with Baldr in his elucidation of the *Second Merseburg Charm*.[222] In the Old High German *Merseburg Charm* Baldr's horse dislocates its foot whereas in a modern Danish charm in a similar context it is Christ's horse that dislocates its foot, a parallel to which he had first drawn attention in 1835.[223] He found confirmation for this parallel in the fact that in Norse the word 'white' is used as an epithet of Christ, *hvíta Kristr*, and of Baldr, *hvíti ás*.

Stephens compared the lament of all creation at Baldr's death with *weop eal gesceaft* at Christ's death, *The Dream of the Rood* line 55. There is a generalizing echo of that in Miss E.E. Wardale's book:[224]

> As in all OE. poetry, nature is in sympathy with the tragedy enacted, it forms a harmonious background; the darkening of the heavens is, of course, taken from the Bible narrative, but in giving the final touch to this scene [*The Dream of the Rood*, lines 51–7] the poet has not been afraid to draw from heathen poetry. 'All creation wept, lamented the fall of the King,' is an echo of the description of the death of Baldor, the sun god, for whose untimely end all nature lamented, and whose death forms the subject of a most telling story in the old mythology.

---

[221] T. Carlyle, *On Heroes, Hero-Worship, and the Heroic in History: Six Lectures* (London, 1841), Lecture I, p. 29, = 'Centenary Edition', V (London, 1897), p. 18.

[222] J. Grimm, 'Über zwei entdeckte Gedichte aus der Zeit des deutschen Heidenthums', *Philologische und historische Abhandlungen der Königlichen Akademie der Wissenschaften zu Berlin. Aus dem Jahre 1842* (Berlin, 1844), pp. 21–2; reprinted in *Kleinere Schriften*, II (1865), p. 24.

[223] Grimm, *Deutsche Mythologie*, 1st edn, Anhang, p. cxlviii.

[224] Wardale, *Chapters on Old English Literature*, p. 181.

Miss Wardale's assumption of borrowing from heathen poetry was made in spite of the note on the passage in Cook's edition of the poem, where he related the description of universal lament for Christ to patristic literature.[225] Miss Wardale's assumption was made in spite of Sophus Bugge's statement, 'The motif of all nature weeping over Baldr is, in my opinion, derived from the medieval descriptions of the death of Christ.'[226]

The edition of the poem by Professors Bruce Dickins and A.S.C. Ross has an ambiguous note on the passage:[227] 'The striking similarity of the Norse story of the lament for Baldr, for whom all things wept save only the giantess Þǫkk, cannot be due to chance.' Unlike Stephens and Miss Wardale, the editors are aware that the borrowing may be in either direction, but they refuse to commit themselves.

That to Stephens as to Miss Wardale it seemed possible for *The Dream of the Rood* to contain such a clear reminiscence of paganism is, of course, the result of their refusal to read a profoundly Christian literature as the Christian writings of a Christian people.

We have seen how scholars of the late nineteenth and early twentieth century emphasized in their reading the incidental to make it the centre of their interest, and so were able to speak, as M.L. Keller did, of 'poems such as the Elene or the Judith dealing principally with battles'.[228] Such common Anglo-Saxon words as *hild* and *wig* were taken as standing for Bellona and Mars.[229] The wolf, the eagle, and the raven were associated in the reader's mind with Woden; as F. Brincker, referring to their appearance in *Judith*, says:[230]

> The appearance of these animals, which were devilish according to Christian conceptions, reminded the Germanic warrior of the presence

---

[225] A.S. Cook (ed.), *The Dream of the Rood* (Oxford 1905), pp. 31–2.
[226] E. Sophus Bugge, translated by O. Brenner, I (Munich, 1881), p. 59, *Studien über die Entstehung der nordischen Götter- und Heldensagen*: 'dieses Motiv vom Weinen der gesammten Natur über Baldr, stammt nach meiner Meinung aus der mittelalterlichen Schilderung von Christi Tod'. Bugge, *Studier over de nordiske Gude- og Heltesagns Oprindelse*, I (Christiania, 1881), p. 55: 'Ogsaa dette Motiv med Alnaturens Graad over Balder hører efter min Mening hjemme i Middelalderens Skildring af Kristi Død.'
[227] B. Dickins and A.S.C. Ross (eds), *The Dream of the Rood* (London, 1934), pp. 27–8.
[228] M.L. Keller, *The Anglo-Saxon Weapon Names Treated Archæologically and Etymologically*, Anglistische Forschungen, xv (1906), p. 13; in part published (1905) as a doctoral dissertation of the University of Heidelberg.
[229] See pp. 19–20 and footnotes 47–9, above.
[230] Brincker, *Germanische Altertümer in ... 'Judith'*, p. 6: 'Das Erscheinen dieser Tiere, die nach christlicher Auffassung teuflisch waren, gemahnte den germanischen Krieger an die Anwesenheit *Woden's*, der die Schlacht leitete. Unwillkürlich denkt man hier an den Gott, von dem Tacitus (Germania 7) sagt: "quem adesse bellantibus credunt".' Cf. Tacitus, *Germania*, 7.1, ed. Hutton, revised Warmington (1970), pp. 141–2, 'whom they suppose to accompany them on campaign'.

of Woden who ruled battles. Involuntarily one thinks of the god of whom Tacitus (*Germania*, ch. VII) says, '*quem adesse bellantibus credunt*' [(the god) whom they suppose to accompany them on campaign].

Involuntarily these scholars were reminded of Tacitus, and involuntarily they identified their interest in a more primitive Germanic age with the interest of the poets. Some scholars thought that Christianity had touched Anglo-Saxon literature only superficially. Yet even men like Edmund Dale, who realized that the influence of the new religion was fundamental, who read Old English literature with understanding and so grasped that a 'deep consciousness of sin was one of the most marked consequences of the conversion, and seems to have made its impress upon much of the literature of the period',[231] nevertheless sought out in that literature all those elements which were regarded as essentially Germanic, or even essentially and perennially English. Thus Dale saw Adam and Eve in *The Later Genesis* as typically Germanic:[232]

> These two sorrowful ones are more than mere Biblical figures. They are of the North, Teutonic and English seekers after God, faithful and devoted though fallen.

And what he means by English he explains in the case of Adam:[233]

> Adam becomes a typical Englishman, slow and cautious in his thought and speech, faithful to his Lord, and distrustful of the beguiling counsels of the stranger spirit, whom he rebuffs with a few gruff words, direct and to the point.

Dale's manner is here that of an English Vilmar, who emphasized not merely the Englishness of Adam – in this originally Old Saxon poem – but the conservatism, the 'blimpishness' almost, of what is looked upon as the national character.

B. *Overt Appearances*

Scholars turned to Germanic literature for evidence of the old religion. The method and its results are well set out by Karl Helm:[234]

---

[231] E. Dale, *National Life and Character in the Mirror of Early English Literature* (Cambridge, 1907), p. 106.
[232] Dale, *National Life and Character*, p. 105.
[233] Dale, *National Life and Character*, p. 104.
[234] K. Helm, *Altgermanische Religionsgeschichte*, I, Germanische Bibliothek, I, V, ii/1 (Heidelberg, 1913), pp. 109–10: 'Die älteste Dichtung christlichen Charakters enthält in Worten, Formeln und Anschauungen manchen, nicht besonders umfangreichen, versteckten, heidnischen Rest.
   'Der Heliand ist (neben anderen) daraufhin untersucht worden von Vilmar.
   'Von den ahd. Dichtungen hat man die Einleitung des Wessobrunner-

The oldest Christian poetry contains a certain, not very extensive, concealed residue of paganism in its vocabulary, formulas and conceptions.

Vilmar and others have investigated the *Heliand* for such residue.

Among Old High German poems, the opening of the *Wessobrunn Prayer* has been looked upon as pagan Germanic. The formulas are certainly very ancient, but their nature is so general that they fit any cosmogony, and do not, therefore, tell us anything specifically Germanic. . . .

The *Hildebrandslied* manifests a Christian milieu, but a few pagan words and concepts tower up also into this monument.

The oldest AngloSaxon poetry yields likewise only little of usable detail. Isolated mention of the gods occurs in the *Gnomic Poems* and in *Solomon and Saturn*. The after-effect of Germanic belief in Fate may well be discernable in the elegiac mood of some of the older Anglo-Saxon poems.

Much of what Helm says has been dealt with above. But two aspects remain: actual mention of pagan deities, and *Wyrd*. The mention of a Germanic deity (other than Wyrd) in *Solomon and Saturn* is based on Saturn. E.V.K. Dobbie, writing in 1942, stated unequivocally:[235]

> It is important to notice that the Saturn represented here is not the pagan divinity of that name or (as some scholars have thought) a native Germanic god, but a 'prince of the Chaldeans' (*Caldea eorl* l. 176), a people traditionally associated with the practice of oriental astrology and magic.

R.J. Menner, on the other hand, took Saturn in the poem to be the Roman god:[236] 'The reason for representing the Roman god Saturn as a Chaldean ruler is the Greek and medieval identification of Saturn–Kronos with Nimrod and Ninus.' He was ready to admit, however, that 'The real reason for this equation is obscure.'[237]

gebetes als heidnisch-germanisch betrachtet; die Formeln sind auch jedenfalls uralt, aber so allgemeiner Natur, daß sie in jede beliebige Kosmogonie passen und deshalb nichts spezifisch Germanisches mitteilen . . .

'Das Hildebrandslied zeigt christliches Milieu, aber einige heidnische Worte und Begriffe ragen auch in dies Denkmal hinein.

'Die älteste angelsächsische Dichtung ergibt ebenfalls wenig Ausbeute an brauchbarem Detail: vereinzelte Nennung von Göttern begegnet in den Gnomen und im Gedicht von Salomo und Saturn. Nachwirkung des germanischen Schicksalsglaubens darf wohl in der elegischen Stimmung einiger der älteren angelsächsischen Dichtungen erblickt werden.'

[235] E.V.K. Dobbie (ed.), *The Anglo-Saxon Minor Poems*, The Anglo-Saxon Poetic Records, VI (New York and London, 1942), pp. liii–liv.
[236] R.J. Menner (ed.), *The Poetical Dialogues of Solomon and Saturn*, The Modern Language Association of America, Monograph Series XIII (New York and London, 1941), p. 107.
[237] Menner, *Solomon and Saturn*, p. 108.

Earlier scholars followed Jacob Grimm who ranged Saturn among Germanic gods.[238] Among these scholars was Kemble:[239]

> I do not think . . . that we must at once reject the name of Saturn as a Teutonic god, merely because the first glance at this poem would induce us to consider it the production of a pedantic monk.

This view held the field when Helm was writing. It was rejected authoritatively by E.A. Philippson in 1929.[240] There is no denying, however, that Woden is mentioned by name in the *Gnomic Poem* (line 132) of the Exeter Book. It is not a mention that redounds to the glory of the god and gives little satisfaction to scholars eager to find the pagan world that was lost to Christendom. The passage in which the line occurs is condemned by them; thus Brandl detected in it 'the acrid tone of the missionary', and Blanche C. Williams had no doubt that these lines are 'obviously the work of a Christian redactor'.[241]

Indeed, there is no reason for thinking that the mention of Woden in the Exeter *Gnomes* – *Woden worhte weos, wuldor alwalda* (Woden brought forth idols, the Almighty brought forth glory) – is in any way different from the mention of Tiw in so indisputably Christian a document as the *Old English Martyrology*:[242] *þone Syxtum nedde Decius se casere to Tiges deofolgilde* (The Emperor Decius compelled Sixtus to the idolatry of Tiw).

In the Old English *Charms*, surprisingly as it must have seemed to those scholars who failed or were reluctant to distinguish the superstitious from the idolatrous, the name *Woden* comes only once,[243] and Thor only as the result of an emendation which is now discredited.[244] W. Bonser says:[245]

---

[238] Grimm, *Deutsche Mythologie*, 2nd edn, pp. 226–8.
[239] J.M. Kemble (ed.), *The Dialogue of Salomon and Saturn*, II, Ælfric Society, No. 13 (London, 1847), p. 127.
[240] E.A. Philippson, *Germanisches Heidentum bei den Angelsachsen*, Kölner anglistische Arbeiten IV (Leipzig, 1929), pp. 176–7.
[241] Brandl, 'Geschichte der altenglischen Literatur', I, Angelsächsische Periode, in Paul (ed.), *Grundriss der germanischen Philologie*, II, 2nd edn, VI/6 § 11, p. 961 (= p. 21 of separate): 'in scharfem Missionarston'; and Williams, *Gnomic Poetry*, p. 93.
[242] G. Herzfeld (ed.), *An Old English Martyrology*, EETS, o.s. 116 (1900), p. 140 line 3.
[243] In 'The Nine Herbs Charm', line 32; Dobbie, *The Anglo-Saxon Minor Poems*, p. 120.
[244] In 'For a Sudden Stitch', line 27, Dobbie, *The Anglo-Saxon Minor Poems*, p. 123; cf. G. Storms (ed.), *Anglo-Saxon Magic* (The Hague, 1948), p. 148.
[245] W. Bonser, 'Survivals of Paganism in Anglo-Saxon England', The Birmingham Archaeological Society, *Transactions and Proceedings for the Year 1932* lvi (1934), p. 44. Cf. W. Bonser, *The Medical Background of Anglo-Saxon England*, Publications of the Wellcome Historical Medical Library, n.s. III (1963), p. 128, where the passage is taken over from the earlier study without any significant change.

We have the testimony of Wulfstan, Bishop of Worcester and Archbishop of York, that Woden and Thor were the most popular of the heathen gods in England, as they were also on the Continent from the time of Tacitus to the final conversion to Christianity. . . . In Anglo-Saxon charms the name of Woden occurs only once – to the writer's knowledge: possibly in other cases it has been cut out by Church influence. Woden was the god of magic and spells in Scandinavia, and his spirit is behind the Anglo-Saxon charms, even though his name no longer occurs.

The possibility that the Pseudo-Wulfstan testimony refers, not to a survival of Anglo-Saxon paganism, but to Scandinavian paganism, is not mentioned by Bonser in spite of the non-English forms *Þor* and *Owðen*;[246] everything is subordinated to the wish of finding pagan divinities, yet for all the strength of that wish the *Charms* yield only the line *Þa genam Woden VIIII wuldortanas* in *The Nine Herbs Charm*, of the pagan implications of which there can be no doubt. As G. Storms says:[247]

> Crowning the achievement of the herbs Woden himself comes to their assistance against the hostile attack of the evil one. He takes nine glory-twigs, by which are meant nine runes, that is, nine twigs with the initial letters in runes of the plants representing the power inherent in them, and using them as weapons he smites the serpent with them. Thanks to their magical power they pierce its skin and cut it into nine pieces. The connection between Woden and the runes is very close in Germanic mythology.

Thunor is never mentioned in the Anglo-Saxon charms, but O. Cockayne supplied that want by emendation,[248] and he was followed, though with a different interpretation, by Joseph Bosworth in his *Dictionary*.[249] The manuscript reading of lines 27–8 of the charm *For a Sudden Stitch* reads *fled þ'r onfyrgen hæfde halwestu*; it is discussed by Storms, who says of the emendation of *þ'r* to *Þor* (among other editorial interventions, namely, *fled* to *fleoh*, and the improved word-divisions on *fyrgen hæfde hal westu*):[250]

---

[246] Bonser, 'Survivals', p. 44, has a footnote giving a reference for the popularity of Thunor and Woden: A.S. Napier, *Wulfstan – Sammlung der ihm zugeschriebenen Homilien*, Sammlung englischer Denkmäler in kritischen Ausgaben IV (Berlin, 1883), Homily XLII, p. 197 lines 19–20: *Þor eac and Owðen, ðe hæðene men heriað swiðe* [Thunor and Woden whom pagans venerate greatly]. For the authorship of Homily XLII, see K. Jost, *Wulfstanstudien*, Swiss Studies in English XXIII (Berne, 1950), pp. 218–21.

[247] Storms, *Anglo-Saxon Magic*, p. 195.

[248] T.O. Cockayne (ed.), *Leechdoms, Wortcunning and Starcraft of Early England*, Rolls Series, 35, III (1866), p. 54.

[249] J. Bosworth (ed.), *An Anglo-Saxon Dictionary*, part I, A–H (Oxford, 1882), s.v. *fyrgen*.

[250] Storms, *Anglo-Saxon Magic*, p. 148.

The emendation to *þor* is most uncertain. Thor is never mentioned in Charms, nor does his name occur in any other text as having any connection with magic, and the translations of Cockayne and the A[nglo-]S[axon]D[ictionary] are as obscure as the manuscript reading.

J.H.G. Grattan and C. Singer rightly say that Cockayne's *þor* is impossible as an expansion of *þ'r*, and do not consider it as an emendation.[251] In the part of their introduction devoted to the 'Sources of Anglo-Saxon Medico-Magic' they say:[252]

> In A.S. literature traces of Thor and Woden are conspicuously few. By the tenth century the names of the days of the week meant no more than they do now. Moreover, when we catch a glimpse of the great gods in England they are devoid of many of the attributes ascribed to them in the Scandinavian cycle.

The wish to see pagan implications in a wide range of Old English writings has yielded to proper scholarly scepticism. Very recently that scepticism has affected even the subject of English rune-magic. R.I. Page ends his notable article on 'Anglo-Saxon runes and magic' with the warning that 'it is wise to hesitate before interpreting OE runic texts as magical.'[253] In the course of his survey of some of the evidence he says:[254]

> Thus the Anglo-Saxon evidence for rune-magic, though not negligible, is slight. The only certain point is Ælfric's unambiguous reference. Without it the existence of rune-magic would hardly have been deduced from the English material alone. . . . Those who argue that OE runes were commonly used for magical purposes must rely on supporting evidence from outside this country, in particular from Scandinavia. They should remember the differences in cultural development between Dark Age Scandinavia and Anglo-Saxon England, especially the early date of the conversion to Christianity and the introduction of Roman script into this country.

This is the very opposite of the attitude of Grimm and those who followed him in regarding Germanic antiquity as a common civilization of all who spoke the Germanic languages, and a civilization to which the Germanic tribes clung tenaciously through the centuries.

---

[251] J.H.G. Grattan and C. Singer, *Anglo-Saxon Magic and Medicine illustrated especially from the semi-pagan text 'Lacnunga'*, Publications of the Wellcome Historical Medical Museum, new series III (London, New York, Toronto, 1952), p. 176.

[252] Grattan and Singer, *Anglo-Saxon Magic and Medicine*, p. 57.

[253] R.I. Page, 'Anglo-Saxon Runes and Magic', *Journal of the British Archaeological Association*, 3rd series xxvii (1964), p. 31.

[254] Page, 'Anglo-Saxon Runes and Magic', p. 30. The reference to the magical power of runes in Ælfric is to B. Thorpe (ed.), *The Homilies of Ælfric*, second series, Ælfric Society, II part IX, No. 11 (1846), pp. 356–9, 'Hortatorius sermo de efficacia sanctae missae'.

11. *Wyrd*

A. *'Event' or 'Fate', Norn or Fortune*

IN THE DISCUSSION of the surviving paganism in Anglo-Saxon literature *wyrd* occupies a central place; views on *wyrd* epitomize the views on the wider issue. There is no need to cite here at length the occurrences of the word in Old English. R. Jente has devoted a whole chapter to the subject.[255] In view of the range of meanings of the word it may, however, be desirable to illustrate this range briefly.

First, in the early Glosses *wyrde* (*uuyrdae*) renders 'parcae' (thus, *Épinal* and *Erfurt* 764, *Corpus* 1480); in the later Glosses 'parcae' is rendered by *gewyrde* (thus, in Napier's Aldhelm Glosses 1^{5480}, 8^{413}, $8B^5$).[256]

Secondly, *wyrd* occurs in accounts of pagan beliefs (probably the uses of the word in the early Glosses belong here); thus in *Boethius*:[257]

> Ða eode he furður, oð he gemette ða graman metena ðe folcisce men hatað Parcas, ða hi secgað ðæt on nanum men nyton nane are, ac ælcum men wrecen be his gewyrhtum; þa hi secgað ðæt walden ælces mannes wyrde. [Then he went on till he met the fierce Fates whom common people call Parcae, who, they say, show respect to none, but each they punish according to his deserts, and they say that they rule each person's *wyrd*.]

In the Latin (*De Consolatione Philosophiae*, III, m. 12. 31 f.) the Furies (*Ultrices*) are referred to, not the *Parcae*, but the translator's amplifying reference to *wyrd* shows that in his mind *wyrd* goes with *Parcae*. Boethius (*De Consolatione Philosophiae*, IV, pr. 6) had a definitilon of Fate (*fatum*) as distinct from Providence (*prouidentia*) which the Old English version renders by *wyrd* and *foreðonc* or *foresceawung*.[258] In the Alfredian *Boethius*

---

[255] Jente, *Die mythologischen Ausdrücke*, pp. 196–234, ch. IV, 'Schicksal und Tod'.
[256] H. Sweet, *The Oldest English Texts*, pp. 86 and 83; A.S. Napier (ed.), *Old English Glosses Chiefly Unpublished*, Anecdota Oxoniensia, IV, Mediaeval and Modern Series XI (Oxford, 1900), pp. 138, 171, 172.
[257] W.J. Sedgefield (ed.), *King Alfred's Old English Version of Boethius De Consolatione Philosophiae* (Oxford, 1899), p. 102 lines 20–5. For the Latin, see H.F. Stewart and E.K. Rand (eds), *Boethius: The Theological Tractates, The Consolation of Philosophy*, The Loeb Classical Library (Cambridge, Massachusetts, and London, 1918, rpt 1946), p. 296.
[258] Sedgefield, *King Alfred's . . . Boethius*, p. 128 lines 10–26.

(as in the Glosses, e.g. Corpus 897) *wyrd* is also used to translate *fortuna* (*De Consolatione Philosophiae*, 1, m. 529).²⁵⁹ In *Solomon and Saturn* lines 426–50 *wyrd* contends with *warnung*, and in this context the two words may be defined by reference to Spenser's 'who can deceiue his destiny, Or weene by warning to auoyd his fate?' (*The Faerie Queene*, III. iv. 27).²⁶⁰ Ælfric's *Epiphany Homily* alludes to conceptions, heretical in a Christian context, of destiny and predestination, and uses the word *gewyrd*:

> sume gedwolmen . . . cwdon þæt se steorra his gewyrd wære. Gewíte ðis gedwyld fram geleaffullum heortum, þæt ænig gewyrd sy, buton se Ælmihtiga Scyppend, seðe ælcum men foresceawað lif be his geearnungum.²⁶¹ [Some heretics . . . said that the star (at Christ's Nativity) was His *gewyrd*. Let this error go away from the hearts of the faithful, that there should be any *gewyrd* except the Almighty Creator who for every person provides life according to his deserts.]

> Þa ðe ne gelyfað, ðurh agenne cyre hí scoriað, na ðurh gewyrd forðan ðe gewyrd nis nan ðing buton leas wena; ne nan ðing soðlice be gewyrde ne gewyrð, ac ealle ðing þurh Godes dom beoð geendebyrde.²⁶² [Those who do not believe through their own choice, they refuse, not through *gewyrd* because *gewyrd* is nothing other than a false expectation (or notion), for truly nothing comes about through *gewyrd*, but all things are put in order through God's decree.]

> Mine gebroðra, ge habbað nu gehyred be ðan leasan wenan, þe ydele men gewyrd hatað.²⁶³ [My brethren, you have now heard about that false expectation (or notion) that the foolish call *gewyrd*.]

Thirdly, *wyrd* occurs not infrequently in collocation with the poetic word *fæge*: for example *Gewurdene wyrda ðæt beoð ða feowere fæges rapas* [*wyrda* that have come about, they will be the four ropes of one about to die; *Solomon and Saturn* lines 334–5]; *Wyrd oft nereð unfægne eorl þonne his ellen deah* [*wyrd* always saves the man not fated to die when his courage avails; *Beowulf* lines 572–3]; *Wyrd ne meahte in fægum leng feorg gehealdan deore frætwe, þonne him gedemed wæs* [*wyrd* could not keep the life, precious treasure, longer in the man doomed to die than was ordained for him; *Guthlac B* lines 1057–9]; *He þa wyrd ne mað, fæges forðsið* [he did not conceal that *wyrd*, the going forth of the one about to die; *Guthlac B* lines 1345–6]. In these contexts the meaning of the word is something like 'final event, final fate, doom, death'.

---

[259] Sedgefield, *King Alfred's . . . Boethius*, p. 10 line 18. For the Latin, see Stewart and Rand (eds), *Boethius: . . . The Consolation of Philosophy*, p. 156.
[260] See *OED*, s.v. *Warning*, vbl. sb.¹, 1. Taking heed, precaution.
[261] B. Thorpe (ed.), *The Homilies of Ælfric*, I, Ælfric Society, I, part 1, Nos. 1–2 (1843), p. 110.
[262] Thorpe, *The Homilies of Ælfric*, I, p. 114.
[263] Thorpe, *The Homilies of Ælfric*, I, p. 114.

Fourthly, as Mrs. Gordon has pointed out in her note on *wyrd* at line 115 of *The Seafarer*, '*Wyrd* is often equated in Christian poetry and homily with the working of God's will, especially with reference to the Doom to come.'[264] She refers to *Blickling Homily* No. X, 'The End of This World is Near', a passage that equates *wyrd* with *hwonne se ælmihtiga God wille þisse worlde ende gewyricean* [when Almighty God wishes to bring this world to its end].[265]

Fifthly, because *wyrd* is etymologically very close to the verb *weorþan*, the meanings of the verb are directly relevant to those of the noun. As the abstract of *weorþan*, *wyrd* may mean no more than 'that which happens or has happened, an event, occurrence, incident, fact'. The word *gewyrd* seems to be used in much the same way as *wyrd* with the same meanings. The meanings of *wyrd* and *gewyrd* are also connected with those of *geweorþan*, which (in addition to the meanings which the verb shares with *weorþan*, 'to come to be, to come to pass, to become') can mean 'to agree upon, to decide, to settle', so that the abstract *gewyrd* could have the meaning 'that which is agreed upon, is decided, is settled; destiny'. This etymological connection may be a further reason why *wyrd* (e.g. *uyrd*, *Leiden* 96) and *gewyrd* (e.g. Napier, *Old English Glosses*, 18B^{32}) glosses *fatus, fata, fatum*.[266]

It is difficult to establish at each occurrence the extent to which *wyrd* is personified. It is difficult also to establish to what extent the personification of *wyrd* is indebted to classical mythology: it is generally accepted that *Wyrd*'s (or rather *Urðr*'s) two sisters, *Verðandi* and *Skuld*, are the result of classical influence, presumably by way of Isidore of Seville's *Etymologiae*, VIII. xi. 93,[267] though it has been suggested that the Germanic triad (instead of the single principle of *wyrd*) may be the result, not of borrowing from the Classics, but of developments analogous with the Parcae.[268] Jente uses the fact that the Parcae are described as spinning and cutting the thread of life, whereas *Wyrd* is associated with the weaving of the web of fate, as proof that this aspect of

---

[264] Gordon, *The Seafarer*, p. 47.

[265] R. Morris (ed.), *The Blickling Homilies of the Tenth Century*, EETS, o.s. 58 (1880), p. 109 lines 32–3.

[266] Sweet, *The Oldest English Texts*, p. 114; Napier, *Old English Glosses*, p. 187.

[267] See E. Mogk, s.v. 'Nornen' § 3, in J. Hoops (ed.), *Reallexikon der Germanischen Altertumskunde* (Strassburg, 1911–19), III, p. 342; Jente, *Die mythologischen Ausdrücke*, p. 199; E.A. Philippson, *Germanisches Heidentum bei den Angelsachsen*, p. 228, reaffirms the belief in pagan origin of *Wyrd* however much reduced that concept might be in Christian times. Cf. W.M. Lindsay (ed.), *Isidori Hispalensis episcopi etymologiarum siue originum libri XX* (Oxford, 1911).

[268] See E. Mogk, 'Mythologie', in Paul's *Grundriss der germanischen Philologie*, 2nd edn, III, section III, V Der Seelenglaube der alten Germanen, § 36 Die Nornen p. 284; F. Kauffmann, 'Über den Schicksalsglauben der Germanen', *Zeitschrift für deutsche Philologie* 1 (1926), pp. 405–6.

Wyrd cannot be derived from the Parcae; while Brandl points out with justice that *Wyrd* in the Anglo-Saxon sources is never actually engaged in weaving or any other sedentary occupation, and that, far from it, *Wyrd* acts entirely in the manner of men within the epic tradition.[269] It is difficult, lastly, to be sure that the conception of *wyrd* in Old English literature is not primarily Christian, that *wyrd* is not derived from Boethius' *Fortuna* rather than from one or all of the Norns.

B. *Early Interpretations of* Wyrd

Doubts such as these only rarely assailed the early scholars, though A.F.C. Vilmar, who took *thiu wurd* in *Heliand* to be the goddess of death, the Norn, conceded that she might have been introduced merely as a trope.[270] Jacob Grimm's views on personification and myth are set out in the crucial and seminal twenty-ninth chapter of the second edition of his *Deutsche Mythologie*; grammatical gender is seen by him as the expression of a personalizing conception of things,[271] serving poets in their turn, and so at once grammatical and poetic: the origins of the myths closest to the genius of a nation are to be sought in this aspect of its fancy:[272]

> Whatever grows deep into language and spoken tradition cannot remain outside mythology; it must have imbibed fitting nourishment

---

[269] R. Jente, *Die mythologischen Ausdrücke*, pp. 199–200; A. Brandl, 'Zur Vorgeschichte der *weird sisters* im "Macbeth"', in M. Förster and K. Wildhagen (eds), *Texte und Forschungen zur englischen Kulturgeschichte – Festgabe für Felix Liebermann* (Halle, 1921), pp. 255–6.

[270] Vilmar, *Deutsche Altertümer im Hêliand*, p. 10.

[271] Grimm, *Deutsche Mythologie*, 2nd edn, pp. 834–51, ch. XXIX Personificationen; J. Grimm, *Deutsche Grammatik*, III, VI (Göttingen, 1831), p. 346.

[272] Grimm, *Deutsche Mythologie*, 2nd edn, pp. 835–6: 'Was in sprache und sage tief verwachsen ist kann der mythologie niemals fremd geblieben sein, es muß auf ihrem grund und boden eigenthümliche nahrung gesogen haben, und jene grammatische, dichterische allbelebung darf sogar in einer mythischen prosopopöie ihren ursprung suchen. Da alle einzelnen götter und göttlichen eigenschaften auf die idee eines elements, eines gestirns, einer naturerscheinung, einer kraft und tugend, einer kunst und fertigkeit, eines heils oder unheils beruhen, die sich als gegenstände heiliger anbetung geltend gemacht haben; so erlangen auch ihnen verwandte, an sich unpersönliche und abgezogene vorstellungen auf vergötterung anspruch. thieren, pflanzen, sternen, die sich auf besondere götter beziehen oder aus verwandlung entstanden sind, wird eine bestimmte persönlichkeit gebühren. Man könnte sagen, die götter des heidenthums seien überhaupt hervorgegangen aus den verschiednen personificationen, die der sinnesart und entwicklung jedes volks zunächst gelegen haben; nur daß den einzelnen gestalten durch vereinigung mehrerer eigenschaften und lang fortgetragne überlieferung höheres ansehn bereitet werden muste.'

on its soil; and the aforenamed universal, grammatical and poetic animation may even trace its origin to a mythical prosopopœia. Since all individual gods and divine attributes consist in the idea of one element, one constellation, one natural phenomenon, one ability and virtue, one skill or art, one good or evil fortune, which has gained prevalence as an object of sacred veneration; therefore concepts related to such a one, even if in themselves impersonal and abstract, attain a right to apotheosis. A definite personality is proper to such animals, plants or stars as have reference to individual gods or originate in metamorphosis. We may go so far as to say that in general the gods of paganism have proceeded from those various personifications which were closest to the genius and development of each nation, except that by uniting several attributes and as a result of long-continued tradition a more exalted status was bound to be conferred upon individual figures.

We have seen an application of this theory in Grimm's interpretation of *hild* as Bellona and the like.[273] No one now takes these interpretations seriously. It is different with Grimm's interpretation of *wyrd*. He recognized Urðr, Verðandi and Skuld as abstracts, and thought that among all the Germanic tribes the three 'must have been known as personalized beings; we can clearly demonstrate from Old Saxon and Anglo-Saxon poetry the personality of the first Norn'.[274] Grimm quoted from Old English poetry; among other citations, these: *Me þæt Wyrd gewæf* [Fate wove this for me; *Rhyming Poem* line 70], *Wyrd oft nereð unfægne eorl þonne his ellen deah* (*Beowulf* lines 572–3), *Him wæs . . . Wyrd ungemete neah, se þone gomelan gretan sceolde, secean sawle horde, sundur gedælan lif wið lice* [Fate was exceedingly close to him that was to assail the aged man, was to seek out the treasure of his soul, was to sever asunder his life from his body; *Beowulf* lines 2419–23]; and he provided the later history of *Wyrd* and the *Weird Sisters* with reference to Gavin Douglas's *Virgil*, *The Complaynt of Scotlande*, Holinshed, William Warner's *Albions England*, and *Macbeth*.[275]

J.M. Kemble largely followed Grimm; his comment on the personalized use of *wyrd* at *Beowulf* line 1056 is a good example of the application of Grimm's theories:[276]

> there are two separate uses of this word, one a more abstract one, in which it is capable of being used in the plural, and which may generally

---

[273] See p. 19 and footnote 49, above.
[274] Grimm, *Deutsche Mythologie*, 1st edn, p. 228, 2nd edn, p. 377: 'eine gothische Vaúrþs, Vaírþandei, Skulds, eine ahd. Wurt, Werdandi, Scult u. s. w. müssen als persönliche wesen bekannt gewesen sein, wir vermögen die persönlichkeit der ersten norn deutlich aus alts. und ags. poesien zu beweisen'.
[275] Grimm, *Deutsche Mythologie*, 1st edn, p. 229, 2nd edn, p. 378.
[276] Kemble, *The Saxons in England*, I, pp. 399–400.

be rendered *eventus*, another more personal, similar to the Oldsaxon *Wurth*, and in which it never occurs but in the singular. In the following most remarkable passage the heathen and Christian thoughts are strangely mingled, Wierd being placed in actual apposition with God,

> swá he hyra má wólde
> nefne him witig God,
> Wyrd forstóde,
> & ðæs mannes mód.

'As he would more of them had not wise God, Wierd forstood him, and the man's courage.' How very heathen the whole would be, were we only to conceive the word *God* as an interpolation, which is highly probable: nefne him witig – Wyrd forstóde!

With these precedents A. Köhler's treatment of the occurrences of *wyrd* in *Beowulf* seems bold, to his contemporaries unacceptably bold:[277]

> Wyrd occurs nine times, 477, 572, 734, 1056, 1205, 1233, 2420, 2526, 2814 [he omits 455 and 2574], in every case as the personification of Fate. All recollection of the venerable figure of the Norn has been lost, and the word has been reduced to a completely abstract term. Thus at line 1056 it is said that Grendel would have perpetrated more misdeeds if the wise God and the man's (i.e. Beowulf's) courage had not defended the men (i.e. Hrothgar's retainers) from such a fate: *nefne him witig god wyrd forstode and þæs mannes mod*, which Simrock translates quite meaninglessly, 'but *Wyrd* warded it off, the wise God and the man's courage'. The completely abstract significance of *wyrd* emerges especially clearly from the use at line 3030 of the genitive plural *wyrda*, which cannot possibly have been formed from the name of the Norn, and which is to be rendered 'facts'.

K. Simrock in his translation (1859) of line 1056 was following the editions and translations of Kemble (1835–7), and Benjamin Thorpe (1855), and the translation of L. Ettmüller (1840); Köhler's punctuation and interpretation is that of Grein's edition and translation, both of

---

[277] Köhler, 'Germanische Alterthümer im Beóvulf', p. 133: 'An 9 Stellen wird *Vyrd* angeführt, v. 477. 572. 734. 1056. 1205. 1233. 2420. 2526. 2814, überall als Personification des Geschickes. Die Erinnerung an die ehrwürdige Gestalt der Norne ist völlig verloren und es hat sich das Wort zu einem ganz abstracten Begriffe abgeschwächt. So wird v. 1056 gesagt, Grendel würde noch mehr Unthaten verübt haben, wenn nicht der weise Gott und des Mannes (d. i. Beóvulfes) Kühnheit den Männern, d. h. Hrôðgârs Mannen, ein solches Schicksal, den Tod, gewehrt hätten, *nefne him vitig god vyrd forstôde and þäs mannes môd*, wo Simrock ganz gedankenlos übersetzt: "aber Wurd wehrt' es, der weise Gott und des Mannes Muth". Ganz besonders deutlich geht die völlig abstracte Geltung von *vyrd* aus v. 3030 hervor, wo sich der Gen. Plur. *vyrda* findet, der von dem Namen der Norne unmöglich gebildet werden konnte und der durch "Thatsachen, Facta" zu übersetzen ist.'

1857.[278] Köhler never doubted that *wyrd* was ultimately a part of Germanic paganism, but at the same time he was convinced that an unprejudiced reading of *Beowulf* does not support the view that the poet used the word *wyrd* as the name of the pagan Norn. Klaeber accepted Köhler's views on *wyrd* in *Beowulf*, and reduced the scope of personification in the poem even further:[279]

> *Wyrd* is no longer thought of as personalized; *hild*, *guð*, *deað*, *heaðoræs*, *ecg(a)* . . . , are at almost the same level. The allusion to the weaving of Fate, *ac him Dryhten forgeaf wigspeda gewiofu* (697) is faded and fossilized in a formula.

As late as 1892 John Earle followed the early editors in their interpretation of line 1056 (because he erroneously thought that *him* in *nefne him witig God wyrd forstode* must be singular) and he translated the lines, 'as he would have killed more of them, had not the providence of God, had not Wyrd, stood in his way; – and the courage of that man.'[280] Earle's note on the passage, however, goes much further than anything Köhler had suggested:[281]

> The passage 1056–62 is not from the repertory of old minstrelsy; it belongs to the reflection and the philosophical studies of the present poet. It cannot be said to rise naturally out of the occasion; on the contrary, it is rather calculated to afford a triumph to those critics who exult over the incongruities of our text. It has certainly the effect of a doctrinal passage rather forcibly inserted; and I would account for it in the following manner. The elder minstrelsy had made Wyrd (Fate) allpowerful, and we have enough of it left to reveal conviction. . . . In the ordinary treatment line 1056 would have closed the allusion to Grendel, with the reflection that he would have slain more men had not Fate opposed him:– somewhat thus, *nefre* [sic (? for *nefne*)] *him*

---

[278] K. Simrock, *Beowulf Das älteste deutsche Epos Uebersetzt und erläutert* (Stuttgart and Augsburg, 1859), p. 55 (fit 16 lines 7–8 = lines 1056–7); J.M. Kemble (ed.), *The Anglo-Saxon Poems of Beowulf, The Travellers Song and The Battle of Finnesburh* (London, 1835), p. 75 lines 2104–7; J.M. Kemble, *A Translation of the Anglo-Saxon Poem of Beowulf*, the 2nd volume of his edition (London, 1837), p. 44; B. Thorpe (ed.), *The Anglo-Saxon Poems of Beowulf, The Scôp or Gleeman's Tale, and The Fight at Finnesburg* (London, 1855), p. 71 lines 2115–18; L. Ettmüller, *Beowulf. Heldengedicht des achten Jahrhunderts* (Zürich, 1840), pp. 107–8 lines 1069–71; C.W.M. Grein (ed.), *Bibliothek der angelsächsischen Poesie*, I, Text I (Göttingen, 1857), p. 283; C.W.M. Grein, *Dichtungen der Angelsachsen stabreimend übersetzt*, I (Göttingen, 1857), p. 251.

[279] Klaeber, 'Die christlichen elemente im Beowulf, IV', p. 172. 'Als persönliches wesen ist *wyrd* nicht mehr gedacht; fast auf derselben stufe stehen *hild*, *guð*, *deað*, *heaðoræs*, *ecg(a)*. . . . Nur abgeblaßt und formelhaft ist die anspielung auf das weben des schicksals, (*ac him Dryhten forgeaf*) *wigspeda gewiofu* 697.'

[280] Earle, *The Deeds of Beowulf*, p. 34.

[281] Earle, *The Deeds of Beowulf*, pp. 144–5.

wealdend Wyrd forstóde. In place of *wealdend* (or other epithet in *w-*) the poet puts *witig god* to correct the heathenism of it; and then gives a free rein to the thoughts which rose when Providence and Fate were brought into juxtaposition. Providence and Fate are not opposed but harmonised by the subordination of the latter; and divine Prescience is no check upon man's activity, but cooperative with it. In this view, and the rest of this train of associations, we can hardly err in recognising a mind fed upon the book of Boethius, *De Consolatione*, especially iv. 6, and onward.

Grimm had a reference to the phrasing of the Anglo-Saxon *Metres of Boethius*, comparing the wording, *wyrd gescraf* (*Metres* 1[29]), with *swa him wyrd ne gescraf* (*Beowulf* line 2574), *wyrd gescreaf* (*Elene* line 1046);[282] but Earle is not likely to have gone to any German work of scholarship for the realization that the poet's conception of *wyrd* is Boethian. In that (though not of course in regarding the passage as an interpolation) Earle looks back to no one, and forward to the scholarship of our time; in A.G. Brodeur's words:[283] 'Wyrd, then, as the poet conceives this force, is not the pagan goddess, and retains no trace of the heathen Norn; the poet's conception of *Wyrd* is purely Boethian.' Brodeur's interpretation of lines 1056–7, however, harks back to other, older strands of scholarship:[284] 'As the poet tells us plainly – God, and the hero's courage, averted fate.'

C. Wyrd *in a Leipzig Ph.D. Thesis*

Earle was exceptional. C.W. Kent was more typical of the scholarship of his time; he objected to Köhler's minimizing of the mythological significance of *wyrd*, and wished to give to the word the fullest force, even if the poets themselves might have implied rather than intended that force:[285]

> Among the appellations of the Deity occurs *wyrda wealdend* E[lene] 80, A[ndreas] 1058 [=1056]. It is easy to translate this by *Controller of Events*, and to contend as Köhler . . . does, that the word has lost all its association with the Norn, Wyrd. . . . but there are uses of this word even in Andreas and Elene, that forcibly recall, if they do not designedly imply, the Wyrd of mythology.

Kent referred to *Andreas* line 1561 where 'there is in my opinion no attempt on the part of the poet to escape a heathen allusion, for the words are put into the mouth of a heathen.[286] Referring to *Andreas* line

---

[282] Grimm, *Deutsche Mythologie*, 2nd edn, p. 378.
[283] Brodeur, *The Art of Beowulf*, p. 218.
[284] Brodeur, *The Art of Beowulf*, p. 76.
[285] Kent, *Teutonic Antiquities in Andreas and Elene*, p. 2.
[286] Kent, *Teutonic Antiquities in Andreas and Elene*, p. 3.

613 he wrote that in a speech 'uttered by the Divine Pilot . . . confounding the devil with Wyrd, or rather supposing Wyrd an emissary or agent of the devil; in either event however it is an unmistakable allusion to the powerful Fate'.[287] Lastly he referred to *Elene* line 1046:[288]

> Cynewulf, . . . recalling the chequered and singular career of Judas, who, from the most ardent of all opponents to surrender to Helen, became a most faithful and steadfast defender of Christianity, exclaims, Verily, Weird decreed that he should become so faithful, etc., recording thus his belief in fatalism, and attributing this to one of the sisters who presided over the destinies of men. Recalling now the expression *wyrda wealdend,* it may be said that had the poet used this expression deliberately and in its full sense, he would not have been heathenizing God, but rather elevating Him above the highest powers of heathen belief, (for even the gods were controlled by the decrees of the Norns,) and giving Him a controlling power over the controlling powers of heathen belief.

D. *Germanic Fatalism Accommodated in Anglo-Saxon Christianity*

From the time of Grimm to the First World War it was part of the central tradition of Germanic scholarship to look upon *wyrd* as a survival of paganism among the Christian Anglo-Saxons, and not a few scholars clung to that view for very much longer. Typical expressions of the view include R.C. Boer's account of the early period of Christianity in England, when 'The pagan conception of Fate has not yet lost its importance.'[289] J. Müller described the cultural background of *Beowulf* in similar terms:[290]

> Quite a number of pagan elements exist side by side with the dominant Christianity, some as religious conceptions, others as customs and

---

[287] Kent, *Teutonic Antiquities in Andreas and Elene*, p. 3.
[288] Kent, *Teutonic Antiquities in Andreas and Elene*, p. 3.
[289] R.C. Boer, *Die altenglische Heldendichtung,* I *Béowulf*, Germanistische Handbibliothek, XI (Halle, 1912), p. 122: 'Der heidnische begriff des schicksals hat aber noch eine nicht geringe bedeutung.'
[290] Johannes Müller, *Das Kulturbild des Beowulfepos*, Studien zur englischen Philologie, LIII (1914, also published in part as a doctoral dissertation of the University of Göttingen), p. 46: 'Neben dem herrschenden Christentum finden sich eine ganze Anzahl heidnischer Elemente, teils als Glaubensvorstellungen, teils als Sitten und Gebräuche. Wirklich lebendig ist das Heidentum noch in dem Glauben an Wyrd, das unabwendbare Schicksal. . . . Meist steht es im Gegensatz zu dem gütigen, ruhmreichen Gott, als die den Menschen feindliche Macht, die ihnen den Tod bringt (477, 1056, 1205), aber gelegentlich zeigt sich eine Überführung ins Christentum, indem Wyrd als die Vorsehung und Vollstreckerin von Gottes Willen erscheint.'

practices. Paganism is truly alive in the belief in *Wyrd*, inevitable Fate. . . . *Wyrd* is mostly contrasted with a bounteous and glorious God and described as a power hostile to man, a bringer of death (lines 477, 1056, 1205); but occasionally *Wyrd*, exemplifying a transitional stage to Christianity, is shown as Providence and the executrix of the Divine Will [lines 2526, 2814].

Müller later in his work widened his field of reference:[291]

> In *Beowulf* pagan *Wyrd* . . . appears several times beside Almighty God. That this relic of ancient paganism was in fact still alive in England follows from the mention of *Wyrd* – always as harsh, unyielding Fate – in secular lyric poetry (*The Seafarer* line 115, *The Wanderer* line 100, Cotton *Gnomes* line 5). In the North the Norns play the same rôle of Fate, especially one of them, *Urðr*, who by the very fact that she has the same name shows herself essentially related to the English *Wyrd*.

The view that *Wyrd* is a part of Germanic paganism explains such somewhat contradictory statements as C.C. Ferrell's on the fatalism in *The Wanderer* and *The Seafarer*:[292] 'Even in that portion of the "Seafarer" which is thoroughly Christian, God seems to be identified with Wyrd (S. 115 f.).' Later in the same article on *The Wanderer* and *The Seafarer* he wrote:[293]

> Both of the poems . . . are bathed in the sad light of fatalism. It is impossible for man to withstand the Wyrd (W. 15, 107, S. 115–116) during this dark life *þis deorce lif* (W. 89).

E. *Germanic Fatalism: a Key to Anglo-Saxon Melancholy*

The 'sad light of fatalism' is a recurring theme. We have met it in Henry Sweet:[294]

---

[291] Müller, *Das Kulturbild*, p. 76: 'Im Bēowulf erscheint neben dem allmächtigen Gott mehrfach die heidnische Wyrd. . . . Dass dieser Rest des alten Heidentums in England tatsächlich noch lebendig war, folgt aus der Erwähnung Wyrds – immer als hartes unbeugsames Schicksal – in der weltlichen Lyrik (Seefahrer 115, Wanderer 100, Cott. Denkspr. 5). Dieselbe Rolle des Fatums spielten im Norden die Nornen, insbesondere eine von ihnen, Urd, die sich schon durch den gleichen Namen als der englischen Wyrd wesensverwandt erweist.'

[292] Ferrell, 'Old Germanic Life in the Anglo-Saxon "Wanderer" and "Seafarer"', col. 402.

[293] Ferrell, 'Old Germanic Life in the Anglo-Saxon "Wanderer" and "Seafarer"', col. 406.

[294] Sweet, 'Sketch of the History of Anglo-Saxon Poetry', p. 6, quoted more fully above, pp. 38–9 and footnote 106.

A marked feature of Anglo-Saxon poetry is a tendency to melancholy and pathos . . . : joined to the heathen fatalism of the oldest poems, it produces a deep gloom.

It comes also in E. Dale's book:[295]

Closely woven into the English character was a dark strain of brooding melancholy, which again and again found its expression in English song. In spite of all the inbred fierceness, the pathos of sorrow lay near to every heart, being, no doubt, the outcome of an experience of dark days of national stress and strain, and of personal hardship and privation. The Englishman long had felt the dread and mysterious forces of existence pressing upon his soul, ever bearing him irresistably whither he would not. To find a key to the problem of life was altogether beyond his power; and he turned for a solution of its mystery to the dark goddess Wyrd or Fate, in whose hands both gods and men were powerless, and by whose arbitrary decisions the fortunes of men were determined.

The connection between the elegiac mood and *Wyrd* is made most clearly and most profoundly by G. Ehrismann:[296]

Melancholy permeates the Anglo-Saxon poets' thoughts on life, toilsome and transient, and a dark fate rules it. A great deal of paganism still projects into this national and Christian epic poetry. Beside the Christian Deity there still exists a pagan power, Fate, *Wyrd*. . . . That such relics of paganism could be retained undisturbed in poetry side by side with Christian teaching significantly reveals the tenacious adherence to older concepts, the freedom and independence of the Anglo-Saxon scop.

And again:[297]

The elegiac mood of the Anglo-Saxons is inherited from paganism. Life is suffused with this mood in a tender sensibility of its painful

---

[295] Dale, *National Life and Character*, pp. 51–2. Marginal notes refer to *The Wanderer* lines 95ff., and (for the end of the statement here quoted) line 107.

[296] Ehrismann, 'Religionsgeschichtliche beiträge', p. 235: 'Von wehmut durchzogen sind die gedanken, die die angelsächsischen dichter vom leben haben, mühselig ist es und vergänglich und über ihm waltet ein düsteres schicksal. In diese national-christliche epik ragt noch viel heidentum herein. Neben dem christengott besteht noch eine macht, eine heidnische, das schicksal, die *Wyrd*. . . . bezeichnend is es doch für das zähe festhalten an den alten begriffen, für die freiheit und selbständigkeit des angelsächsischen scop, dass reste des heidnischen wesens in der dichtung so ungestört neben der christlichen lehre beibehalten werden konnten.'

[297] Ehrismann, 'Religionsgeschichtliche beiträge', pp. 238–9: 'Die elegische stimmung der Angelsachsen ist eine erbschaft des heidentums. Sie ist über das leben verbreitet in einem weichen empfinden für die schmerzgefühle, welche dieses bietet, und in dem gedanken an die vergänglichkeit und an den tod, die auch der freude überall drohen. Sie ist ausgesprochen in der weltanschauung, die von dem pessimistischen glauben an ein starres fatum noch nicht ganz losgekommen ist.'

afflictions, and in thoughts of mutability and death, likewise threatening all joy, this mood is expressed in a view of life that has not yet entirely escaped from a pessimistic belief in immutable Fate.

In 1929 E.A. Philippson, reviewing past work in the field, expressed himself in fundamental agreement with it, and, like Baesecke after him,[298] he believed in the existence of a Germanic ethic, of which, according to Philippson, belief in Fate forms part:[299]

> The belief in *Wyrd*'s Power of Destiny or in the Order of Things (*orlæg*) provides the key, on the one hand, to contempt of death which is a part of the Germanic ethic, and, on the other hand, to the pessimism of pagan Germanic philosophy and to the remarkable tenderness of the Old English Elegies.

Philippson's survey of work on the subject begins at this point with the 'direction-giving remarks of Grimm and Kemble', and continues with Ehrismann's article of 1909.

F. Wyrd: *the Mark of Heathenism*

Scholars who saw in Fatalism a key to pessimism were obviously more sophisticated than those to whom the occurrence of *wyrd* in a text was a clear sign that that text was pagan. Thus to M.B. Price *wyrd* was simply 'the mark of heathenism'.[300] Klipstein (writing on *The Wanderer* line 100: *Wyrd se mæra*) provides an early example of this particular search for paganism at its crudest:[301]

> '*Wyrd se máera*,' *Fate the powerful*. The use of 'wyrd' proves the antiquity of the older part of this poem, and generally that of all others in which it is found. The word was rejected from the poetry of the

---

[298] See pp. 27–8 and footnote 74, above.
[299] Philippson, *Germanisches Heidentum bei den Angelsachsen*, pp. 227–8: '. . . weil hier im Glauben an die Schicksalsmacht der *Wyrd* oder an das Urgesetz (*orlæg*) der Schlüssel für die Todesverachtung der germanischen Ethik einerseits, den Pessimismus der heidnischen Weltanschauung und die auffällig weiche Stimmung der altenglischen Elegien andrerseits zu finden ist. Nach Grimms und Kembles wegweisenden Bemerkungen sind zu nennen die Arbeiten von Ehrismann . . . .''
He goes on to list A. Keiser, *The Influence of Christianity on the Vocabulary of Old English Poetry*, Illinois Studies in Language and Literature, V.1 and 2 (Urbana, Illinois, 1919), Alfred Wolf (see p. 107 n. 339, below), R. Jente, *Die mythologischen Ausdrücke* (1921), *Die Bezeichnungen für Schicksal* (1919), and Friedrich Kauffmann, 'Über den Schicksalsglauben der Germanen', *Zeitschrift für deutsche Philologie* 1 (1926), 361–408.
[300] Price, *Teutonic Antiquities in the Generally Acknowledged Cynewulfian Poetry*, p. 7.
[301] Klipstein, *Analecta Anglo-Saxonica*, II, p. 432.

nation belonging to the period succeeding the introduction of the Gospel as savoring too much of heathenism.

The books by Blanche C. Williams and Ernst Sieper treat *wyrd* in very much the same way.[302] Miss Williams's discussion of the Old English Gnomic Poems is derived from Brandl's, who considered them to belong to pagan ritual literature;[303] and Miss Williams, following Brandl, based her arguments for the early date of the Cotton *Gnomes* in the first place on the occurrence of the word *wyrd*:[304]

> First, there are tokens of the old religion. *Wyrd, enta, þyrs,* – all relate directly to the beliefs and practices of heathen times, and in a vital fashion.

Miss Williams applied her belief in *wyrd* as a 'token of the old religion' to *Deor* line 32, where *witig dryhten* occurs in a passage which is obviously, though, according to Miss Williams not irreparably, Christian:[305] '*Wītig dryhten* may be a single substitution in a heathen passage for *Wyrd* and a corresponding modifier.'

Sieper, in a chapter devoted to the psychology of the Germanic tribes, lists 'constant reference to Wyrd' among those things which 'prove the pagan character of these poems' (*scil.* the Elegies).[306] This view is fundamental to the whole argument of his book; it provides him with the reason for ascribing these poems to heathendom, and also, conversely, for the decay of elegiac writing in Christian times:[307]

> Certainly, all that gave rise to the pagan Elegies, death, exile, solitude, desertedness, decrepitude, mutability, was experienced also in Christian times. But the spirit no longer confronts in moving incomprehension the dark ways of the absolute Weird Sister: God is mightier than Wyrd.

But, at least now and then, Sieper seems to be aware that Old English poetry is not easily subjected to neat proofs. He points to phrases and ideas in the 'spurious' parts of *The Seafarer* and *The Wanderer* which he

---

[302] Williams, *Gnomic Poetry*; Sieper, *Die altenglische Elegie*.
[303] Brandl, 'Geschichte der altenglischen Literatur', I, Angelsächsische Periode, in Paul (ed.), *Grundriss der germanischen Philologie*, II, 2nd edn (1908), VI/6, § 11, pp. 959–61 (= pp. 19–21 of separate).
[304] Williams, *Gnomic Poetry*, p. 110.
[305] Williams, *Gnomic Poetry*, p. 52.
[306] Sieper, *Die altenglische Elegie*, p. 119: '. . . die beständige Bezugnahme auf Wyrd . . . beweist den heidnischen Charakter dieser Gedichte.'
[307] Sieper, *Die altenglische Elegie*, p. 16: 'Gewiß ist alles das, was zu den heidnischen Klagen Anlaß gab – Tod, Verbannung, Einsamkeit, Verlassenheit, sieches Alter, Vergänglichkeit – auch in christlicher Zeit empfunden worden. Aber nicht länger steht der Geist in erschütternder Fassungslosigkeit den dunkeln Wegen der "unberatenen Schicksalsschwester" gegenüber. Gewaltiger als Wyrd ist Gott.'

thinks are very similar, perhaps indebted to the 'genuine' poetry of *Beowulf*, *Christ*, the Gnomic Poems, and *Elene*. That may explain why Sieper showed no surprise that in *The Wanderer* 'there are references to Wyrd both in the Introduction (line 5) and in the spurious second half (lines 100 and 107)'.[308] He merely noticed these references, but did not allow them to curb his theories.

G. *Fate and Providence*

In 1921 Brandl wrote his article on the ancestry of the Weird Sisters in *Macbeth*, beginning with the Anglo-Saxons. Though he conceded that the religion of the Anglo-Saxons was Christian, he still sought to preserve for them some of their pagan theology:[309]

> The *Beowulf*-poet, because he was a man with predominantly secular interests still conversant with the pagan cults of the grove and of cremation, retained a conception of *Wyrd* that was correspondingly archaic. . . . Even though *Wyrd* denies glory in battle with the more powerful dragon to the aged Beowulf, best of men (line 2574), she does not do so wantonly, nor of course maliciously, but in the execution of a judicial or penitentiary office, as is indicated by the expression *forscrifan* 'condemnare'. It is in character with her very

---

[308] Sieper, *Die altenglische Elegie*, p. 201: '. . . daß der Hinweis auf Wyrd sowohl in der Einleitung als in der zweiten, unechten Hälfte des Gedichtes wiederkehrt, vgl. V. 5, ferner v. 100 und 107'.

[309] Brandl, 'Zur Vorgeschichte der *weird sisters* im "Macbeth"', pp. 253–4: 'Dem Beowulfdichter als einem vorwiegend weltlich orientierten Manne, dem der heidnische Hain- und Verbrennungskult noch vertraut war, ist ein entsprechend altertümlicher Begriff der Wyrd noch eigen. . . . Wenn sie auch Beowulf, dem Besten, im Alter beim Kampf mit dem übermächtigen Drachen den Ruhm verweigert (2573), so tut sie dies nicht aus Willkür oder gar aus Bosheit, sondern in Ausübung eines Richter- und Bußamtes . . . , wie durch den Ausdruck *forscrifan* "condemnare" angedeutet wird. Gesetzmäßigkeit ist ihre Wesenseigenschaft; die fatalistische Weltanschauung der alten Germanen gewinnt dadurch etwas wie eine naturphilosophische Grundlage.

'Aber zugleich denkt der Beowulfdichter die Wyrd in einem Dienstverhältnis zu Gott, der ebenfalls ein solches Amt zu üben pflegt (106, 980). . . . Beowulf sagt es seinen Gefährten vor dem Drachenkampf, daß die Entscheidung von der Wyrd kommen werde, und nennt sie dabei "metod manna gehwæs" (2527); und daß die Wyrd alle seine Verwandten bis auf Wiglaf bereits dahinraffte gemäß der Weltlauffügung = "to metodsceafte" (2815). Dieser Begriff *metod* ist offenbar aus der Ritualsprache der Heiden übernommen; er setzt ein anordnendes Schicksal voraus, im Gegensatz zum ausführenden, das der Wyrd zusteht: er weist nicht in jüdisch-christlichem Sinn auf Gott als einen reinen Geist hin, sondern auf eine Vernunft in den Dingen selbst: dieser ist die Wyrd gehorsam. Aus keiner Missionarstheologie konnte der Beowulfdichter solches lernen: es war ein Erbteil außerchristlicher Überlegung.'

being to act in conformity to laws; the Germanic fatalistic view of life gains something of a foundation in natural philosophy as a result of this characteristic.

But at the same time, the *Beowulf*-poet thinks of *Wyrd* as subservient to God, who himself is wont to execute an office of the same kind (lines 106, 979). . . . Before the fight with the dragon Beowulf says to his companions that the decision rests with *Wyrd* and he calls her *metod manna gehwæs* (line 2527); he says also that *Wyrd* has snatched away all his kin except Wiglaf, in accordance with the ordinance of the world, *to metodsceafte* (line 2815). It appears that the term *metod* has been taken over from the diction of pagan ritual; it presupposes an ordering Fate, as opposed to an executing Fate such as is proper to *Wyrd*; it does not look upon God, in the Judaeo-Christian sense, as a pure spirit, but rather points to Reason in the things themselves; *Wyrd* obeys that Reason. The *Beowulf*-poet could not have learnt that from the theology of any missionary; it formed part of a heritage of contemplation which lay outside Christianity.

The hard core at the centre of Brandl's woolly texture is the phrase *swa him wyrd ne gescraf* (line 2574) – the verb *gescrifan* was somehow identified and confounded by Brandl with the verb *forscrifan* – a phrase in which etymologically the old religion may be in collocation with the new, *-scrifan* being a Latin loanword. With all its imprecision Brandl's view is interesting as an attempt to understand some of the spiritual difficulties which in the early years of English Christianity must have beset the Anglo-Saxons. Brandl, it seems, thought that differences between the old religion (of which our knowledge is, in fact, largely the result of inference and surmise) and the new religion were resolved by accommodation rather than reconciliation.

Brandl was not the first to suggest that the old and the new religions held in common some ideas on Fate and Predestination; thus F. Brincker, in his programme on the Germanic antiquities in *Judith,* wrote:[310]

> There is no occurrence in *Judith* of the pagan goddess of Fate, *Wyrd*, who plays a great part in the fatalistic view of the world held by the Anglo-Saxons and the Germanic tribes in general, and whom we meet in most Anglo-Saxon poems. There are, however, several allusions to the fact that no one can escape from her governance. Christian and

---

[310] Brincker, *Germanische Altertümer in . . . 'Judith'*, p. 8: 'Die heidnische Schicksalsgöttin *Wyrd*, die in der fatalistischen Weltanschauung der Angelsachsen und der Germanen überhaupt eine große Rolle spielt und uns in den meisten angelsächsischen Dichtungen begegnet, fehlt im Gedichte von Judith. Wohl aber sind Anspielungen darauf vorhanden, daß sich ihrem Walten niemand entziehen kann. Hier stimmen christliche und heidnische Anschauungen überein. Nach beiden ist das Leben ein Lehen, das dem Menschen für eine bestimmte Zeit geliehen ist.'

pagan conceptions are at one in this. According to both, life is granted to man in fee for a limited time.

Nor was Brandl the last to see in Anglo-Saxon Christian references to *Wyrd* a merging of the old and the new. Dame Bertha S. Phillpotts, in her well-known paper on 'Wyrd and Providence in Anglo-Saxon Thought', believed, like Brandl, that some aspects of pagan thought are carried over into Anglo-Saxon Christianity; thus in her opening words:[311]

> However much scholars may differ in the dates they assign to *Beowulf* and to *Widsith*, and however much – or little – Christianity they may ascribe to the authors of the poems, they would doubtless agree on one point, that those authors are still influenced to some extent by the pagan attitude to life.

She saw *Wyrd*, though pagan in origin, as the executrix of divine justice:[312]

> These ideas of Heaven, Hell, and the justice of God, are the three ideas connected with the new faith which we find clearly indicated in *Beowulf*, and they were no doubt specially characteristic of the first few generations after the conversion. How did they blend with the old heathen philosophy of life?

Dame Bertha Phillpotts looked to Boethius for the blending of the old and the new religions, and she thought that the *De Consolatione* 'might never have been translated by Alfred but for paganism'.[313] She went on to say:[314]

> W.P. Ker said that Boethius saved the thought of the medieval world. But he could only save it because the ideas of which he treated were fermenting in the minds of the converted barbarians 'What the onefold Providence of God is, and what Fate is, what happens by chance, and what are divine intelligence, divine predestination, and human free will' [footnote: *Consolation of Philosophy*, Book VI, Alfred's version, tr. Sedgefield] – were not these questions which every thoughtful Anglo-Saxon must have pondered . . . ? . . . We may well owe the preservation of this work, and with it the best thought of the Middle Ages, to the fact that it made a bridge between the ancient philosophy of the Nordic peoples and their new religion.

---

[311] B.S. Phillpotts, 'Wyrd and Providence in Anglo-Saxon Thought', *Essays and Studies by Members of the English Association* XIII (1928, for 1927), p. 7.

[312] Phillpotts, 'Wyrd and Providence', p. 16.

[313] Phillpotts, 'Wyrd and Providence', p. 25.

[314] Phillpotts, 'Wyrd and Providence', p. 25. The reference is to Sedgefield (ed.), *King Alfred's . . . Boethius*, p. 127 lines 18–21, as translated by Sedgefield, *King Alfred's Version of the Consolations of Boethius – Done into Modern English, with an Introduction* (Oxford, 1900), p. 148.

H. *Metod*

Older ideas on *wyrd* persist. F. Norman's comment on *Waldere* I¹⁹ *ðy ic ðe metod ondred* supports the view that '*metod* is fate',[315] a view found, as Norman says, in Grein's *Sprachschatz* s.v. *meotud*:[316]

> Epithet of God (used only in verse); usually supposed to mean 'Creator'; it seems to me more probably to have had (in pagan times) a meaning analogous to Latin *fatum*, and this meaning seems in fact to be preserved not only in the compound *meotudwang* [*Andreas* line 11], but also at *Waldere* I¹⁹.

T.N. Toller repeated Grein's view, but introduced the significantly cautious word *may*:[317]

> The earlier meaning of the word in heathen times may have been *fate, destiny, death* (cf. metan), by which Grein would translate *metod* in Wald. l. 34 [= *Waldere* I¹⁹].

As early as 1869 Sophus Bugge, pointing to a rather unconvincing parallel, *ic ondræde me God* (Ælfric's *Old Testament*, Genesis xlii:18), had translated *metod* convincingly by 'God',[318] a translation that has the support of E.V.K. Dobbie,[319] but not of Norman, who refers to Bugge's interpretation without making use of it in his glossary.[320] The interpretation by Grein, Vilmar's pupil, is a good example of the search for paganism, wilfully pursued and gladly imitated, as for example by R. Jente, who says:[321]

---

[315] F. Norman (ed.), *Waldere* (London, 1933), p. 37, confirmed in the glossary, p. 52.

[316] C.W.M. Grein, *Sprachschatz der angelsächsischen Dichter*, Bibliothek der angelsächsischen Poesie, IV, Glossar II (Cassel and Göttingen, 1864), p. 240 (retained, virtually unchanged, in the edition, revised by J.J. Köhler [Heidelberg, 1912–14], p. 461), s.v. *meotud*: 'Epitheton Gottes (nur bei den Dichtern vorkommend), nach der gewöhnlichen Annahme Schöpfer bedeutend; eher scheint es mir in der Heidenzeit einen dem lat. *fatum* analogen Begriff gehabt zu haben, und diese Bedeutung scheint sich in der That nicht bloß in dem Compositum *meotudwang* [*Andreas* 11] erhalten zu haben, sondern auch in der Stelle Vald. 1¹⁹.'

[317] T.N. Toller (ed.), in J. Bosworth's *An Anglo-Saxon Dictionary* (Oxford, 1882–98), s.v. Cf. Brandl's discussion, quoted p. 98 and footnote 309, above.

[318] E. Sophus Bugge, 'Spredte iagttagelser vedkommende de oldengelske digte om Beowulf og Waldere', *Tidskrift for Philogi og Paedagogik* viii (1868), p. 74. Cf. S.J. Crawford (ed.), *The Old English Version of The Heptateuch, Aelfric's Treatise on the Old and New Testament and his Preface to Genesis*, EETS, o.s. 160 (1922), p. 187.

[319] Dobbie, *The Anglo-Saxon Minor Poems*, p. 138.

[320] Norman (ed.), *Waldere*, pp. 37 and 52.

[321] Jente, *Die mythologischen Ausdrücke*, p. 218: 'Eine andere sehr gewöhnliche Bezeichnung für "Schicksal" war ags. *metod*, ein poetisches Wort, das häufig auch als Bezeichnung des Christengottes vorkommt.'

Another very common term for 'Fate' was OE *metod*, a poetic word, which occurs frequently also to denote Christ.

I. *More Recent Pagan Interpretations of* Wyrd

Miss E.E. Wardale, writing in 1935, has little to offer to modern readers of Anglo-Saxon literature in her interpretation of pagan remains attached to *wyrd*, and what seems least acceptable today goes back to the beginnings of modern Anglo-Saxon scholarship. She comments on the tolerance of the Christian missionaries to some pagan ideas and practices:[322]

> One result of this tolerance . . . is the curious jumble of Christian and heathen elements which is constantly met with in our oldest poems, as when one of the Gnomic verses tells us 'the powers of Christ are great', and then goes on to add 'Fate is strongest'. It is also to be seen in the part played by 'Wyrd' or Fate in the older O.E. literature generally.

Her view of the part played by Fate, characteristically, ascribes to Fate the gloom that prevails throughout Old English literature:[323]

> The cheerful company of the gods and goddesses of the old Germanic mythology had been lost behind the one relentless figure of Fate, and the general tone of O.E. literature was coloured by this idea.

Miss Wardale's method is well exemplified by her treatment of *The Wanderer*:[324]

> in reading the Wanderer, one is at once struck with the difference in spirit between the opening lines and final passage which are clearly Christian, and the rest which is essentially heathen in its unrelieved gloom and its belief in fate, in spite of a Christian term interpolated here and there.

Then she remembers that the 'clearly Christian' opening includes the half-line *wyrd bið ful aræd*:[325]

> It may be suggested that the second half of verse 4 [*sic* for 5] 'Fate is full inexorable', must belong to the original poem. The sentiment is purely heathen and the scribe's object in his addition was to introduce some Christian element. The poem cannot, however, have begun in the middle of a line. The scribe may have worked over an existing passage, leaving, in a surprising way, this definitely heathen half-line.

---

[322] Wardale, *Chapters on Old English Literature*, p. 6.
[323] Wardale, *Chapters on Old English Literature*, p. 8.
[324] Wardale, *Chapters on Old English Literature*, p. 58.
[325] Wardale, *Chapters on Old English Literature*, p. 59 footnote 1.

Surprise at the results, not doubt in her method, was as far as Miss Wardale's learning took her, and that in spite of the explicit statement by Klaeber on the parallel case, the disintegration of *Beowulf*:[326]

> If . . . we were to remove the doubtful passages by simple *excision* we should find that . . . as a rule the alliteration of at least one line, often of two, would be disturbed.

G.K. Anderson, as late as 1949, wrote in a strain similar to Miss Wardale's:[327]

> We see the pagan spirit surviving in the unquenchable fatalism which permeates most of the Old English literature, whether the subject matter be Christian or pagan.

His account of the rôle of Fate in *Beowulf* owes little to the scholarship of Klaeber and those who followed him:[328]

> In many passages Fate (*Wyrd*) and her warriors, both the doomed and the undoomed, wrestle with the Christian God for supremacy. Such inconsistencies, however, are easily enough understood when we remember that *Beowulf* as we have it today has a story many features of which belong to the pagan Germanic world of the sixth century or earlier and a form which belongs to Christian England of the eighth century as regards language and of the early eleventh century as regards manuscript.

Karl Helm, the historian of Germanic religion, based his remarks about fatalism among the West Germanic tribes on the interpretation of lines 4–5 of the Cotton *Gnomes*, which Brandl and Blanche C. Williams[329] had also isolated as a particularly striking heathendom. Perhaps the lines are ambiguous; they are if we allow that their author associated *Wyrd* with the pre-Christian religion of the English, but that is very far from certain. The author is more likely to have associated *wyrd* with the Divine Will, as did all the other Christian poets. He presumably intended *wyrd byð swiðost* as a variation of *Þrymmas syndan Cristes myccle*, and authoritative modern editors (thus Grein–Wülcker and Dobbie) punctuate the lines:[330]

---

[326] Klaeber, 'Die christlichen elemente im Beowulf, IV', p. 180: 'Wollten wir . . . die fraglichen stellen durch einfache a u s s c h a l t u n g beseitigen, so zeigt sich . . . , daß in der regel in mindestens einem, oft in zwei versen die alliteration gestört werden würde.'

[327] Anderson, *Literature of the Anglo-Saxons*, p. 109.

[328] Anderson, *Literature of the Anglo-Saxons*, p. 68.

[329] See pp. 61–2 and footnotes 178–82, above.

[330] R.P. Wülcker (ed.), *Das Beowulfslied nebst den kleineren epischen, lyrischen, didaktischen und geschichtlichen Stücken*, Bibliothek der angelsächsischen Poesie begründet von C.W.M. Grein, I (Kassel, 1883), p. 338; Dobbie, *The Anglo-Saxon Minor Poems*, p. 55. See the facsimile in Williams's *Gnomic Poetry*, frontispiece.

> þrymmas syndan Cristes myccle,
> wyrd byð swiðost.

The punctuation of the manuscript is, of course, no help. It is metrical, marking off each half-line; Miss Williams, however, has a full stop after *myccle*, thus making it impossible to consider *wyrd* as varying *Þrymmas Cristes*. She is explicit on the subject:[331]

> 4b and 5a are distinct, Christ and Fate being put in opposition to each other, the predominance of the latter testifying to remote heathen origin.

Brandl, on the other hand, connects the two half-lines:[332]

> In the manner typical of the missionaries, the poem stresses the 'great miracles' in the case of Christ. *Wyrd* appears together with Him and is described as 'very mighty' (*swiðost*); as in *Beowulf*, *Wyrd* occurs together with the Deity; she does not perform miracles but is part of their execution.

Helm agreed with Miss Williams, not with Brandl in spite of his reference to him; like her he was sure that *wyrd* is unconnected with Christianity, and is stronger than Christ; unlike Brandl he gave *swiðost* its full superlative force:[333]

> The West Germanic sources of the pagan era once again give no information about the relationship of the power of the gods and that of Fate; there is no indication anywhere that, succumbing to Fate, the gods too will perish one day, as in the North. But in the Anglo-Saxon *Gnome* on Fate, interpreted by Brandl, we find this remarkable passage: 'The powers of Christ are great, *Wyrd* is strongest.' Since according to the Christian view God is the Lord of Fate, the postulate according to which *Wyrd* is placed above Christ must be a remnant of the pagan conception according to which Fate is stronger than the gods.

---

[331] Williams, *Gnomic Poetry*, p. 107.
[332] Brandl, 'Zur Vorgeschichte der *weird sisters* im "Macbeth"', p. 254: '... und zwar sind an Christus in echter Missionarsweise die "starken Wunder" betont. Neben ihm erscheint die Wyrd als "sehr mächtig" (swiþost); sie steht, wie im Beowulf, neben der Gottheit; sie tut nicht die Wunder, gehört aber zu deren Ausführung.'
[333] K. Helm, *Altgermanische Religionsgeschichte*, II, 2 (1953), p. 284: 'Über das Verhältnis zwischen der Macht der Götter und der Schicksalsmacht geben westgermanische Quellen heidnischer Zeit wiederum keine Auskunft, und daß auch die Götter dem Schicksal unterliegend einst wie im Norden untergehen wird nirgends angedeutet. Aber in dem von Brandl interpretierten angelsächsischen Schicksalsspruch steht die merkwürdige Stelle: Christi Kräfte sind groß, *Wyrd* ist am stärksten. Da in christlicher Auffassung Gott Herr des Schicksals ist, kann dieser Anspruch, der die *Wyrd* über Christus stellt nur ein Rest heidnischer Auffassung sein, nach der das Schicksal stärker ist als die Götter.'

J. *Wyrd* in *Solomon and Saturn*

The occurrences of the word *wyrd* in *Solomon and Saturn* offer difficulties which are peculiar to that poem. R.J. Menner's edition of the poem is of course very far from naïve paganization. Even so, he connected *wyrd* closely with Germanic paganism:[334]

> The central themes of the second dialogue are . . . 'the last things', Wyrd, Old Age, Death, and Doomsday. Of these it is Wyrd, the mythological personification of inexorable destiny, that most clearly reflects Germanic beliefs. This mighty power, 'Wyrd sēo swīðe' (434 [= 444]), accomplished the predetermined events of the whole world of nature, and governed the course of man's life, bringing him death and the end of earthly joys. In a poem as late as *Solomon and Saturn* the heathen conception of Wyrd is naturally influenced by both classical and Christian views of Fate. Saturn's question about which is mightier, Wyrd or Providence (*wyrd ðe warnung*, 419 [= 429]), is almost Boethian, and his further characterization of Wyrd the mighty as the daughter of death and the source of all wickedness and woe, though ostensibly a pagan characterization, has been fundamentally influenced by Christian beliefs. . . . But even Solomon, who, as the champion of Christianity, must be expected to give a Christian interpretation of Wyrd, shows the influence of the ancient Germanic belief when he says that Wyrd is hard to change (427 [= 437]).

A difficulty, for which Menner's explanatory note does not provide a solution, is that in Saturn's view (434–40 [= 444–50]) *wyrd* is *eallra fyrena fruma, fæhðo modor, frumscylda gehwæs fæder and modor* [(*wyrd* is) the cause of all sins, the mother of strife, the father and mother of every one of the capital sins]. Menner, misled by his belief in the Germanic pagan origins of *wyrd* in this poem, thought the poet was muddled:[335]

> the poet himself probably had no clear conception of the original heathen belief in Wyrd and intends Saturn's speech to be merely a pagan's inquiry concerning the reason for the existence of the evil in the world brought to men by fate.

Of course, Saturn's is a pagan's speech, and the clue to it lies in Boethius, though not in any of the passages quoted by Menner. *De Consolatione Philosophiae* IV. prose vii, *Omnem, inquit, bonam prorsus esse fortunam* [she (Philosophy) said, 'In every way all fortune is good'] is translated by King Alfred, 'Ða cwæð he: Ic wille secgan þæt ælc wyrd bio good, sam hio monnum good þince, sam hio him yfel þince' [Then he (Wisdom) said: I would say that whatever happens is good, whether it seems good

---

[334] Menner, *Solomon and Saturn*, pp. 62–3.
[335] Menner, *Solomon and Saturn*, p. 139.

to human beings or seems evil to them'].³³⁶ The whole chapter underlies this particular Dialogue, but the sentence quoted has a wider application. The speaker is *Se Wisdom*; and Wisdom's teaching is that *Wyrd* is good regardless of what man may think. To the heathen, who see only immediate effects and know nothing of their ultimate cause, *wyrd* seems baleful, a subject for gloomiest speculation and darkest fear; Christians, and among them the Old English poets, recognize in *wyrd* the executive aspect of an ultimately beneficent divine power.

K. *Current Views on* Wyrd

It is no longer as fashionable as it once was to look upon the occurrences of the word *wyrd* in Old English literature as survivals of Germanic paganism, or even to claim that we know anything about Germanic, that is pre-Christian, fatalism.

Klaeber was among the first to feel at least some slight doubt that the Anglo-Saxon ideas on Fate were not merely survivals of paganism:³³⁷

> The conception of the governance of Destiny (*wyrd*) derives from Germanic antiquity; it is presented almost without exception as a baleful, nay, mortal, power (a conception, however, that may perhaps have been influenced already by Christianity).

In 1916 Enrico Pizzo of Padua made a notable contribution to *Beowulf* criticism in which he took Klaeber's views on the unity of the poem a stage further. He rejected the last remnants of paganism in *wyrd*:³³⁸

---

[336] Sedgefield, *King Alfred's . . . Boethius* (1899), p. 137 lines 2–4. For the Latin, see Stewart and Rand (eds), *Boethius: . . . The Consolation of Philosophy*, p. 356.

[337] F. Klaeber, 'Die christlichen elemente im Beowulf, IV', p. 171. 'Aus germanischer vorzeit stammt die anschauung von dem walten des geschickes (*wyrd*) das (vielleicht doch schon unter christlichem einfluss?) fast ausnahmslos als eine verderbliche, ja tod bringende macht vorgeführt wird.'

[338] E. Pizzo, 'Zur frage der ästhetischen Einheit des Beowulf', *Anglia* xxxix (1916), pp. 11–12: 'Wenn wir jedoch das lied unvoreingenommen lesen, wenn wir erfahren, daß das schicksal Grendels tun ein ende setzt (v. 735f.), daß das schicksal die seele am ende des lebens vom körper trennt (v. 2421 ff.), daß Beowulf in seiner letzten rede sagt: *Ac unc feohte sceal / weorðan æt wealle, swa und Wyrd geteoð, / metod manna gehwaes* (v. 2526 ff.); wenn wir uns dabei vor augen halten, daß die anschauung von der allmacht gottes aus jeder zeile des gedichtes spricht, so können wir ohne weiteres von einer (undenkbaren) dualistischen auffassung absehen und annehmen, daß auch *wyrd* in dieser fassung des gedichtes ganz in den dienst der christlichen weltanschauung getreten ist. . . . Sagt man aber, gott widerspreche sich selbst, so berührt man allerdings einen widerspruch, der aber nicht im kontrast zwischen christlichem und heidnischem, sondern in der gottesauffassung des ganzen mittelalters begründet ist.

'Dieser widerspruch zwischen der allmacht gottes und der verantwortlichkeit

If, however, we read the poem without prejudice, when we learn that fate puts an end to Grendel's deeds (734–6), that fate separates the soul from the body at the end of life (2420–3), and that Beowulf says in his last speech,

> Ac unc [feohte] sceal
> weorðan æt wealle, swa unc wyrd geteoð,
> metod manna gehwæs
>
> (2525–7),

when we remember at the same time that the conception of God's omnipotence informs every line of the poem then we can ignore without more ado the (unthinkable) notion of a dualistic conception, and assume that in the extant form of the poem *wyrd* too has been subordinated to a Christian philosophy.... If, on the other hand, we say, God contradicts Himself, we have indeed lighted upon a contradiction, a contradiction, however, that has its basis in the medieval idea of God, and not in the contrast between Christianity and paganism.

This contradiction between God's omnipotence and man's responsibility, between the infinite power of God and the existence of Evil is to be observed also in our poem.

A.P. Wolf similarly denied that in the extant literature *wyrd* is pagan. He summarized the long chapter on the word in his dissertation on fate in Old English verse:[339]

> In Anglo-Saxon poetry the word *wyrd* retains nowhere the meaning 'fatum' nor that of the goddess of fate or death. *Wyrd* has been shown ... rather to mean 'event', as defined by 'happening, occurrence, fact'; this sense develops further into an event which is experienced by man individually or collectively, in other words it develops into the weakened sense 'fate', and finally into an unhappy event affecting the individual human being or life more generally, that is, in the weakened sense of 'destiny', which may be further subdivided into 'misfortune' and 'mortal calamity'.

---

der menschen, zwischen der unendlichen gewalt des guten und der existenz des bösen macht sich auch in unserem liede bemerkbar.'

[339] Alfred (Paul) Wolf, *Die Bezeichnungen für Schicksal in der angelsächsischen Dichtersprache* (Breslau, 1919), a doctoral dissertation of the University of Breslau, p. 48: 'Fasst man das Ergebnis der Untersuchungen über wyrd zusammen, so ist wyrd nirgendsmehr in der a[n]g[el]s[ächsischen] Poesie in der B[e]d[eu]t[un]g "fatum" oder als Schicksals- und Todesgöttin erschienen. Vielmehr hatte wyrd ... die B[e]d[eu]t[un]g eines Geschehens in den Def[initionen] "Ereignis", "Vorgang", "Tatsache"; diese wurde weitergeleitet in ein Geschehen, das den einzelnen Menschen oder das gesamte Leben trifft, also in den verblassten Begriff, "Schicksal", und schliesslich in ein unglückliches Geschehn für den einzelnen Menschen oder das gesamte Leben, in den verblassten Begriff "Verhängnis" im Sinne eines "unglücklichen Schicksals", das wiederum spez[iell] sich in "Missgeschick" oder "Todesverhängnis" gliederte.'

Theodora Idelmann, writing in 1932, allowed only a very much weakened meaning to *wyrd* in the Old English Elegies; she rejected specifically Siepcr's simple connection of *wyrd* with paganism, and considered it 'completely mistaken to point to the frequent references to *wyrd* as proof that those lines of the Elegies which are described as genuine are pagan in character'.[340]

Clear expression is given by Walter Baetke to what I take to be the current view:[341]

> We try to form a picture of the Germanization of Christianity mostly from works like *Heliand* or the earliest Anglo-Saxon poems, because it is thought that we have in them testimony of characteristically Germanic religious thought. But that is justified only in a very restricted sense. . . . Ever since Vilmar's famous interpretation of *Heliand* the attempt has been made time and again to characterize that Old Saxon Messianic poem as a monument of German piety. Scholars have looked for, and have even believed that they have found, in the poem substantial evidence of Germanic faith, of German religious feeling, of northern fatalistic religion, and of who knows what else. And Anglo-Saxon poems have been subjected to similar treatment. Not only has all sorts of stuff been read into these works by misinterpretations, things quite alien to their authors, but the underlying conceptions of the nature of Old Saxon religion and of Germanic

---

[340] Theodora Idelmann, *Das Gefühl in den altenglischen Elegien* (Bochum, 1932), a doctoral dissertation of the University of Münster, p. 106: 'Ganz verfehlt ist vor allem der Hinweis auf die beständige Bezugnahme auf Wyrd als Beweis für den durchaus heidnischen Charakter der als echt bezeichneten Verse in den genannten Elegien.'

[341] W. Baetke, 'Die Aufnahme des Christentums durch die Germanen', *Die Welt als Geschichte* ix (1943), pp. 153–4; republished in *Die Aufnahme des Christentums durch die Germanen*, Libelli XLVIII (Darmstadt, 1959, rpt 1962), pp. 27–8: 'Man sucht bei uns ein Bild von der Germanisierung des Christentums meist aus Werken wie dem Heliand oder den frühesten angelsächsischen Dichtungen zu gewinnen, weil man in ihnen Zeugnisse arteigener germanischer Religiosität zu haben meint. Aber das ist nur in sehr bedingtem Sinne berechtigt. . . . Man hat seit Vilmars berühmter Heliand-Interpretation sich immer wieder bemüht, die altsächsische Messiade zu einem Denkmal deutscher Frömmigkeit zu stempeln, hat in ihr altgermanisches Glaubensgut, deutsches Gottgefühl, nordische Schicksalsfrömmigkeit und wer weiß was alles gesucht und zu finden gemeint. Und mit der angelsächsischen Dichtung ist man ähnlich verfahren. Man hat dabei aber nicht nur alles mögliche in diese Werke hineininterpretiert, was ihren Verfassern ganz fern gelegen hat, man ist auch von falschen Vorstellungen über die Religion der alten Sachsen und die germanische Religion im allgemeinen ausgegangen. So ist z.B. das meiste, was man über den Schicksalsglauben in diesen Dichtungen geschrieben hat, unhaltbar. Wir wissen ja über den germanischen Schicksalsglauben überhaupt sehr wenig. Ob wir den Fatalismus, der uns in einigen eddischen Heldenliedern und in gewissen Sagas entgegentritt, zurückdatieren und in ihm einen Wesenszug germanischer Frömmigkeit sehen dürfen, ist zum mindesten fraglich.'

religion in general have been false. For example, most of what has been written about the fatalism in these poems is untenable. We know very little indeed about Germanic fatalism. It is, to say the least, questionable if it is permissible to antedate the kind of fatalism we find in some of the Eddaic heroic lays and in certain sagas, and to regard it as a characteristic trait of Germanic piety.

Professor Dorothy Whitelock's remarks about the survival of pagan fatalism in Anglo-Saxon verse is similar in direction:[342]

> It is often held that Anglo-Saxon poetry is permeated by a strong belief in the power of fate, inherited from heathen times, and some have even seen a conflict between a faith in an omnipotent Christian God and a trust in a blind, inexorable fate. To me, this view seems exaggerated. The word used for fate can mean simply 'event', 'what happens', and though there are passages where some degree of personification is present, such as 'the creation of the fates changes the world under the heavens' or 'woven by the decrees of fate', I doubt if these are more than figures of speech by the time the poems were composed. If they are inherited from the heathen past, they may indicate that men then believed in a goddess who wove their destiny, but the poet who says 'to him the Lord granted the webs of victory' is unconscious of a heathen implication in his phrase. It would be natural enough that, even while yet heathen, the Anglo-Saxons should feel that man's destiny is outside his own control, but stronger evidence would be necessary before we could assume a belief in the fate-weaving Norns at the foot of the world-tree Yggdrasil, as described in the much later, poetic, mythology of the Scandinavians.

Still more recently Morton W. Bloomfield has repeated Dr Idelmann's warning in a footnote in which he draws attention to the valuable surveys of the late B.J. Timmer:[343]

> The widespread tendency to use the word 'wyrd' as evidence of Germanic Paganism seems to be dangerously simplistic, for *wyrd* was soon given a Christian meaning. After all, there is a Christian meaning to fate well summed up in the term 'providence'.

---

[342] D. Whitelock, *The Beginnings of English Society*, The Pelican History of England, II (1952), pp. 27–8.

[343] M.W. Bloomfield, 'Patristics and Old English Literature: Notes on Some Poems', *Comparative Literature* xiv (1962), p. 37; rpt in Greenfield (ed.), *Studies in Old English Literature in Honor of Arthur G. Brodeur*, p. 37. The studies referred to by Bloomfield, among which he singles out the two by Timmer, are: Phillpotts, 'Wyrd and Providence', B.J. Timmer, 'Wyrd in Anglo-Saxon Prose and Poetry, *Neophilologus* xxvi (1940–41), pp. 24–33, 213–28, and B.J. Timmer, 'Heathen and Christian Elements in Old English Poetry, *Neophilologus* xxix (1944), pp. 180–5.

12. Conclusion

IN THIS MONOGRAPH I have sought to anatomize a prejudice which turned into a predilection. Some kind of chronological order has been followed, but I make no pretence that the deliberate selections presented here amount to a chapter in the history of the scholarship of Anglo-Saxon literature. In one view, however, the history of scholarship is a history of error, and looked at that way the search for paganism comes near the centre of any historical account of the Anglo-Saxon scholarship of the last hundred and fifty years. In that period the unknown – as I think, the unknowable unknown – was so firmly used to explain the known that scholars felt no doubt in their methods or results.

That is no longer so. At a factual level the search for Anglo-Saxon paganism is, if conducted at all, no longer conducted naïvely; but some of the attitudes to literature and learning characteristic of those earlier scholars, who, like the Wife of Bath, were (*mutatis mutandis*) on the side of the elves rather than of the limiters, still prevail. Tracing to its origins the error on which these attitudes are based may perhaps help to eradicate them.

PART II

ANGLO-SAXON TRIAL BY JURY

Trial by Jury and How Later Ages Perceive its Origin Perhaps in Anglo-Saxon England

The First Trial by Jury, by Charles West Cope, 1847

B.M. 1854–12–11–135, © Copyright The British Museum

1. Jury: this *palladium* of our liberties, sacred and inviolate

The striving for liberty has been regarded as the special endeavour of the English, vigorously pursued from time immemorial, and liberty was achieved, it has been thought, by the Anglo-Saxons, and assuredly by the time of the Glorious Revolution of 1688 and thereafter. So it seemed to Voltaire, who said of the English:[1] 'They are not only jealous of their own Liberty, but even of that of other nations.' That striving for liberty was founded on a legal system based on truth, and bound in conscience as its constant and sure foundation. This is a model of which England herself has reason to be proud, a model for all the English-speaking peoples to make their own, and for all Europe to emulate, as it seemed to learned writers of modern times, among them Milton, Voltaire, Blackstone, Kant and Hegel. These noble ideals were traced back to Anglo-Saxon times, and trial by jury, with the institution of the jury itself, twelve good men and true from the vicinage, to bear witness on oath to the truth presented by a party in a dispute, was central to this historical conception. How wonderful to trace it back, and to associate its beginnings with no less a person than Alfred the Great, king of the West Saxons, who was credited with so much that is greatest in the governance of England as it was before the Norman Conquest, and as, in the opinion of many, it was slowly restored in later ages.[2]

---

[1] The translation, by John Lockwood, appeared before the French original, *Letters Concerning the English Nation by Mr. de Voltaire* (London: for C. Davis and A. Lyon, 1733); I quote p. 55. Voltaire's French reads, 'Ce peuple n'est pas seulement jaloux de sa liberté; il l'est encore de celle des autres'; *Lettres Ecrites de Londres sur les Anglois et autres sujets Par M. D. V**** ('Basle', i.e. London, 1734), p. 52. Cf. other early editions: *Lettres Philosophiques Par M. de V . . .* (Rouen: Jore, 1734), p. 33; and with the same title (Amsterdam: E. Lucas, 1734), p. 58. Cf. G. Bengesco, *Voltaire – Bibliographie de ses œuvres*, II (Paris, 1885), 9–21 (no 1558). A modern edition is by N.E. Cronk, *Voltaire Letters Concerning the English Nation*, The World's Classics (Oxford, 1994), p. 34. In the great Kehl edition the *Lettres* are split up and presented alphabetically: *Oeuvres Completes de Voltaire* ([Kehl]: Imprimerie de la Société Littéraire-Typographique), XLII (1785), *Dictionnaire Philosophique* VI, p. 256.

[2] See E.G. Stanley, 'The Glorification of Alfred King of Wessex (from the publication of Sir John Spelman's *Life*, 1678 and 1709, to the publication of

Trial by jury is traditionally regarded as the ancient bulwark of the civil liberty of the English; in the words of Sharon Turner, the historian of Anglo-Saxon England at the beginning of the nineteenth century, opening his chapter, 'The Trial by Jury':[3]

> IN considering the origin of the happy and wise institution of the ENGLISH JURY, which has contributed so much to the excellence of our national character, and to the support of our constitutional liberty, it is impossible not to feel considerable diffidence and difficulty. It is painful to decide upon a subject on which great men have previously differed. It is peculiarly desireable to trace, if possible, the seed bud, and progressive vegetation of a tree so beautiful and so venerable.

Turner, aware of the difference between twelve jurymen and twelve sworn witnesses, nevertheless quotes from 'De contentione inter Gundulfum & Pichot', which occurred between 1077 and 1097,[4] and is preserved in Textus Roffensis of the twelfth-century:[5]

> But since the bishop of Bayeux, who presided at that lawsuit, did not believe them well, he ordered that, if they knew what they said to be true, they should elect twelve from among themselves, who should confirm with an oath what all had said. They, however, when they had withdrawn in counsel and were there frightened by the sheriff through a messenger, came back and swore that what they had said was true.

This occurrence does not well support the contention that the beginnings of trial by jury are to be seen among the Anglo-Saxons: the dispute between Gundulf and Pichot involved Bishop Odo, brother of William the Conqueror, too late for certainty that it follows Anglo-Saxon legal practice; it uses compurgators,[6] or better oath-helpers, to

---

Reinhold Pauli's, 1851)', *Poetica* (Tokyo) 12 (1981), pp. 103–33, reprinted in E.G. Stanley, *A Collection of Papers with Emphasis on Old English Literature*, Publications of the Dictionary of Old English, 3 (Toronto, 1987), pp. 410–41.

[3] S. Turner, *The History of the Manners, Landed Property, Government, Laws, Poetry, Literature, and Language, of the Anglo-Saxons* = *The History of the Anglo-Saxons*, IV (London, 1805), p. 335.

[4] Gundulf was consecrated bishop of Rochester in 1077 and Odo bishop of Bayeux died in 1097.

[5] Turner, *History of the Manners*, pp. 335–6, used J. Thorpe, *Registrum Roffense: or A Collection of Ancient Records, Charters, and Instruments of Divers Kinds* (London, 1769), pp. 31–2, which is based on T. Hearne, ed., *Textus Roffensis* (Oxford, 1720), pp. 149–52. I quote from P. Sawyer, ed., *Textus Roffensis Rochester Cathedral Library Manuscript A. 3. 5*, II, Early English Manuscripts in Facsimile XI (Copenhagen, 1967), fol. 175v: 'Sed cum eis Baiocensis episcopus, qui placito illi preerat, non bene crederet, precepit ut, si uerum esse quod dicebant scirent, ex seipsis duodecim eligerent, qui quod omnes dixerant iureiurando confirmarent. Illi autem cum ad consilium secessissent & inibi a uicecomite per internuntium conterriti fuissent, reuertentes uerum esse quod dixerant iurauerunt.'

[6] That term is an anachronism when applied by legal historians writing in English to

swear to the truth of a statement made by one of the litigants; and it does not use those chosen from among the people to pronounce guilty or not guilty, which is the essential function of the modern jury. A few years later, Francis Palgrave, in a marginal note on trial by jury in his constitutional history, neatly sums up the difference:[7]

> Trial by Jury, according to the old English Law, [is] essentially different from the modern Jury; the ancient Jurymen being the Witnesses of the fact, and not the judges or triers of the truth of the evidence given by other Witnesses before them.

He goes on:[8]

> Many of those who have descanted upon the excellence of our venerated national franchise, seem to have supposed that it has descended to us unchanged from the days of Alfred;[9] and the Patriot who claims the Jury as the 'Judgment by his Peers,' secured by Magna Charta, can never have suspected how distinctly the trial is resolved into a mere examination of Witnesses.

And in another marginal note:[10]

> Juries in criminal cases [are] sometimes, but erroneously, supposed to be an Anglo-Saxon institution. The Twelve sworn Thanes of the Wapentake . . .[11] possessed the power of accusation, but not of trial. The Attesting Jurats . . . were only empowered to give a verdict respecting the transactions which they had been required to witness.

Anglo-Saxon and early Norman England; see *OED* s.v. *compurgator*, 1.b. Felix Liebermann, *Die Gesetze der Angelsachsen*, 3 vols (Halle, 1898–1916), II/2 'Rechts- und Sachglossar', pp. 377–80, s.v. *Eideshelfer*, does not use the term *compurgator*, except to state that it is not to be found in the Anglo-Saxon laws; he uses *Eideshelfer*, never its doublet *Eidhelfer* of which Modern English *oath-helper* is a loan-translation first used in the late nineteenth century. As is shown by *OED*, *compurgator* was the term used by David Hume and William Blackstone. The section 'Of the Compurgators' in William Forsyth's *History of Trial by Jury* (London, 1852), pp. 73–84, ch. IV section VI, may have lent authority to the use of the word in technical literature, though, in fact, Forsyth was not an expert in Anglo-Saxon law.

[7] F. Palgrave, *The Rise and Progress of the English Commonwealth: Anglo-Saxon Period* (London, 1822), I, p. 243.
[8] Palgrave, *Rise and Progress*, I, p. 244.
[9] For the myth that King Alfred instituted trial by jury, see E.G. Stanley, 'The Glorification of Alfred King of Wessex', pp. 105, 107, 113 and 119, reprinted in E.G. Stanley, *A Collection of Papers*, pp. 412, 414, 420 and 427. I do not know who first stated that Alfred instituted trial by jury.
[10] Palgrave, *Rise and Progress*, I, p. 250.
[11] Palgrave seems to be referring to what is, in Liebermann, *Gesetze der Angelsachsen*, I, p. 228, 'III Æthelred: zu Wantage' [*III Atr.* 3, 1]; but the reference 'Ethelred II., § 8' is not clearly to D. Wilkins (ed.), *Leges Anglo-Saxonicæ Ecclesiasticæ & Civiles* (London, 1721), p. 117, the corresponding law in the edition available to Palgrave.

I do not know whether Sir Francis Palgrave had an interest in poetry – as did his son, the famous anthologist Francis Turner Palgrave, – but his words 'unchanged from the days of Alfred; and the Patriot who claims the Jury as the "Judgment by his Peers," secured by Magna Charta' may be a slightly ironic reference to the long poem *Alfred* by Henry James Pye, the Poet Laureate from 1790 to 1813 and not much venerated by the intellectuals of the time. In that poem THE JUDGMENT OF HIS PEERS is one of only two phrases to be singled out by small capitals (in a poem occupying nearly 240 pages):[12]

> One legislator England's sons shall see,
> From aught of pride, and aught of error free;
> One code behold a patriot mind employ,
> To shield from fraud and force domestic joy.
> Though through the creviced wall, and shatter'd pane,
> Sings the chill blast, or drives the drizzly rain,
> The cot, more guarded than the embattled tower,
> Stands a firm fortress 'gainst despotic power.
> The poorest hind, in independance strong,
> Is free from dread, if innocent of wrong,
> Firm o'er his roof while holy Freedom rears
> That sacred shield, THE JUDGMENT OF HIS PEERS.

The last lines of the poem enshrine thoughts of patriotic learning (suitable expressions perhaps for a Poet Laureate but hardly factual enough for Palgrave, if he knew the poem and got to its end):[13]

> While patriot worth this godlike mandate taught,
> 'Free be the Briton's action as his thought.'
> Such the true pride of Alfred's royal line,
> Such of Britannia's kings the right divine.
>   As in his mind revolving thus, he stood,
> The thoughts congenial of the wise and good,
> Along the blue serene, with distant voice,
> Again Heaven's thunder consecrates his choice;
> While Britain's throne applauding angels saw
> Rear'd on the base of Liberty and Law.
>
> [Footnote:] V. 688. 'Et mecum tota nobilitas Westsaxonicæ gentis pro recta jure consentiunt, quod me oportet dimittere

---

[12] H.J. Pye, *Alfred: An Epic Poem, in Six Books* (London, 1801), p. 232 (book VI lines 479–90); these words, part of long address to the king, are spoken by 'Cornubia's Druid'.

[13] Pye, *Alfred*, p. 243, book VI lines 687–96. The footnote refers to F. Wise (ed.), *Annales rerum gestarum Ælfredi Magni, auctore Asserio Menevensi* (Oxford, 1722), p. 80; Wise published Alfred's will pp. 73–80, at the end of Asser's life of the king. Wise has . . . pro recto jure consentiunt; quod me oportet dimittere eos ita liberos, sicut in homine cogitatio ipsius consistit. Another edition that would have been available to Pye is [Thomas Astle (ed.),] *The Will of King Alfred* (Oxford 1788).

> eos ita liberos sicut in homine cogitatio ipsius constitit.'
> *Testamentum Regis Ælfredi*, printed at the end of Asser, p. 80.

Thus Pye in his patriotic effusion adduced an important royal document, not 'the base of Liberty and Law' for the English people in general, but demonstrating King Alfred's understanding of the need for a free nobility to exercise their judgement unconstrained by the king's absolute power.

Henry Hallam, a few years later, expressed himself cautiously on the supposed Alfredian origin of trial by jury, with reference to an important passage in the Laws of Alfred involving twelve oath-helpers:[14]

> & gif man cyninges ðegn beteo manslihtes, gif he hine ladian dyrre, do he þæt mid XII cininges ðegnum; gif ma ðone man betyhð, ðe bið læssa maga ðone se cyninges ðegn, ladige he hine mid XI his gelicena & mid anum cyninges ðægne – swa ægehwilcre spræce ðe mare sy ðone IIII mancussas –; & gyf he ne dyrre, gylde hit ðrygylde, swa hit man gewyrðe.
>
> (And if one accuses a king's thegn of manslaughter, if he dare to clear himself by oath, let him do so with twelve king's thegns; if one accuses someone who is less powerful than a king's thegn, let him clear himself with eleven of his peers and with one king's thegn – and so in every lawsuit that is of more than four mancuses –; and if he dare not (clear himself by oath), let him pay threefold compensation, as it is assessed.)

Hallam says:[15]

> It has been a prevailing opinion that trial by jury may be referred to the Anglo-Saxon age, and common tradition has ascribed it to the wisdom of Alfred.

Hallam continues (p. 146), denying that the numerical equivalence, twelve oath-helpers and twelve jurymen, is sufficient to establish the institution of trial by jury as Anglo-Saxon in origin:[16]

> in searching for the origin of trial by jury, we cannot rely for a moment upon any analogy which the mere number affords. I am induced to make this observation, because some of the passages which have been alledged by eminent men for the purpose of establishing the existence of that institution before the conquest, seem to have little else to support them.

---

[14] H. Hallam, *View of the State of Europe during the Middle Ages* (London, 1818), II. In doing so he refers to the '*Foedus* Ælfredi & Guthruni *Regum*' in Wilkins's edition of *Leges Anglo-Saxonicæ*, p. 47; corresponding to Liebermann (ed.), *Gesetze der Angelsachsen*, I, pp. 126–9, 'Ælfred und Guthrum', on clearing oneself by oath (*A Gu.* 3).

[15] Hallam, *View of the State of Europe*, II, pp. 142–3.

[16] Hallam, *View of the State of Europe*, II, p. 146.

Somewhat later than Hallam, the distinguished German jurist F.A. Biener rebutted, not without irony, that the Alfredian institution of the system of jury goes back to King Alfred, in a particularly good historical account of the facts, as far as they are known, of the origins of that system:[17]

> BLACKSTONE's remark, from which it appears that he regards the jury as a creation of Alfred the Great, is mythical in character, in that the English like to trace back all good institutions to this ruler.

A quarter of a century earlier, Biener had not been so bold as to reject Blackstone's attribution of the jury to King Alfred:[18]

> BLACKSTONE has in his excellent, well-known work treated the historical background only incidentally. According to his remarks in Book III xxiii and Book IV xxxiii, he regards the jury as an Anglo-Saxon institution that probably belongs among the creations of Alfred the Great.

The reference is, of course, to Blackstone's *Commentaries*,[19] first presumably on 'peace', that is, *grið* appertaining to the Danelaw; and secondly, the reference is to Blackstone on the origin of jury,[20] 'which wise institution has been preserved for near a thousand years unchanged from Alfred to the present time'.

What the oath-helpers have in common with modern jurymen is that they are twelve in number and that they are chosen from among the people of the vicinage. If we begin with the definition, that jurymen return the verdict 'guilty' or 'not guilty' the Anglo-Saxon twelve are not jurymen, for they do not fulfil the essential function of the modern jury, that they return a verdict of 'guilty' or 'not guilty'. It is not what in German is called an *Urteiljury*, a 'jury of trial', but it confirms by oath the truth of the evidence of a party to a case: it is a *Beweisjury*, a 'jury of proof'. When the party is the accuser the twelve constitute a 'jury of accusation', in German an *Anklagejury* or *Rügejury*. Especially in

---

[17] F.A. Biener, *Das englische Geschwornengericht* (Leipzig, 1852), ch. I, p. 11: 'Blackstone's Aeußerung, zufolge deren er die Jury als eine Schöpfung Alfreds des Großen ansieht, trägt einen mythischen Charakter an sich, indem die Engländer überhaupt alle guten Einrichtungen gern auf diesen Regenten zurückführen.'

[18] F.A. Biener, *Beiträge zu der Geschichte des Inquisitions-Processes und der Geschwornen-Gerichte* (Leipzig, 1827), p. 234: 'Blackstone hat in seinem vortrefflichen, allgemein bekannten Werke das Historische nur beiläufig behandelt. Nach seinen Aeußerungen in III. 23. IV. 33. hält er die Jury für eine angelsächsische Einrichtung, welche wahrscheinlich zu den Schöpfungen Alfred des Großen gehörte.'

[19] W. Blackstone, *Commentaries on the Laws of England*, III (London, 1768), pp. 349–85, at p. 349 he refers to Wilkins (ed.), *Leges Anglo-Saxonicæ*, 117, that is, Liebermann, *Gesetze der Angelsachsen*, I, pp. 228–30 [*III Atr. Prol.*–6,2], specifically on *grið* at *III Atr.* 1–1.2.

[20] Blackstone, *Commentaries*, IV (London, 1769), pp. 400–36, at pp. 403–4.

popular history, the jury used to be firmly traced back to Anglo-Saxon law; as Patrick Wormald says at the beginning of his encyclopaedia entry 'jury',[21] 'Traditionally the talisman of English liberties and once traced back to Old English times.' Learned authorities deny that trial by jury goes back to Anglo-Saxon times; among them the standard works by Liebermann, and by Pollock and Maitland echoed in *OED*.[22]

It would be easy to produce a long list of writers on Anglo-Saxon law who distinguished clearly between pre-Conquest *Beweisjury* and post-Conquest *Urteiljury*, though, of course, those who wrote in English did not use these German terms. Benjamin Thorpe's statement, based on the work of a German writer, J.M. Lappenberg, is sufficient illustration of informed opinion (before it received the strongest confirmation through Heinrich Brunner's learning and clarity). There are some questionable details in the Lappenberg–Thorpe account, such as that the rank of the accused was always (or usually even) that of the lowest freeman, the *ceorl*, and that unanimity was not required of the oath-helpers if they were to succeed in exculpating the accused who had called them; but then Thorpe warns the reader to proceed with caution:[23]

> It has often been supposed that the origin of trial by jury is to be traced to the earliest periods of Anglo-Saxon history, some finding it in their courts of law, others in the compurgators. But among the Anglo-Saxons there was no tribunal composed of sworn individuals, whose province it was to decide on the credibility of accusations, and the value of the proof adduced in support of them. The compurgators

---

[21] P. Wormald, in M. Lapidge, J. Blair, S. Keynes and D. Scragg (eds), *The Blackwell Encyclopaedia of Anglo-Saxon England* (Oxford and Malden, Massachusetts, 1999), p. 267.

[22] Liebermann, *Gesetze der Angelsachsen*, II/2 Rechts- und Sachglossar, p. 466 s.v. *Geschworene*; F. Pollock and F.W. Maitland, *The History of English Law before the Time of Edward I* (Cambridge, 1895), the second edition of which appeared in 1898 (and reprinted with introduction and revised bibliography by S.F.C. Milsom, 1968) with different pagination (1895 p. 118 = 1898 p. 139). *OED* s.v. *jury*, refers to 'Pollock & Maitland *Hist. Eng. Law* I. 118'. The *OED* entry *jury* first appeared in *A New English Dictionary on Historical Principles*, V, fascicule *Jew–Kairine* issued June 1901; it is repeated unchanged in the so-called second edition of *OED* published in 1989. (The bibliography to *OED*, published in the *Supplement* of 1933, lists only the first edition of Pollock and Maitland; the bibliography to the 1989 edition of *OED* refers to no edition of Pollock and Maitland other than the first.) Presumably, what *OED* refers to is the last sentence of the footnote on p. 118 (= 1898 edn p. 139): 'that the jury should originally have grown out of a body of doomsmen seems almost impossible'.

[23] B. Thorpe, *A History of England under the Anglo-Saxon Kings, Translated from the German of Dr. J.M. Lappenberg* (London, 1845), II, pp. 347–8. This corresponds to J.M. Lappenberg, *Geschichte von England*, I Angelsächsische Zeit, in A.H.L. Heeren and F.A. Ukert (eds), Geschichte der europäischen Staaten (Hamburg, 1834), pp. 605–6.

appeared for the purpose of strengthening the allegation, but were not judges. It is in the latter only that we can perceive any resemblance to the modern jury, and they furnish us only with the most general features of sworn examiners from the neighbourhood of the accused ceorl; they were authorized accusers, witnesses and judges at the same time; unanimity in their verdict was not required. Two circumstances have especially changed this, as well as other old legal institutions, that every attempt at comparison should be made with the utmost caution: viz. the entire change in the process of proof after the abolition of the God's judgements and compurgation; and, in a still greater degree, the introduction of a written law, framed on abstract principles, instead of that existing as matter of fact, and attested only by the judges. The period and manner of this transformation will be shown in the history of the first Norman kings.

Many jurists from the Renaissance onwards have been in fundamental agreement with that. The difference, at once apparent to lawyers, between twelve men who on oath confirm evidence and the twelve jurors who return the verdict of 'guilty' or 'not guilty' is too fundamental for the function of the latter to be derived from the former: what the two sets have in common is that they consist of twelve and that they are on oath.

The best account of the origin of jury, and the historiography of the matter, is that by Heinrich Brunner.[24] Great jurist that he was, he imposed order and clarity on the multifaceted and obscure, early history of jury. He rejects any attempt to combine into a single theory of origination two or more of the facets that may be discerned in the legal history of England from the earliest mention of oath-helpers to the emergence of trial by jury a century and more after the Norman Conquest. His clear lead was gladly followed, and Pollock and Maitland (in fact, mainly Maitland), whose work has been for many years, and may be still, the standard history of English law, cautiously walk on the path swept so clean by Brunner:[25]

> The essence of the jury – if for a while we use the term 'jury' in the widest sense that can be given it – seems to be this: a body of neighbours is summoned by some public officer to give upon oath a true answer to some question.
> . . .

---

[24] Heinrich Brunner, *Die Entstehung der Schwurgerichte* (Berlin, 1871), especially pp. 11–19 'Die nationale Herkunft', and pp. 19–30 'Der juristische Ursprung'. An important earlier paper was concerned with the definition of jury, but it was confined to continental, not English institutions: 'Zeugen- und Inquisitionsbeweis in deutschen Gerichtsverfahren karolingischer Zeit', *Sitzungsberichte der kaiserlichen Akademie der Wissenschaften*, Philosophisch-historische Classe LI, for the year 1865 (Vienna, 1866), pp. 343–505.

[25] *The History of English Law* (1895), I, pp. 117, 118–19, 120–1; 2nd edn (1898), pp. 138, 139–40, 140–1.

But what the jurors or recognitors of our twelfth century deliver is no judgment; they come to 'recognise,' to declare, the truth: their duty is, not *iudicia facere*, but *recognoscere veritatem*. No less deep is the gulf which separates them from witnesses adduced by a litigant. If all that we wanted were witnesses, if all that we wanted were a fixed number of witnesses, for example, twelve, there would really be no problem before us. But the witnesses of the old Germanic folk-law differ in two respects from our jurors or recognitors:– they are summoned by one of the litigants, and they are summoned to swear to a set formula; the jurors are summoned by a public officer and take an oath which binds them to tell the truth whatever the truth may be. In particular they differ from oath-helpers or compurgators; the oath-helper is brought in that he may swear to the truth of his principal's oath.

. . .

Such is now the prevailing opinion [that jury is of continental, especially royal Frankish origin], and it has triumphed in this country over the natural disinclination of Englishmen to admit that this 'palladium of our liberties' is in its origin not English but Frankish, not popular but royal.[26] It is certain that of the inquest of office or of the jury of trial the Anglo-Saxon dooms give us no hint, certain also that by no slow process of evolution did the doomsman or the oath-helper become a recognitor.

Lady Stenton has suggested[27] that Maitland's acceptance of Brunner's view of the origins of the English jury[28] is not expressed in terms that sound like 'the words in which a man who is fully convinced accepts an argument or embraces a new opinion'. But it could well be that Maitland is merely expressing his opinion cautiously: that the Scandinavian sources are too late and the continental evidence contemporary with Anglo-Saxon and Norman England not certain enough for there not to be room for further work and thought.

The phrase 'palladium of our liberties' presumably derives from Blackstone's famous discussion of trial by jury, both grand jury and petty jury as prevalent in eighteenth-century England (and comparable with legal institutions as they have developed in the United States):[29]

[26] Cf. H. Brunner, 'Zeugen- und Inquisitionsbeweis der karolingischen Zeit' (see n. 15, above), in which the early Frankish legal material was surveyed by him. He returns to the subject in *Die Entstehung der Schwurgerichte*, pp. 70–126, ch. v 'Das fränkische Königsgericht als Billigkeitsgerichtshof', ch. vi 'Das fränkische Frageverfahren in Civilsachen'. He deals with the evidence for Norman jury, pp. 127–233, ch. vii 'Entwicklungsgang des normannischen Rechtes', ch. viii 'Grundzüge der normannischen Gerichtsverfassung', ch. ix 'Das normannische Gerichtsverfahren', ch. x 'Das Inquisitionsrecht des Fiscus'.

[27] Doris M. Stenton, *English Justice between the Norman Conquest and the Great Charter, 1066–1215*, Jayne Lectures for 1963 (London, 1965), p. 16.

[28] At Pollock and Maitland, 2nd edn, p. 143 (= 1st edn, p. 122).

[29] Blackstone, *Commentaries*, IV (1769), ch. xxvii, pp. 342–3. When he read a draft

The trial by jury, or the country, *per patriam*, is also that trial by the peers of every Englishman, which as the grand bulwark of his liberties, is secured to him by the great charter . . .

But the founders of the English laws have with excellent forecast contrived, that no man should be called to answer to the king for any capital crime, unless upon the preparatory accusation of twelve or more of his fellow subjects, the grand Jury: and that the truth of every accusation, whether preferred in the shape of indictment, information, or appeal, should afterwards be confirmed by the unanimous suffrage of twelve of his equals and neighbours, indifferently chosen, and superior to all suspicion. So that the liberties of England cannot but subsist, so long as this *palladium* remains sacred and inviolate, not only from all open attacks, (which none will be so hardy as to make) but also from all secret machinations, which sap and undermine it.

of this paper, Dr Patrick Wormald rightly thought that I had not made clear that the grand jury cannot be said to be exercising a function that constitutes a defence of civil liberty of the subject; the trial jury, later in origin, may perhaps be recognized as exercising a function that could be so interpreted.

2. Delivering the truth not the same as judging

Not all commentators on trial by jury took so idealistic a view of that institution as Blackstone. Pope, with characteristic cynicisms whenever he adverted to some hallowed organization of supposed virtue, enshrined his doubts in the oft-quoted couplet:[30]

> The hungry Judges soon the Sentence sign,
> And Wretches hang that Jury-men may Dine;

a couplet in which Pope, in fact, ascribes to the judges of his time a greater concern for the welfare of jurymen than seems warranted, makes it appear, mistakenly, that judge and jury are acting together as if a combined magistracy operating against the interests of the accused, the wretches.

The scholarly, juridical perception of the fundamental distinction between *iudicia facere* and *recognoscere veritatem* has a long history. In the nineteenth century Brunner, in his earlier study of Carolingian law, had mentioned the terminological imprecision that blurred the distinction:[31] 'The factual distinction between "declaring the truth" and "declaring the law" was not strictly adhered to in expression.' For this blurring of a fundamental legal distinction he has a reference to Jacob Grimm, by the 1860s the *Altmeister* of the study of Germanic Antiquity; *veritatem dicere* is shown in Carolingian documentary use in support of Grimm's distinction between, on the one hand, 'das abgelegte gültige zeugnis *entschied* die sache' (the valid testification *decided* the charge) and 'der zeuge indem er die *wahrheit sagte*' (the witness in *delivering the truth*), and on the other hand, '*urtheilend*' (*judging*):[32]

---

[30] Alexander Pope, *The Rape of the Lock and Other Poems*, ed. Geoffrey Tillotson, The Twickenham Edition of the Poems of Alexander Pope, II, 3rd edn (London and New Haven, 1962), p. 170, *The Rape of the Lock*, Canto III, lines 19–20. First published in *The Rape of the Lock an Heroi-Comical Poem: In Five Canto's. Written by Mr. Pope* (London: Bernard Lintot, 1714), p. 20.

[31] In the section on 'Zeugenverfahren der Capitularien' in 'Zeugen- und Inquisitionsbeweis in deutschen Gerichtsverfahren karolingischer Zeit', p. 363 n. 2: 'Der sachliche Unterschied von *veritatem dicere* und *legem dicere* wurde im Ausdruck nicht strenge festgehalten.'

[32] J. Grimm, *Deutsche Rechts Alterthümer* (Göttingen, 1828; = 2nd edn, *Deutsche*

This throws light on a conjunction between those judging and those testifying, which is unmistakable especially in the earliest period when there were no permanent *Schöffen*.[33] In such cases truth *de facto* and truth in law were the same.

Brunner's own clarity of exposition has obscured the essential conjunction of witness and juryman in the early stages of the development of the jury, a conjunction recognized by Grimm, who had studied law and was as fully aware as Brunner of the modern distinction between judging and testifying.

As someone, who is not a jurist or legal historian yet ventures to write on the history of English law, let me be bolder still and try to rescue the origin of jury from the lawyers. In the public mind the following are the salient features of that institution:

1. The jurymen are twelve in number.
2. They speak truth on oath and, therefore, upon their conscience; and for anyone with even a smattering of etymological knowledge, the word *verdict* itself transparently enshrines the jurors' duty that they speak truth (a transparency reinforced when the etymological spelling and, somewhat later, spelling pronunciation were imposed on earlier *verdit*, *vardit* from medieval Latin *verdictum*.[34]
3. They are chosen, not from those in authority nor from those learned in the law, but from among the peers of the litigants, and dwelling in their vicinage.
4. As such, they are the representatives of the people, the governed, whereas the judge and the court, that is, the whole panoply of the law, are the authorities, that is, in a modern misconception, the government.

These conceptions – and misconceptions – have the result that the institution of jury is perceived by Englishmen as the 'palladium of our liberties', and that is the reason also why the jury, but not trial by jury, may be said to owe something to Anglo-Saxon institutions.

Such perceptions (though no historical account of the origins of trial by jury, no mention even of the Anglo-Saxons) feature in the Kantian

---

Rechtsalterthümer [Göttingen, 1854], with identical pagination), pp. 858–9: 'hieraus leuchtet ein zusammenhang zwischen urtheilern und zeugen hervor, der besonders für die älteste zeit, wo es noch keine ständigen schöffen gab, unverkennbar ist. Factische wahrheit und rechtwahrheit waren in solchen fällen eins.'

[33] I make no attempt to define the concept *Schöffe*. That institution has no direct parallel in Anglo-Saxon procedure, but, as applied to early continental institutions, is analogous to but not identical with some later institutions in England, *juryman* and *lawman* especially.

[34] See E.J. Dobson, *English Pronunciation 1500–1700* (2nd edn; Oxford, 1968), § 303 and § 442 s.v.

metaphysical fundamentals of jurisprudence, whereas they have no place in Brunner's juridical essentials of trial by jury. Kant writes (with reference to disputes of civil property):[35]

> After all, neither the sovereign nor the governor of a state can *judge*: he can only appoint judges as magistrates. A people judges itself through those of its fellow citizens that have been, in a free choice, designated as its representatives for that purpose, and have moreover been designated specifically for each act in a legal process. For a verdict (a sentence) is the individual act of public justice (*iustitiae distributiuae*) of an administrator of the state (a judge or a court of justice) to adjudicate (to allot) what is his to the subject – i.e. to someone who is of the people and who therefore is not invested with any authority. Now since every individual of the people is, in this relationship (to the authorities), merely passive, either of these two authorities [the legislature or the executive] could, in a case of controversy over an individual subject's property, do an injustice in what they determine concerning that subject, because not the people itself pronounced *guilty* or *not guilty* upon a fellow citizen. But after the facts in that lawsuit have been established, the court of justice has the judicial authority to apply the law, and, by means of its executive authority, to accord to each individual what is his. Thus only the *people* can pass judgement on one of the people, though only indirectly, through their representatives (the jury) whom they have deputed.

[35] I. Kant, *Metaphysische Anfangsgründe der Rechtslehre*, part 1 of Kant's *Die Metaphysik der Sitten* (Königsberg, 1797), § 49 pp. 171–2; cf. *Kant's gesammelte Schriften*, VI, Werke VI (Berlin, 1914), p. 317: 'Endlich kann, weder der Staatsherrscher noch der Regierer, richten, sondern nur Richter, als Magisträte, einsetzen. Das Volk richtet sich selbst durch diejenigen ihrer Mitbürger, welche durch freye Wahl, als Repräsentanten desselben, und zwar für jeden Act besonders, dazu ernannt werden. Denn der Rechtsspruch (die Sentenz) ist ein einzelner Act der öffentlichen Gerechtigkeit (*iustitiae distributiuae*) durch einen Staatsverwalter (Richter oder Gerichtshof) auf den Unterthan, d. i. einen, der zum Volk gehört, mithin mit keiner Gewalt bekleidet ist, ihm das Seine zuzuerkennen (zu ertheilen). Da nun ein jeder im Volk diesem Verhältnisse nach (zur Obrigkeit) bloß passiv ist, so würde eine jede jener beyden Gewalten in dem, was sie über den Unterthan, im streitigen Falle des Seinen eines jeden, beschließen, ihm unrecht thun können; weil es nicht das Volk selbst thäte, und, ob schuldig oder nichtschuldig, über seine Mitbürger ausspräche; auf welche Ausmittelung der That in der Klagsache nun der Gerichtshof das Gesetz anzuwenden, und, vermittelst der ausführenden Gewalt, einem jeden das Seine zu Theil werden zu lassen die richterliche Gewalt hat. Also kann nur das Volk, durch seine von ihm selbst abgeordnete Stellvertreter (die Jury), über jeden in demselben, obwohl nur mittelbar, richten.' My translation has been greatly helped by M.J. Gregor (ed. and trans.), *Cambridge Edition of the Works of Immanuel Kant*, IV (Cambridge, 1996), pp. 460–1. Kant's German does not distinguish 'sentence' from 'verdict', unlike of course Blackstone's English in dealing with the subject in *Commentaries*, III (1768), pp. 378–9, on which Kant may be basing his statement, directly or indirectly.

The very neatness of Brunner's view, his advocacy of a singleness of origination of jury together with his rejection of theories that look to more than a single origin, may be less subtle than the multifactorial matter requires. Brunner appears to be driven by definitional logic; but in the long course of the historiography of English law the word 'jury' has been applied to various categories, and he fails to see that divergent factors may combine to produce something not much like that category alone to which, in his opinion, the word should be applied strictly. In dealing with the rise of trial by jury in England and the concomitant weakening of the system of *Beweisjury* (jury of proof), Brunner himself offers no documentary support for his bold assertion:[36]

> The history of trial by jury may certainly record as a remarkable fact that *Beweisjury* existed side by side with the remains of a defunct procedure of evidence, whereas the confirmation of evidence by oath-helpers was not only maintained without diminution but encroached upon the area of evidence by witnesses. Everyone who is accessible to general considerations will conclude from this fact alone which of these two evidential institutions was deprived of its life-blood by the developing jury system.

Though condemned by Brunner as untenable,[37] some *Combinationstheorien* seem attractive, precisely because of their lack of clarity of origination, which is not necessarily the same as a lack of reasoning in understanding it, but lies in the nature of the development of the institution of trial by jury. No one who has lived through the many changes that have occurred in the political and racial attitudes held in the course of the twentieth century can have much faith in any explanation of the divergent developments of legal institutions in the various countries in which a Germanic language is spoken by attributing the changes or lack of changes in legal institutions to a virtually unchanging national character. An ever steadfast Germanic national character was regarded in former times as a fundamental and axiomatic truth in any explanation, especially by German jurists, of origins and subsequent development of any institution including trial by jury. Significant among such jurists was C.S. Zachariä:[38] 'The influence of the *national character*

---

[36] Brunner, *Die Entstehung der Schwurgerichte*, pp. 195–6: 'Die Geschichte der Schwurgerichte muß es als eine beachtenswerte Thatsache verzeichnen, daß die Beweisjury die Reste eines abgestorbenen Zeugenverfahrens zur Seite hat, während sich der Eideshelferbeweis neben ihr nicht bloß ungeschwächt erhalten, sondern zum Theil auch in das Gebiet des Zeugenbeweises hinübergegriffen hat. Für jeden, der allgemeinen Erwägungen zugänglich ist, ergiebt sich hieraus von selbst, welchen der beiden Beweisinstitute die aufkeimende Jury die Lebenssäfte entzogen hat.'

[37] Brunner, *Die Entstehung der Schwurgerichte*, pp. 27–9.

[38] In Zachariä's review of Owen Flintoff, *The Rise and Progress of the Laws of*

is to be overlooked least of all in the attempt to explain the origin and development of the law of a nation.' At the end of the twentieth century it looks, however, as if legal institutions, like systems of government are imposed; they do not arise, as if by nature, from a *Volksgeist*.

Brunner could not accept Reinhold Köstlin's view of the origin of jury, perhaps partly because it is allied to that liberal historian's longing for legal reforms in criminal proceedings within at least some of the German states; for Köstlin was writing a short time before the events of 1848.[39] He states that public opinion demands the introduction of trial by jury, held in public and conducted orally. He did, however, advocate at the same time that trial by learned judges operating in courts attended by learned lawyers should be maintained.[40] He thinks that among foreign examples for such reforms 'das klassische Beispiel von England' should be considered strongly, for in England Germanic legal and political institutions developed undisturbed by foreign interference.[41] He surveys the legal scene with an eye on the past and with hopes for the future:[42]

> If one wishes to pursue the subsequent development of criminal procedure in the Germanic countries the general, earlier history has to be firmly kept in mind. For a time the development runs uniformly till the varying national characters begin to develop their national

England and Wales (London, 1840), *Kritische Zeitschrift für Rechtswissenschaft und Gesetzgebung des Auslandes* xiii (1844), p. 65: 'Bei dem Versuche, die Entstehung und Ausbildung eines Nationalrechts zu erklären, darf man am wenigsten den Einfluß des Nationalcharakters übersehn.'

[39] [Christian] Reinhold Köstlin, 'Die Zukunft des Strafverfahrens in Deutschland', *Deutsche Vierteljahrs Schrift*, 1846, I, pp. 315–47.

[40] Köstlin, 'Die Zukunft des Strafverfahrens in Deutschland', p. 321, 'gelehrte Gerichte'.

[41] Köstlin, 'Die Zukunft des Strafverfahrens in Deutschland', p. 326. The foundations that led to modern British democracy were seen to lie in ancient Germanic institutions: R. Schmid, *Die Gesetze der Angelsachsen* (Leipzig, 1832), p. lxix, speaks of 'Das demokratische Element in den germanischen Verfassungen' (the democratic element in the Germanic constitutions).

[42] Köstlin, 'Die Zukunft des Strafverfahrens in Deutschland', p. 326: 'Will man nun die Entwicklung des Strafverfahrens in den germanischen Staaten weiterverfolgen, so muß man die allgemeine Geschichte wohl im Auge behalten. Man wird die Entwicklung noch eine Zeitlang gleichförmig finden, bis die verschiedenen Volksgeister ihre Eigenthümlichkeit zu entwickeln und hiernach den Staat verschieden zu gestalten beginnen. Insbesondere trennt sich denn die Entwicklung in England bald von der des Continents ab, wo Frankreich mit Deutschland noch einige Zeit gleichen Schrittes geht. Jedermann weiß nun, daß in England das germanische Staatsprinzip sich am frühesten, und sofort am stetigsten und ungestörtesten entwickelte; dasselbe ist mit dem germanischen Strafverfahren auf englischem Boden der Fall. Das erste rohe Beweissystem geht dort naturgemäß bei steigender Kultur in ein angemässeneres über, aus welchem als seine Blüthe die Jury hervorwuchs, ohne daß je fremdartige Elemente in den Entwicklungsgang sich eingemischt hätten.'

peculiarities and accordingly to give differing shape to their polity. The development in England especially soon diverges from that of the continent, where the kingdom of the Franks for some time keeps pace with Germany. Everybody knows that in England the Germanic system of government developed soonest, at once most steadily and with the least disturbance; that is the case also with the development of Germanic criminal procedure on English soil. In that country the first crude evidential system quite naturally advances to one appropriate for a rising culture, out of which, as its flowering, grows the jury, without that foreign elements ever interfered with that progress.

3. Guilt and innocence a matter of conscience

A little later,[43] Köstlin considers

> ... the Germanic, fundamental principle of evidence in criminal cases. That proceeds from the idea that establishing the truth concerning a committed crime has of course to draw on sources revealing their history, such as the statements of witnesses, circumstantial evidence, etc., but that indeed the main point, the criminal's guilt, being a purely inward matter, can only be established by an inward method. We must refer to the treatises cited above[44] for how this view was expressed even in the earliest, crude systems of evidence (with oath-helpers, duel, and ordeals), naive and barbaric though they were.

Köstlin's *rein Innerliches* may go back to Georg Ludwig von Maurer's insistence that guilt and innocence are matters of conscience as is the truth of an oath, and the title of Maurer's treatise[45] shows the importance he attaches programmatically to public and oral procedure. He distinguishes oath-helpers from jurymen who return the verdict:[46]

---

[43] Köstlin, 'Die Zukunft des Strafverfahrens in Deutschland', p. 327: '. . . die germanische Grundidee über den Beweis in Criminalsachen. Sie geht davon aus, daß die Ermittlung der Wahrheit über ein begangenes Verbrechen zwar auch zunächst aus historischen Quellen, wie Zeugenaussagen, Indizien etc., zu schöpfen habe, daß aber gerade die Hauptsache, die Frage nach der Schuld des Thäters, als ein rein Innerliches, nur auf innerlichem Wege entschieden werden könne. Wie sich diese Ansicht schon in dem ältesten, rohen Beweissysteme (mit Eidhelfern, Zweikampf und Gottesurtheilen) freilich auf naive und barbarische Weise aussprach, darüber muß wieder auf die oben angeführten Aufsätze verwiesen werden.'
[44] The most prominent among the studies referred to are those by K.J.A. Mittermaier, especially *Die Mündlichkeit, die Oeffentlichkeit und das Geschworenengericht* (Stuttgart, 1845).
[45] G.L. (von) Maurer, *Geschichte des altgermanischen und namentlich altbairischen oeffentlich-muendlichen Gerichtsverfahrens, dessen Vortheile, Nachtheile und Untergang in Deutschland ueberhaupt und in Baiern insbesondere* (Heidelberg, 1824).
[46] Maurer, *Geschichte des altgermanischen . . . Gerichtsverfahrens*, pp. 108–10:
> Aus den Eidhelfern des Klägers sind nun nach und nach die Geschwornen hervorgegangen.
> . . .
> Aus eben diesem Ursprung der Geschwornen aus den Eidhelfern erklärt sich
> . . . warum die zwölf Geschwornen in England *einstimmig* seyn

The system of jurors arose gradually from the oath-helpers of the accuser. . . . The fact, precisely, that the system of jurors arose from oath-helpers explains: why in England the twelve jurors have to be unanimous, for otherwise the charge or the evidence would not have been conducted through twelve oath-helpers; and why they (the jurors) are not tied to any rules of evidence but have to follow solely the voice of their conscience, for, as with the oath-helpers of former times, everything depends on their opinion, on their conviction. That is how the number of the jurors is to be explained: *twelve*, which was very customary also for oath-helpers; and why the jurors are *judges only of the fact*, and not also of *the law*, which indeed was similarly foreign to the consideration of the oath-helpers. . . .

The result of these historical investigations is therefore that the institution of jurors has been developed and formed from oath-helpers, that is, it has grown from ancient Germanic seeds yet not on German soil.

Maurer's stress on both conscience and public and oral procedure must go back to Hegel's *Philosophie des Rechts*, §§ 227–8, on jury, as justified by Hegel; he, like Kant, is always difficult to translate into English, and my attempt may not entirely represent his thought, but may perhaps serve in a sketch of the history of nineteenth-century ideas on trial by jury:[47]

The right of apperception, the important factor of *essential liberty*,[48] may be regarded as the substantial point of view on the

> müssen, denn sonst wäre ja die Anklage oder der Beweis nicht durch zwölf Eidhelfern geführt gewesen. . . .
>
> . . . warum sie sich an keine Beweisregeln zu binden, sondern einzig der Stimme ihres Gewissens zu folgen haben, denn, wie bei den früheren Eidhelfern, kommt alles auf ihre Meinung, auf ihre Ueberzeugung an. Eben daher erklärt sich
>
> . . . die auch bei den Eidhelfern sehr gewöhnliche Zahl *zwölf* der Geschwornen, und
>
> . . . warum dieselben *bloße Richter der That*, und nicht auch *des Rechtes* sind, welches ja auch den Eidhelfern fremd war.
>
> . . .
>
> Das Resultat dieser historischen Untersuchungen ist demnach, daß sich das Institut der Geschwornen aus den Eidhelfern, also aus altgermanischen Keimen, allein nicht auf Deutschem Grund und Boden entwickelt und gebildet hat.

[47] G.W.F. Hegel, *Grundlinien der Philosophie des Rechts*, alternative title: *Naturrecht und Staatswissenschaft im Grundrisse* (Berlin, 1821), pp. 223–4 § 228: 'Das Recht des Selbstbewußtseyns, das Moment der **subjectiven Freyheit**, kann als der substantielle Gesichtspunkt in der Frage über Nothwendigkeit der öffentlichen Rechtspflege und der sogenannten **Geschwornengerichte** angesehen werden. Auf ihn reducirt sich das Wesentliche, was in der Form der **Nützlichkeit** für diese Institutionen vorgebracht werden kann.'

[48] My translation may be compared with T.M. Knox, *Hegel's Philosophy of Right Translated with Notes* (Oxford, 1942), pp. 144–5 § 228: 'The right of self-

question of the necessity of public procedure at law and the necessity of *trial by jury*. To this point of view the essence is reducible of what may be presented on behalf of these institutions as bestowing knowable reality to their *utility*.

consciousness, the moment of subjective freedom, may be regarded as the fundamental thing to keep before us in considering the necessity for publicity in legal proceedings and for the so-called jury-courts, and this in the last resort is the essence of whatever may be advanced in favour of these institutions on the score of their utility.' Knox's introductory remarks on translating Hegel show that he is well aware of the difficulty and the resulting insufficiency of any translation. His use of 'self-consciousness' for Hegel's *Selbstbewußtseyn* is misleading, except when understood as the equivalent in philosophy of *apperception*; see G.W.F. Hegel, *Encyclopädie der philosophischen Wissenschaften im Grundrisse* (Heidelberg, 1817), pp. 229–34 §§ 344–59 s.v. To translate Hegel's *subjective Freyheit* as 'subjective freedom' may mislead; but my 'essential freedom' is not an exact translation. Hegel's *öffentliche Rechtspflege* refers, of course, to public (and oral) legal procedure, and again Knox's 'publicity in legal proceedings' may mislead because of the recent development in the use of publicity for advertising purposes. Knox translates for readers interested in philosophy; I have attempted to translate for readers interested in the history of Anglo-Saxon law and how later ages perceived it.

4. 'England's great and glorious Revolution' (1688), its debt to Henry II's revival of ancient institutions fostering liberty

Shortly before the events of 1848, Josef Ignaz Gundermann published a treatise on the origin of the jury in England.[49] He outlines a more single-stranded development than Köstlin's 'Combinationstheorie', a development that breaks at the Norman Conquest, unlike the gradual emergence from the oath-helpers of Germanic antiquity to the jurors of the age of Henry II to modern times described by G.L. von Maurer. Nevertheless, like Köstlin and Maurer, Gundermann looks to developments in the laws of Anglo-Saxon and Norman England as relevant to the legal situation of modern Germany, and, in a spirit of Germanic nationalist superiority, involves the French Revolution, in a vague phrase. More clearly he involves the steady English striving to advance civil liberty culminating in what Dickens[50] called 'England's great and glorious Revolution' of 1688. Gundermann says:[51]

> There are questions which at some time must occupy every citizen as he educates himself and every German man. The one that forms our subject is of that kind.

---

[49] Ignaz Gundermann, *Geschichte der Entstehung der Jury in England und deren leitender Gedanke. Ein germanistischer Versuch* (Munich, 1847).

[50] C. Dickens, *A Child's History of England*, III (London, 1854), p. 317, last sentence of ch. XXXVI; first published in *Household Words*, No. 192 (26 November 1853), p. 312.

[51] Gundermann, *Geschichte der Entstehung der Jury*, opening of the preface: 'Es gibt Fragen, die jeden sich bildenden Staatsbürger und deutschen Mann einmal beschäftigen müssen. So die unsere. Es handelt sich hier nicht darum, irgend ein fremdartiges gleichgültiges Rechtsinstitut zu begreifen, sondern mit ihm die Verfassung eines Landes, das einzig unter den germanischen eine stete nationale Entwicklung zeigt . . . , das den Feudalstaat überwunden, nicht gestürzt hat, dessen Revolution, zumal für das Recht, eine von der französischen wohl geschiedene That ist. Hier ein Niederreißen und Aufbauen wegen und nach der Vernunft; dort ein Freimachen und wiederherstellen nach Forderung der Geschichte und, was dasselbe, des germanischen Volksgeistes. In England waren die Formen der Freiheit und des Rechtes nicht untergegangen, aber der innewohnende Geist des Friedens war dahin. Ihn wiederfinden sollte und that das Zeitalter der Revolution.'

It is not our concern here to understand some foreign and uninteresting legal institution, but to understand by that means the constitution of a country that alone among the Germanic countries has manifested a steady national development . . . , and that has overcome feudalism without overthrowing it, whose Revolution was an act very different, especially in respect of its legal system, from the French Revolution. In France, a tearing down and rebuilding because of and according to reason. In England a *liberation* and reinstatement in accordance with the demands of history and in accordance with, it amounts to the same thing, the Germanic national character. In England the conformations of liberty and law never perished, but the indwelling spirit of peace was past. The Age of Revolution was meant to find that peace again, and so it did.

Gundermann was indebted to Dahlmann's *Geschichte der englischen Revolution*, a work that traced from 1485 to 1689 the spirit that culminated in the Glorious Revolution.[52] Gundermann's firm rejection of a 'Combinationstheorie' of the origin of jury anticipates and is agreeable to Brunner; Gundermann says:[53]

Not as a result of the gradual combination of the institution of *Schöffen* with the institution of oath-helpers did the institution of 'recognition' and jury emerge, which is supposed to have received statutory force through Henry II, as Phillips supposed,[54] but the very nature of giving evidence was changed with the result that the *vicinetum* court of justices in eyre received the stereotyped form of

---

[52] F.C. Dahlmann, *Geschichte der englischen Revolution* (Leipzig, 1844), p. 12, '[die] stetig zur Freiheit fortschreitend[e] Entwickelung'. An English translation by H. Evans Lloyd. *The History of the English Revolution by F.E.* [sic] *Dahlmann* (London, 1844), says of the author (p. vii, the last words of the Preface): 'Professor Dahlmann, who is no less esteemed for the depth of his erudition, than for the soundness of his judgment, and the liberality of his views'. He renders (p. 10) Dahlmann's phrase (quoted by me), 'the continually progressive advance to freedom'.

[53] Gundermann, *Geschichte der Entstehung der Jury*, Zweites Buch. Nach der Eroberung, p. 56 § 2: 'Nicht aus einer allmählichen Vereinigung des Instituts der Schöffen mit den Eidhelfern ist das Institut der Recognitiones und der Jury hervorgegangen, welches durch Heinrich II. gesetzliche Kraft erhalten hätte, wie Phillips meinte, sondern das Zeugniß hat sich in seiner Natur geändert und so hat das *vicinetum* bei der Kurie der reisenden Justitiare die stereotype form der Assise erhalten, welche die Jury in sich aufnahm, und formal immer noch das Zeugniß der Nachbarschaft, der Heimat (*vicinetum, patria*), wie früher ist, und gleich den Zeugen gibt ihr Ausspruch (*veredictum*) die Wahrheit an, wie stets der germanische Beweis (*sooth* bei den Ordalien).'

[54] A footnote refers to G. Phillips, *Englische Reichs- und Rechtsgeschichte seit der Ankunft der Normannen*, II (Berlin, 1828), pp. 129 and 285 ff. Gundermann adds 'Uebrigens gab es in England gar keine Schöffen, wie wir sie durch Karl den Großen erhielten' (Incidentally, there were no *Schöffen* in England, such as we received through Charlemagne).

the assizes which absorbed the jury that, as before, is still the evidence of the neighbourhood (the *vicinetum*)[55] and the home region (the *patria*) and brings in its verdict (*veredictum*, the utterance of the truth), as always in Germanic evidence (*soþ* in the ordeals).

There is an element of contradiction here: the gradual combination of legal institutions is not at variance with a change in the nature of the institutions, except that in this case the change amounts to the switch from *Beweisjury* to *Urteiljury*, and that in legal definition is an essential difference. Truth is of the essence with both kinds of jury, though they are summoned differently. That they have truth in common gives them, for all their institutionally important differences at law, a shared inwardness of which Köstlin wrote so attractively in the first half of the nineteenth century. In the second half of the century Brunner's view of an essential difference was such that, when once seen, one is blinded to the institutional and spiritual elements they have in common.

Many theories of evolution see change, not as so gradual as to make it virtually imperceptible, but as proceeding in leaps. The legal institutions of the reign of Henry II seemed to Freeman the result of such a leap, when he wrote:[56] 'The greatest step made at any one time in the developement of the Jury system was when the practice of recognition was organized by the great Assize of Henry the Second.' Perhaps that statement, in tune with what some of the most distinguished legal historians wrote in the third quarter of the nineteenth century, seems to hark back a hundred years to the historian J.L. de Lolme of Geneva, a city, a canton and a country whose citizens valued their liberty:[57] 'Under Henry the Second, liberty took a farther stride; and the ancient *Tryal by jury*, a mode of procedure which is at present one of the most valuable parts of the English law, made again, though imperfectly, its appearance.'

De Lolme was, no doubt, indebted to the Chevalier Louis de Jaucourt's much more Romantic account of trial by jury in the article Wantage – which constitutes a long, glowing tribute to King Alfred, whose birthplace it celebrates – in the *Encyclopédie*:[58]

---

[55] The 'neighbourhood' from which inhabitants are chosen to give a sworn verdict in litigation. See Sir Henry Spelman (ed.), *Glossarium Archaiologicum* (London, 1664), p. 556 s.v. vicinetum.

[56] E.A. Freeman, *The History of the Norman Conquest of England*, V (Oxford, 1876), ch. XXIV, pp. 452–3.

[57] J.L. de Lolme, *Constitution de l'Angleterre* (Amsterdam, 1771), p. 20: 'Sous Henri second la liberté fit un pas de plus, & l'on vit renaître, quoique d'une maniére imparfaite, l'ancienne *Epreuve des Jurés* [a footnote explains, *Trial by a Jury*]: procédure qui fait aujourd'hui une des belles parties de la jurisprudence Angloise.' For the English translation, see J.L. de Lolme, *The Constitution of England* (London, 1775), p. 28.

[58] *Encyclopédie, ou Dictionnaire Raisonné des Sciences, des Arts et des Métiers*, XVII

> It was Alfred who introduced the way of judging by jury, that excellent part of the laws of England, and the best that yet has been devised in order that justice shall be administered impartially. That great man, convinced that the spirit of tyranny and oppression is natural to powerful people, sought to prevent its sinister effects. It was he who began to decree that the king's thanes or barons were to be judged by twelve of their peers; other thanes by eleven of their peers together with one king's thane; and a commoner by twelve of his peers.

Jaucourt gives a brief account of pre-Alfredian legal procedure, from Tacitus onwards, and continues:

> Alfred replaced that [earlier procedure] by the practice that is in force still in England, that is, that twelve free persons from the vicinage, having given an oath and having heard the witnesses, pronounce if the accused is guilty or not guilty. It seems that Alfred had extended to civil cases that kind of procedure, which had only taken place in criminal cases.

(Neuchâtel, 1765), col. 587b: 'C'est Alfred qui introduisit la maniere de juger par les jurés, belle partie des lois d'Angleterre, & la meilleure qui ait encore été imaginée, pour que la justice soit administrée impartialement! Ce grand homme convaincu que l'esprit de tyrannie & d'oppression est naturel aux gens puissans, chercha les moyens d'en prévenir les sinistres effets. Ce fut ce qui l'engagea à statuer que les thanes ou barons du roi seroient jugés par douze de leurs pairs; les autres thanes par onze de leurs pairs, & par un thane du roi; & un homme de commun par douze de ses pairs. . . . Alfred y substitua l'usage, qui subsiste en encore en Angleterre: c'est que douze personnes libres du voisinage, après avoir prêté serment, & oui les témoins, prononcent si l'accusé est coupable ou non. Il semble qu'Alfred ait étendu cette sorte de procédure, qui n'avoit lieu que dans les causes criminelles, aux matieres civiles.' Jaucourt (1704–79) had studied in Geneva, Cambridge and Leyden, and was one of the most productive of the contributors to the *Encyclopédie*; see T. de Morembert's article on him in *Dictionnaire de Biographie Française*, fasc. CV (1991), cols. 518–19.

5. Trial by jury not a Proto-Germanic nor perhaps an Anglo-Saxon institution; but what of the twelve leading thegns of the Wapentake?

It appears that for a considerable time now the Proto-Germanic origin of trial by jury has been insisted on less than long ago, and that bulwark of English liberty cannot be comfortably traced back to Anglo-Saxon times, nor, of course, to the statecraft of Alfred the Great to whom it was once so readily ascribed. Perhaps it is wiser to say that one knows what, at various times in the history of legal historiography, the scholarly consensus has been on the origin of trial by jury, than that one knows what the facts are. That is how Sir Frank Stenton sums it up with his usual care:[59]

> In spite of the vague reporting of early pleas, it is clear that the Norman kings established the jury as a regular part of the machinery of English government. In the opinion of most scholars the jury was introduced into England as a Norman institution, ultimately derived from the sworn inquests which the later Carolingian sovereigns had used for the determination of their rights. That the jury, in this sense, had been known to the early Norman dukes is possible, though it has not yet been proved.[60] On the other hand the 'twelve leading thegns' of the wapentake, who swore that they would neither protect the guilty nor accuse the innocent, were members of a society which had grasped the essential principle of the jury seventy years before the Norman Conquest.

Some difficult and complex legal cases of the period of the Norman Conquest have been studied carefully in the second half of the twentieth

---

[59] F.M. Stenton, *Anglo-Saxon England*, Oxford History of England, II, 3rd edn (Oxford, 1971), p. 651.
[60] Stenton has a footnote, 'There does not seem to be any clear case of the employment of a jury in Normandy between the Norman Settlement and 1066.' A note added, after Stenton's death, to the footnote in the third edition extends further the statement that there is no evidence of the jury in Normandy: 'nor, indeed in the period covered by the recently published volume of ducal charters ed. Marie Fauroux, *Receuil des Actes des Ducs de Normandie* (911–1066) Memoires de la Société des Antiquaires de Normandie, Caen (1961).'

century, among them the fenland case of Ramsey versus Thorney, that is, in a part of the Danelaw not very far from the Five Boroughs to which, as we shall see, the code called 'III Æthelred: zu Wantage' by Liebermann had special application, according to its first paragraph [*III Atr* 1, 1]. Both Ramsey versus Thorney and III Æthelred provide evidence that leads to the view that a form of jury (not of oath-helpers merely) may, from the end of the tenth century, have been in existence in that part of the Danelaw at least. The number of jurors in this case is not stated as having been twelve. The background and the documentary evidence is too obscure for me to venture upon in the hope of forming an opinion other than to accept the account and the cautious conclusions presented by Lady Stenton:[61]

> Nowadays, there is no need to be so tentative [as was Maitland in perhaps not being fully convinced by Brunner]. The strength of the Scandinavian influence in England is one of the great imponderables in Anglo-Saxon England, Nevertheless, during the sixty years since 1912 when Liebermann published his glossary to the *Gesetze*, traces of Scandinavian ideas and institutions have multiplied in Eastern England to an extent which has made the Danelaw a reality. To say the least, there is no longer any inherent improbability in the suggestion that the jury, common to the Scandinavian peoples on either side of the North Sea, rising to the surface for a moment under Æthelræd II, may have persisted in England to become incorporated into the fabric of the Anglo-Norman state.
>
> . . .
>
> For my own part, I believe that the rich stream of English case-law flowing through the Anglo-Saxon period reflects the minds and spirits of a people responsive to reason, ready to welcome a generous settlement of a plea, with a clear understanding of the sacral virtue of an oath. It was in this atmosphere that the seeds of the English jury grew and flourished.
>
> The establishment of the jury as an integral part of English civil procedure belongs to the Norman rather than to the Anglo-Saxon age.

It is very unlikely that Anglo-Saxon legal institutions remained untouched by those of the continent. And thus the German scholarly tradition, which goes back to Jacob Grimm and earlier and is well exemplified by Brunner and Liebermann after Grimm, tended to seek common Germanic origins for Anglo-Saxon and also for continental, Germanic institutions, rather than to regard continental, Carolingian institutions as partly innovative or Rome-based perhaps, that is, to see them as different from continuations mainly of *urgermanisch* law. It could be said without much exaggeration that many, perhaps most,

---

[61] Stenton, *English Justice Between the Norman Conquest and the Great Charter*, pp. 13–17; I quote from pp. 16–17.

German scholars of the nineteenth century and the first half of the twentieth, once they got a whiff of what they thought was *urgermanisch* or *kerndeutsch*, 'German to the core', in their nostrils, lost much of their common sense to myth. Among them Liebermann tended to seek Germanic origins in Anglo-Saxon institutions; as James Campbell has said (referring to a dissertation of 1912, for a higher degree):[62]

> At the same time Liebermann's *Gesetze* were appearing and his inclination was to find early or common Germanic origins for institutions where he could, while he was only marginally concerned with some of the relevant evidence. The strange consequence has been that for sixty years the question of the relationship between English and Carolingian institutions has been only rarely and barely considered. In seeking the origins of English institutions scholars have preferred to look north and to later texts, rather than south and to earlier.

Indeed, long before Liebermann, scholars had been looking around for institutions analogous to trial by jury with less avidity in the kingdom of the Franks than in Normandy, where the Norman Settlement provided a noble prospect of finding originally North-Germanic institutions, and looking around also in Scandinavia, as did, for example, T.G. Repp:[63] 'It cannot be said of the Norwegian Jury that it was empanelled, but still it was enclosed; and other regulations respecting it bear a considerable analogy to those of the English Jury.' If that analogy were to carry weight it would have to be more firmly based. The underlying perception may well go back to another branch of mythical Germanic legal history as practised in Germany in the first half of the nineteenth century (and perhaps later), that the constitution of Norway preserves without alloy its ancient Germanic, free constitution. Thus early in the century Rühs writes:[64] 'Indisputably the free Germanic constitution was maintained

---

[62] J. Campbell, 'Observations on English Government from the Tenth to the Twelfth Century', in J. Campbell, *Essays in Anglo-Saxon History* (London and Ronceverte, 1986), pp. 159–60; originally published in *Transactions of the Royal Historical Society*, 5th series, 25 (1975), p. 44. Campbell is referring to H.M. Cam's London MA dissertation of 1912, *Local Government in Francia and England*, p. 156, and it is hardly surprising that even so good a scholar as Helen Cam did not at that stage in her career question what must have seemed a fundamental orthodoxy.

[63] T.G. Repp, *A Historical Treatise on Trial by Jury, Wager of Law, and Other Co-ordinated Forensic Institutions, Formerly in Use in Scandinavia and in Iceland* (Edinburgh, 1832), p. 48. Repp appears to misunderstand the term *empanel*, which means 'entered in a list (of jurors)', not, as he seems to suggest, 'placed in an enclosure'.

[64] (Christian) Friedrich Rühs, *Handbuch der Geschichte des Mittelalters* (Berlin, 1816), p. 771: 'Unstreitig hatte sich in Norwegen die freie germanische Verfassung am reinsten und längsten erhalten.' For the scholarly opinions expressed by Rühs, see also my preface to the present book, p. xi.

most purely and the longest in Norway.' Wilda, to whom I owe this reference – in fact, he quotes Rühs inaccurately – and who in his own writings strenuously advanced the myth of the common Germanic legal heritage, makes explicit that Icelandic law is comprehended in Norwegian law, and in the manner of the age ignores the inconvenient dating of the *Gragas* manuscript, now regarded as of the second half of the thirteenth century with a dating of its contents as of the tenth-century or earlier nothing more than a hope and a wish.[65]

Whether an ancient institution, or, as seems more likely, an institution evolved for the Danelaw, 'the "twelve leading thegns" of the wapentake, who swore that they would neither protect the guilty nor accuse the innocent' are no myth, but perhaps, as Stenton says, 'derived from the juries of twelve familiar in the Scandinavian north'.[66]

---

[65] W.E. Wilda, *Das Strafrecht der Germanen*, Geschichte des deutschen Strafrechts, I (Halle, 1842), p. 12. For the current dating of the *Gragas* manuscripts and of its contents, see H.P. Naumann, *Grágás*, in H. Beck, H. Steuer and D. Timpe (eds), the 2nd edition of J. Hoops, *Reallexikon der Germanischen Altertumskunde*, XII (Berlin and New York, 1998), pp. 569–73.

[66] Stenton, *Anglo-Saxon England* (3rd edn), p. 511. The reference is to Liebermann, *Gesetze der Angelsachsen*, I, pp. 228–9 [*III Atr.* 3, 1–3].

6. Why promulgated at Wantage?

The laws, III Æthelred: zu Wantage 3, 1–3,[67] were promulgated at the very end of the tenth century in the north of Wessex near the border with Mercia, at Wantage celebrated for a thousand years and more as Alfred the Great's birthplace. The evidence for the place of promulgation goes back to the manuscript of the twelfth century.[68] The evidence for the date rests on Æthelred's charter to the Old Minster, Winchester.[69] That is now regarded as authentic by those competent to judge.[70] The evidence that Alfred was born at Wantage goes back ultimately to the single statement at the beginning of Asser's life of the king.[71] One historian has recently expressed doubts that Alfred was born at Wantage, but these are based on not much other than that, in particular, Wantage 'would then [in 849] have provided a most unsafe place for the lying-in of the wife of a West Saxon king', though we know little about the arrangements for women, royal or other, during their confinement, and, in general, that single doubter's hope that 'the status of Asser was to become a major political issue in Anglo-Saxon studies'.[72]

---

[67] III Æthelred: zu Wantage is one of several Old English law codes contained only in Textus Roffensis (Quadripartitus contains a Latin translation). The name in that form was given to it by Liebermann; see *Gesetze der Angelsachsen*, I, pp. 228–32.

[68] For the place (Wantage) and date (AD 997) of promulgation, as well as for the important discussion and voluminous bibliography of [*III Atr.* 3, 1–3], see Liebermann, *Gesetze der Angelsachsen*, III 'Einleitung zu jedem Stück; Erklärungen zu den einzelnen Stellen', pp. 156–9.

[69] P.H. Sawyer, *Anglo-Saxon Charters*, Royal Historical Society Guides and Handbooks, 8 (London, 1968), no. 891.

[70] See the authoritative statement by D. Whitelock in her *English Historical Documents c. 500–1042*, 2nd edn (London, 1972), p. 439: 'I no longer doubt the authenticity of this charter.' The authenticity of the charter underlies Simon Keynes's discussion in *The Diplomas of King Æthelred 'The Unready', 978–1016*, Cambridge Studies in Medieval Life and Thought, 3rd Series, 13 (Cambridge, 1980), pp. 101–2, and n. 56, pp. 196–7 and 255.

[71] See W.H. Stevenson (ed.), *Asser's Life of King Alfred* (Oxford, 1904), p. 1, and the notes pp. 154–5; for the debt of later medieval writers to Asser on Wantage, see J.A. Giles (ed.), 'Harmony of the Chroniclers, during the Life of King Alfred', in J.A. Giles (ed.), *Memorials of King Alfred* (London, 1863), pp. 6–7 ('Florence' [i.e. John] of Worcester and Simeon of Durham).

[72] See A.P. Smyth, *King Alfred the Great* (Oxford, 1995), pp. 3–8.

It is unlikely that Wantage would have been invented as the place of promulgation (or, for that matter, as the place of Alfred's birth); at least no reason for a false localization is known to us. It is at once noticeable that the language of this part of the Laws of Æthelred has many Scandinavian loanwords. Perhaps historians and philologists do not take sufficient account of the ease of travel from the north of England to the south. A nobleman on his horse and even a cleric, perhaps on foot if he thought of riding a horse as a symbol of the sin of Pride, would have taken no longer for that journey than it would have taken centuries later, in fact, till the construction of railway lines and roads in the course of the nineteenth century. Isaac D'Israeli may be called to witness for the abysmal state of the roads at the end of the eighteenth century which he contrasts with the roads of the Romans:[73]

> These *Roads*, of which some still remain, were high, broad, solid . . ., which the subverting hand of Time seems yet to respect. *Our Roads*, on the contrary, are in a variety of places in so pitiful a condition, that three or four days of rain frequently interrupt the intercourse of commerce, and delay the journeys of the best equipages.

We are dependent for much of our knowledge of the language of Northumbria in late Anglo-Saxon times on Aldred the scribe, of the community of St Cuthbert of Lindisfarne, Chester-le-Street and Durham. We learn that, probably in 970, he attended Bishop Ælfsige of Chester-le-Street (968–90) at Oakley, south of Woodyates, among the West Saxons, and did some writing there in Northumbrian, not in West Saxon.[74] It would not have taken an Anglo-Saxon long to travel from Wantage to the Five Boroughs.

---

[73] [I. D'Israeli,] *Curiosities of Literature* (London, 1791), pp. 424–5.
[74] See T. Julian Brown *et al.* (eds), *The Durham Ritual*, Early English Manuscripts in Facsimile XVI (Copenhagen, 1969), pp. 23–5.

7. The twelve of the wapentake probably an institution for the Danelaw only

Liebermann is good on the Scandinavianisms in this part of this code of Æthelred II, which is designed for the Danelaw or a part of it, namely the Five Boroughs:[75]

> The region where III Æthelred is effective is the Danelaw (or part of the Danelaw), at any rate the district of the Five Boroughs and perhaps that only. The currency is Anglo-Scandinavian, in hundreds of silver (= 8 pounds),[76] the *healfm(e)arc* and *ora*; the lowest court is called *wæpentac*, the reeve at one point *eorl*; the vocabulary sounds strongly Norse: *grið, lagu, bicgean lage, lahcop, landcop, sammæle, þrinna XII, costas, uncwydd & uncrafod, sac, sacleas, botleas* . . . The institution of jurors to support the accuser, and much else, is Norse.

Consideration of III Æthelred 3, 1 is very relevant for the history of trial by jury:

> & þæt man habbe gemot on ælcum wæpentake, 7 gan ut þa yldestan XII þegnas & se gerefa mid, 7 swerian on þam haligdom, þe heom man on hand sylle, þæt hig nellan sacleasan man forsecgean ne nænne sacne forhelan.

---

[75] Liebermann, *Gesetze der Angelsachsen*, III, p. 156: 'Der **Geltungsbereich** von III Atr ist die (oder ein Teil der) D e n a l a g u, jedenfalls das Gebiet der Fünfburgen und vielleicht nur dieses. Die Geldrechnung ist die Anglo-Skandinavische nach Hundert (= 8 £), Halbmark und Ör; das unterste Gericht heisst Wapentake, der Graf einmal *eorl;* der Wortschatz klingt stark Nordisch; *s. grið, lagu, bicgean lage, lahcop, landcop, sammæle, þrinna XII, costas, uncwydd & uncrafod, sac, sacleas, botleas* . . . Das Institut der Rügegeschworenen und manches andere ist Nordisch.' He gives bibliographical references to those to whom his account of the Scandinavian element in these laws is heavily indebted, including K. Maurer, 'Das Beweisverfahren nach deutschen Rechten', *Kritische Ueberschau der deutschen Gesetzgebung und Rechtswissenschaft*, 5 (Munich, 1857), pp. 180–249, 332–93 (on *III Atr.* 3–3,4 specifically p. 389), which had been cited in Brunner, *Die Entstehung der Schwurgerichte*, p. 403 note 2. I am indebted to Patrick Wormald for drawing my attention to a fuller, more recent treatment: C. Neff, 'Scandinavian Elements in the Wantage Code of Æthelred II', *Journal of Legal History* x (1989), pp. 285–318.

[76] MS 'lecge an C to wedde', *Quadripartitus* 'ponat unum hundretum in uadio' [*III Atr.* 7], Liebermann 'hinterlege er Ein Hundert (Silbers) als Pfand' (he is to lay down one hundred [of silver] as pledge).

(And that one shall hold a meeting in each wapentake, and that the most prominent twelve thegns and the reeve with them are to come forward and swear on the holy relic, which is to be given into their hands, that they will not wrongly accuse anyone innocent nor wrongly conceal anyone guilty.)

Those who write on medieval Scandinavian law are, of course, aware of the fact that there is no Scandinavian manuscript evidence for a period as early as the late tenth century. Presumably, the legal institutions of the Danelaw are Scandinavian institutions when they are not English. How far they were by then traditional in Scandinavia and how far the legal traditions of Scandinavia are *urgermanisch* are difficult, perhaps unanswerable problems; but it is unwise to believe that innovation without borrowing (from Carolingian or Roman law, for example) is impossible or unlikely for the nations of Scandinavia and Britain.

In III Æthelred: zu Wantage we have documentary confirmation that the legal institutions of the two parts of the kingdom, the part administered in accordance with the laws of the English and the part administered in accordance with the laws of the Danes, were not uniform. Simon Keynes, in his account of the matter, has a footnote in which he indicates that the interpretation of this Scandinavian element is not undisputed:[77] 'I incline more towards the traditional interpretation of III Æthelred as the codification of existing provincial custom . . . than I do towards its interpretation as "a flagrant encroachment on the legal autonomy of the Danelaw" by the extension to it of English practices.' 'The traditional interpretation' accepted by Keynes is likely to be right since this code is so much more heavily Scandinavianized than the rest of the laws of Æthelred, and the suggestion of 'encroachment' shows an unwarranted belief that the Danes under the English kings were unfairly used. As Keynes says (in the passage to which the footnote is appended):

> The code sets out in particular to define some of the customs relating to legal procedure in the Danelaw, and the degree of Norse influence on the terminology and practice of the law shows clearly how it was legislation sympathetic to the distinctly Anglo-Danish community that had grown up in eastern England during the course of the tenth century. Its provisions in many ways complement those for legal procedure given in Æthelred's so-called 'first' code of laws, . . . specifically said to have followed English custom.

The words *æfter Engla lage* 'according to the law of the English', of I Æthelred: zu Woodstock' [*I Atr. Prolog*], are central to this argument because they are echoed in *þa laga . . . to friðes bote* 'the laws . . . for the

---

[77] Keynes, *The Diplomas of King Æthelred*, pp. 196–7. Footnote 159 gives the source of the theory of encroachment: N. Lund, 'King Edgar and the Danelaw', *Medieval Scandinavia* ix (1976), pp. 181–95, 'flagrant encroachment' at p. 194.

improvement of peace', of III Æthelred: zu Wantage [*III Atr. Prolog*] followed by *Ðæt is, þæt his grið stande swa forð swa hit fyrmest stod on his yldrum dagum* (That is, that his [the king's] peace holds good henceforth as it held good most widely in the days of his forebears). The promulgation at Woodstock for the English used the English word *frið* for the king's peace, the promulgation at Wantage for the Danes used the Scandinavian word *grið* for the king's peace. Liebermann wants it spelt out, and hypothesizes a lost original wording for the Prologue of III Æthelred, *æfter Dena lage (according to the law of the Danes).[78] There is no need of greater explicitness for the Danes who were to be governed by this code: *his grið stande* says it all. It uses the Scandinavian word for the king's peace, used nowhere in the codes of Æthelred except in this code for the Scandinavians. There is linguistic sensitivity in that use; and more than that, it shows rare administrative respect for ethnic difference, a respect that goes back to the days of the king's forebears when the Danelaw was established. The council met at Wantage, the very birth-place of the greatest of his forebears: it could not have met there without those *witan* present piously remembering that. Æthelred 'the Unready'[79] is not usually praised for administrative sensitivity, and with good reason; but whoever suggested that the parliament meet at Wantage and whoever formulated the code showed imagination and tact.

In a history of Scandinavian law, III Æthelred: zu Wantage must have a high place near the beginning of such a work. It provides an early record of Scandinavian legal custom, perhaps specifically Danish custom. And as Lady Stenton has shown,[80] if one looks at Anglo-Saxon law in the hope of tracing to its beginnings the English trial by jury this particular code designed for the Danelaw may not be an

---

[78] Liebermann, *Gesetze der Angelsachsen*, vol. I, p. 228 col. 1 note **, and vol. III, p. 157 *Erklärung* of *III Atr Pro* note 4.

[79] The king's sobriquet does not go back to Anglo-Saxon times; see C. Sisam, '"Ready" and "Unready" in Middle English', in E.G. Stanley and D. Gray (eds), *Five Hundred Years of Words and Sounds: A Festschrift for E.J. Dobson* (Cambridge: 1983), pp. 137–43, with further references to discussions on this much-discussed sobriquet, the meaning of which is not quite certain, 'ill-advised' perhaps, or 'undecided', or 'unfortunate in the outcome of his actions'. The description in the Anglo-Saxon Chronicle of the events of 1011 may be relevant in that it uses the word *unrædas* which is translated 'bad policy' by Whitelock, *English Historical Documents*, 2nd edn, p. 244, and 'lack of prompt decision' by M. Ashdown (ed.), *English and Norse Documents Relating to the Reign of Ethelred the Unready* (Cambridge, 1930), p. 59: *Ealle þas ungesælða us gelumpen þuruh unrædas* (All these catastrophes befell us through lack of sound decisions), see G.P. Cubbin (ed.), *MS D, The Anglo-Saxon Chronicle A Collaborative Edition* (Cambridge, 1996), p. 56.

[80] Stenton, *English Justice Between the Norman Conquest and the Great Charter*, pp. 13–17.

irrelevance whenever it is different from pre-Conquest English legal custom. There is, however, no clear evidence that the laws of the Norman kings continued the traditions specifically of Scandinavian legal customs, and the use made of this particular code in Quadripartitus and, perhaps via Quadripartitus, in later codes (including the codes of Norman kings)[81] does not include those stipulations of paragraph 3,1 that have been regarded as having a place in the early history of the jury. What exactly that place is on the way to the institutionalization of the jury is unclear, but it is clear that the jurors involved in Ramsey versus Thorney and the twelve involved in III Æthelred 3,1 are quite unlike those in attendance at an ordeal, for example, II Æthelstan: 'æt Greatanleage' 23,2:[82]

> & ofga ælc mon his tihtlan mid foreaðe . . . ; & beo þæra ælc fæstende on ægþera hond se ðær mid sy on Godes bebode & ðæs ærcebiscopes; & ne beo ðær on naþre healfe na ma monna þonne XII. Gif se getihtloda mon ðonne maran werude beo þonne twelfa sum, þonne beo þæt ordal forod, buton hy him from gan willon.
> (And let each man exact his charge with a preliminary oath . . . ; and let each of those present on both sides be fasting in accordance with the command of God and the archbishop; and let there not be on either side more persons than twelve. If the accused is then one of a greater company than twelve in all,[83] then the ordeal fails, unless they are willing to go away from him.)

---

[81] See Liebermann, *Gesetze der Angelsachsen*, III, p. 156, 'Zu III. Æthelred. Einleitung', 5.

[82] Liebermann, *Gesetze der Angelsachsen*, I, pp. 162–3, MS H (Textus Roffensis).

[83] Whitelock, *English Historical Documents*, 2nd edn, p. 421 footnote, regards the formulation as ambiguous; she is not sure if the defendant is one of the twelve. The wording in itself is clear; *twelfa sum* is inclusive of the defendant: he is the *sum* 'the one' who has up to eleven others with him. Thus also Liebermann, *Gesetze der Angelsachsen*, III, p. 106 Erklärung of II As 23,2 note 7. The number probably matters in so ritualistic a paragraph; twelve certainly mattered in the eyes of scholarly commentators on oath-helpers and jury. The ambiguity arose through usage of the *sum* formula in the course of the Anglo-Saxon period: 'one of so many' came to be used occasionally as if it meant 'one with so many', perhaps through contamination with the prefix *sam-* 'together'; see E. Einenkel, *Das englische Indefinitum* (Halle, 1903), pp. 76–7, §§ 80–1, = *Anglia* xxvi (1903), pp. 537–8; Liebermann, *Gesetze der Angelsachsen*, II/1, Wörterbuch, s.v. *sum*; J. Hoops, *Kommentar zum Beowulf* (Heidelberg, 1932), pp. 45–6.

8. Conclusion

Trial by jury is important in the historical perception of English law. In that perception civil liberty was for a long time regarded as the supreme political aim of the English over the centuries. The meaning of 'civil liberty' has not been static since the term was first used in the seventeenth century. Milton's well-known use in the opening paragraph of *Areopagitica* almost amounts to a pragmatical definition of the concept:[84]

> when complaints are freely heard, deeply consider'd, and speedily reform'd, then is the utmost bound of civill liberty attain'd, that wise men looke for.

Perhaps what Milton has in mind would now be referred to as 'civil liberties' in the plural; and where he says 'complaints' more recent advocates of civil liberties might think and speak of 'protests'. How fully civil liberty, in the singular, has been achieved and whether a country without written constitution can fully achieve civil liberty or civil liberties are questions that may not receive identical answers from within England and from without. England's partners in Europe and, very probably, the descendants of English settlers in what were once colonies in North America, especially the United States, may now give an answer different from that given as a matter of course in England. But on the whole foreign commentators have over the centuries admired the liberty enjoyed in England. Wise men and women, as they look for liberty, need look no further than English trial by jury. The jury was in 1997, when the Conservatives were in office, under scrutiny in the hope of saving money on the administration of justice in England, and so it is again in 2000 under the Labour government. It is, however, traditionally regarded as the bulwark of England's liberty. To an Anglo-Saxonist it would be pleasing to think of this 'palladium of our liberties' – to vary the old metaphors – as going back to Anglo-Saxon legal institutions, and perhaps it does so in part. There have of course been many changes at various times. Most important among them is the institution (and

---

[84] John Milton, *Areopagitica: A Speech Of M^r. John Milton For the Liberty of Vnlicend'd Printing, To the Parlament of England* (London, 1644); see *The Complete Prose Works of John Milton*, II (New Haven and London, 1959), p. 487.

subsequent demise) of two classes of jury, the grand jury (which in no sense defended civil liberty) and the petty jury, a primary principle of legal administration, the roots of which may go back to before the reforms of Henry II, and which did not reach its firm shape till after his reign.[85] The modern jury includes both men and women. An important break with ancient tradition is the introduction of majority verdicts where earlier practice required unanimity. Unanimity had been the subject of a short monograph by Gundermann, who saw it as fundamental and believed it to have been in existence before trial by jury proper had come into being:[86] 'As with the history of the English jury as a whole, we must begin the account of unanimity with the law of the age of the Anglo-Saxons, even though at that time there can as yet be no question of jurymen proper.' The jurist and conservative politician Carl S. Zachariä (von Lingenthal) had predicted that unanimity might at some future time be abandoned:[87] 'Lastly, ... it is not beyond the realm of possibility that in time the requirement of unanimity will be given up.'

Some essential features have remained. The twelve good men and true, who from Anglo-Saxon times onwards have been summoned from the vicinage to speak truth on oath, are not learned in the law. Their conscience based on faith assures their truth: at the end of the twentieth century the faith of the twelve is less firm than it was in Anglo-Saxon times and long thereafter. We may hope that truth based on a sense of duty owed to the community may take over, or may already have taken over, from truth based on faith. If so, trial by jury may remain a living institution.

---

[85] This highly important development lies at the centre of trial by jury as understood from the thirteenth century onwards; for the standard account see Pollock and Maitland, *The History of English Law*, 2nd edn (Cambridge, 1898) (and subsequent editions and issues), II, pp. 642–50.

[86] I. Gundermann, *Ueber die Einstimmigkeit der Geschwornen* (Munich, 1849), pp. 46–7: 'Wie bei der Geschichte der englischen Jury überhaupt, so gehen wir auch bei der Einstimmigkeit von dem Rechte zur Zeit der Angelsachsen aus, obwohl hier von wahren Geschwornen noch keine Rede sein kann.' He devotes pp. 48–109 to unanimity in Anglo-Saxon law. For the standard discussion of unanimity see Pollock and Maitland, *The History of English Law*, 2nd edn (and subsequent editions and issues), II, pp. 625–7.

[87] C.S. Zachariä, *Kritische Zeitschrift für Rechtswissenschaft und Gesetzgebung des Auslandes* xxv (1853), p. 208: 'Endlich ... liegt es nicht ausser den Gränzen der Möglichkeit, dass man mit der Zeit die Forderung der Einstimmigkeit aufgibt'.

INDEXES

THE FOOTNOTES are indexed only when they contain bibliographical and other information and references not available via the body of the text. Page numbers are in roman, *footnote numbers are in italic*. In the alphabetization ä, ö, and ü are treated as if ae, oe, and ue, ð and þ are treated as if th.

I. Index of sources

The titles of Old English poetic texts are usually given in the form as in Krapp, G.P., and Dobbie, E.V.K. (eds), *The Anglo-Saxon Poetic Records*, 6 vols (New York and London, 1931–1953). References to the Anglo-Saxon laws are listed together under 'Laws', and the abbreviations used for their titles are as in F. Liebermann (ed.), *Die Gesetze der Angelsachsen*, 3 vols (Halle, 1898–1916).

Ælfric: xi; Preface to Genesis, 14; Genesis, 101; Catholic Homily (*Hortatorius sermo de efficacia sanctae missae*), 84 *254*; Catholic Homily (*Epiphania Domini*), 86
Æthelred II, the Unready: charter to the Old Minster, Winchester, 140
Aldhelm glosses: 85; 87
Alfred the Great, king of the West-Saxons: his will: 116–17. Old English translation of Boethius, *De consolatione philosophiae*, 85–6; 105–6; *The Meters of Boethius*: 92. See also Boethius, below
Andreas: 15–18; 36; 40; 63; 67–9; 71; – ll. 1–11a, 67; – l. 11, 101; – l. 613, 92–3; – l. 1056, 92; – l. 1561, 92
Asser's life of King Alfred: 140

Battle of Finnsburh, The, see *Finnesburh Fragment*, below
Bede: 15; 62
Bede's Death Song: 11
Beowulf: 6; 8; 10; 13; 15; 17; 35; 36; 37; 40; 41–50; 51; 70–1; 90–2; 98–9; 100; 103; 106–7; *Beowulf*-lays, 51; biblical or classical influence, 48; Christian elements, 41; 46–8; civilization depicted, 64–5; the dragon, 98–9; imagery, 68; a 'literary' *Beowulf*, 48; nature elements, 4; 38–9; a secular poem, xv; – l. 73, 65; – l. 106, 99; – ll. 178b–88, 44; 49; – l. 452, 19; – l. 477b, 94; – ll. 572–3, 86; 89; – ll. 696b–697a, 91; – ll. 734–6, 107; – l. 979, 99; – ll. 1055b–62, 91–2; – ll. 1055b–1057a, 89–92; 94; 104; – l. 1123, 19; – l. 1205, 94; – ll. 1357b–1376a (Grendel's mere), 38–9; – l. 1481b, 19; – ll. 1724b–1781 (Hrothgar's 'sermon'), 44–5; – ll. 2420–3a, 107; – ll. 2525b–2527a, 94; 107; – l. 2536b, 19; – l. 2574b, 92; 99; – ll. 2814b–2815, 94; 99; – l. 3030a, 90. Germanic antiquities, the Germanic past recalled, see Index III s.vv. Germanic antiquities, Germanic antiquity
Blickling Homilies: 87
Boethius, *De consolatione philosophiae*: 88; 100. See also s.v. Alfred the Great, above

Cædmon, Cædmonian poetry: 8; 12; 15; 17; 20; 27; 36; 39; 48; 70; 73; 74
Chaucer, Geoffrey, Wife of Bath: 110
Christ: xiv; 98; *Christ* C: 71
Complaynt of Scotlande, The: 89
Corpus Glossary: 85–6
Cynewulf, Cynewulfian poetry: 5; 12; 13; 63; 70–2; 73

149

INDEX OF SOURCES

Daniel: 20; – ll. 188–485, 20; – l. 231, 20; – l. 413, 20
Deor: 6; 12; 43; 52; 56–7; 60; 97
Douglas, Gavin: 89
Dream of the Rood, The: 12; 67; 78–9

Edda: x; 16; 109
'elegies', Old English: 40; 50–61; 63; 96; 97; 108
Elene: xiv; 15; 16–17; 36; 40; 63; 67; 77; 79; 98; – ll. 18–68 (battle of the Huns, Goths, and Franks), 66; – l. 80a, 92; – l. 1046b, 92; 93
Épinal Glossary: 85
Exeter Book: xiv; 61; 82
Erfurt Glossary: 85
Exodus: 11; 63; 66; – l. 168a, 69–70; – l. 398b, 20; – l. 401b, 20
Finnesburh Fragment, The: 12; 43

Genesis: 17; 36; 63; *Genesis A* l. 1194a, 64; – l. 1862b, 64; – ll. 1982–93a, 50; – l. 1991a, 69; – ll. 2047–86a (the deliverance of Lot), 66; – l. 2817a, 64; – ll. 2856b–2857a, 2904b, 2930b, 20; – *Genesis B* , 39; Adam and Eve, 80
Gifts of Men, The: 62
Gnomic poems, Old English, and gnomes in other Old English poems: 40; 60; 61–3; 81; 98; Exeter Gnomes (*Maxims* I), l. 132a, 82; Cotton Gnomes (*Maxims* II), 52 *149*; – ll. 1–13, 61–2; – ll. 4b–5a, 102–4; – l. 5a, 94; – ll. 5a and 41b, 97
Gragas: 139
Guthlac: xiv; *Guthlac* A, ll. 191b–199, 75–6; – ll. 209b–214, 76 *Guthlac* B, ll. 1057b–1059, 86; – ll. 1276b–1282a, 5; – ll. 1314b–1315a, 77; – ll. 1345b–1346a, 86

Heliand: 9; 16–17; 20–3; 24; 40; 63; 67; 74; 76; 81; 108; *thiu uurd* 'Fate', 88; – l. 151 (Zachariah and Elizabeth deprived of strength by age), 21; – ll. 4865b–4882a (Peter's sword-stroke), 66
Hildebrandslied: 27–8; 81
Holinshed, R.: 89
Homiletic Fragment I: 63
Husband's Message, The: 10–11; 60–1

Isidore of Seville: 87

John ('Florence') of Worcester: 140 *71*
Judgment Day I (perhaps Judgment Day II): 5
Judith: 11; 17; 63; 73–5; 79; 99–100; – ll. 205b–212a, 75
Juliana: xiv; 72–3

Laws: [*A Gu.*3] 117 *14*; [*II As.* 23,2] 145; [*I Atr.*] 143; [*I Atr. Prolog*] 143–4; [*III Atr.*] 142–4; [*III Atr. Prolog*–6,2] 118 *19*; [*III Atr. Prolog*] 144; [*III Atr.* 1–1, 1] 118 *19*; [*III Atr.* 1, 1] 137; [*III Atr.* 3, 1] 115 *11*; 142; 145; [*III Atr.* 3, 1–3] 139 *66*; 140
Leiden Glossary: 87

Martyrology, Old English: 82
Maxims I and II, see Gnomic poems, above
Merseburg Charms : 78
Meters of Boethius, The: 92
Metrical Charms: 82–4; *For a Sudden Stitch*, 55; 82–3; *The Nine Herbs Charms*, 82–4
Milton, J.: *Areopagitica*, 146
Muspilli: 9

Nibelungenlied: 68

Otfrid: 9; 16; 48

Phoenix, The: 5

Quadripartibus: 145

Riming Poem, The: 89
Ruin, The: xiv

Saxo Grammaticus: 47
Seafarer, The: 4–5; 12–13; 54–61; 63; 94; 97; – ll. 39–43, 55; – l. 58, 55; – ll. 80b–93, 54; – ll. 115b–16, 94; – l. 115b, 87; 94
Shakespeare, Wm, the Weird Sisters in *Macbeth*: 88 *269*; 89; 98
Simeon of Durham: 140 *71*
Solomon and Saturn: 63; 81–2; 105–6; ll. 334–5, 86; – ll. 426–50, 86; 105
Spenser, Edmund, *The Faerie Queene* III. iv. 27: 86

INDEX OF SOURCES

Tacitus, *Germania*: 64; 83; and Old English poetry, 64–5; 80; and Old Norse poetry, 65
Textus Roffensis: 114; 140 *67*

Vainglory: 63
Vercelli Book: 68–9

Waldere: 41; 43; 101
Wanderer, The: 52–8; 60–1; 63; 75; 94; 95 *295*; 96; 97–8; – l. 5b, 102; – l. 15b, 94; – l. 89a, 94; – l. 100b, 94; 98; – l. 107a, 94; 95 *295*; 98; – ll. 111–15, 56; – l. 112a, 62
Warner, Wm, *Albions England*: 89
Wessobrunn Prayer: 81
Widsith: 6; 40–1; 43; 47; 100
Wife's Lament, The: 57; 60–1
William of Malmesbury: 52
Wulf and Eadwacer: 60–1
Wulfstan, homily ascribed to him: 83

II. Index of scholars, critics, and authors not regarded as sources in Index I

Allen, J.: 25–7
Anderson, G.K.: xiv; 5; 6; 12; 28; 41; 56; 103

Baesecke, G.: 27–8; 36; 76; 96
Baetke, W.: 108–9
Baker QC, His Honour Judge Paul V.: xii
Bartels, A.: 64
Beck, H.: viii *3*
Bentham, Jeremy: 31
Biener, F.A.: 118
Blackstone, W.: 113; 114–15 *6*; 118; 121; 123; 125 *35*
Bloomfield, M.W.: 47; 109
Boase, T.S.R.: xii *14*
Boer, R.C.: 93
Bonser, W.: 82–3
Bosworth, J.: 83
Boyd, Zachary: 11 *30*; 12
Bradley, H.: 43; 44; 48
Brandl, A.: 11; 46; 52; 56–7; 61–2; 82; 97; 98–100; 103–4
Brewer, D.S.: xv
Brincker, F.: 63; 74–5; 79–80; 99–100
Brink, B. ten: 11; 45; 50; 58–9; 73
Brodeur, A.G.: 47; 92
Brunner, H.: 119; 120; 121 *26*; 123; 124–7; 133; 134; 137
Bütow, H.: 12
Bugge, E.S.: 79; 101
Bunyan, John: xiii

Campbell, A.: vii
Campbell, J.: 138
Carlyle, Thomas: x; 78
Chadwick, H.M.: 48
Chadwick, H.M., and Chadwick, N.K.: 49–50
Chambers, R.W.: 41
Clarke, M.G.: 43
Cockayne, (T.) O.: 83–4
Cook, A.S.: 74–5; 79
Cooper, C.P.: xii
Cope, C.H.: xii *14*
Cope, C.W.: xii; his 'The First Trial by Jury', 112
Craigie, (Sir) W.A., and Onions, C.T.: 30 *84*

Cronk, N.E.: xii; 113 *1*

Dahlmann, F.C.: 133
Dale, E.: 80; 95
de Lolme, J.L.: 134
de Selincourt, E.: 24
Dickens, Charles: 132
Dickins, B.: 11–12; 30; 31 *88*
Dickins, B., and Ross, A.S.C.: 79
D'Israeli, Isaac: 27; 141
Dobbie, E.V.K.: 81; 101
Donoghue, Daniel: xii

Earle, J.: 41–3; 45–6, 47; 91–2
Ebel, E.: viii *3*
Ebert, A.: 26–7; 45–6; 47; 71–4; 75–6
Edinburgh Review: (1815) 25–6; (1845) 36–7; (1848) 36–7; (1849), 24
Ehrismann, G.: 59–60; 95–6
Ekholm, G.: 64
'Eliot, George': xiii
Encyclopédie, ou Dictionnaire Raisonné des Sciences, des Arts et des Métiers: 134–5
Ettmüller, L.: 8; 14–15; 42; 90

Ferrell, C.C.: 5; 63–5; 69; 94
Forsyth, W.: 115 *6*
Freeman, E.A.: 134

Gervinus, G.G.: 6; 27; 28; 30; 33; 48
Girvan, R.: 65
Gneuss, H.: xii
Goethe, J.W. von: 7
Gollancz, (Sir) I.: xiv
Gooch, G.P.: 6; 14
Gordon, E.V.: 61
Gordon, I.L.: 12–13; 87
Gradon, P.O.E.: xiv
Grattan, J.H.G., and Singer, C.: 84
Green, J.R.: 39; 40
Grein, C.W.M.: 23; 30; *Bibliothek der angelsächsischen Poesie* (1857–1858), 90–1; part II, *Sprachschatz* (1861–1864), 101; *Dichtungen der Angelsachsen* (1857–1859): xv; 50 *139*
Grein, C.W.M., and Wülcker, R.P.,

INDEX OF SCHOLARS, CRITICS, AND AUTHORS

(eds): *Bibliothek der angelsächsischen Poesie* (1883–1898), 103
Greverus, J.P.E.: 33–5
Grimm, Jacob: viii; ix–x; 31; 33; 84; 93; 96; 137; review of C.F. Rühs (1812), xi; *Deutsche Grammatik*, I (1st edn 1819, 2nd edn 1822), viii *5*; 10; 29; *Deutsche Grammatik*, II (1826), x *8*; *Deutsche Rechts Alterthümer* (1828), 123; *Deutsche Grammatik*, III (1831), 88 *271*; *Deutsche Mythologie* (1st edn 1835, 2nd edn 1844), x; 19–20; 78; 82; 88–9; 92; *Andreas und Elene* (1840), 15–23; 36–7; 40; 63; 67–9; 77; 'Deutsche Grenzalterthümer', 70 and *201*; 'Über das Verbrennen der Leichen' (1849), 20
Grimm, Jacob, and Grimm, Wilhelm, viii *3*; ix; x–xi; 30–1; 67
Grimm, Wilhelm: review of Rühs (1813), xi
Grubl, E.D.: 12
Gummere, F.B.: 51
Gundermann, J.I.: xii; 132–4; 147

Hallam, H.: 117–18
Hegel, G.W.F.: 5; 113; 130–1
Heinzel, R.: 51
Helm, K. 80–2; 102; 103–4
Heusler, A.: viii *3*; 60–1; 66–7
Hickes, G.: 29
Hodgkin, R.H.: 12
Hölderlin, Friedrich: ix
Holborn, Guy: xii
Hoops, J.: viii *3*
Hume, David: 115 *6*
Hurd, Richard: 3

Idelmann, T.: 108; 109

Jaucourt, L. de: 134–5 and *59*
Jente, R.: 69; 85; 96 *299*; 101–2

Kant, I.: 113; 124–5; 130
Kauffmann, F.: 87 *268*; 96 *299*
Keiser, A.: 96 *299*
Keller, M.L.: 79
Kemble, Frances Ann (Fanny): 30–1
Kemble, J.M.: 18; 29–33; 68–9; 70; 82; 89–90; 96
Kent, C.W.: 63; 67–8; 92–3
Ker, W.P.: viii–ix; 43; 46; 47; 100

Keynes, S.D.: xii; 143
Kingsley, Charles: 28; 35
Klaeber, F.: 41; 46–8; 60; 91; 103; 106
Klipstein, L.F.: 10–11; 52–3; 96–7
Kluge, F.: 4; 54
Köhler, A.: 63; 90–1; 92
Köstlin, C.R.: 127–30; 132; 134

Lachmann, K.: 9
Langenfelt, G.: 40
Lapidge, M., Blair, J., Keynes, S., and Scragg, D.: xii *12*
Lappenberg, J.M.: 119
Lawrence, W.W.: 46; 48–9
Legouis, E.: 6; 26; 57
Leo, H.: 7–8; 14–15
Levison, W.: 14–15
Liebermann, F.: 114–15 *6*; 119; 137–8; 142; 145
Lingard, J.: 24–7
Lloyd, H. Evans: 133 *52*

Maitland, F.W., see Pollock, F., and Maitland, F.W
Massmann, H.F.: 35–6
Maurer, G.L. von: 129–30; 132
Maurer, K. (von): 142 *75*
Menner, R.J.: 81; 105
Migne, J.P.: xv
Mill, James: 31
Milton, John: 39; 113
Mittermaier, K.J.A.: 129 *44*
Mogk, E.: 52
Müllenhoff, K.: 41–2 and *113, 115*; 56
Müller, J.: 64–5; 93–4

Napier, A.S.: 85
Neckel, G.: 52
Neff, C.: 142 *75*
Norman, F.: 101–2

OED, see *Oxford English Dictionary*, below
Olszewska, E. Stefanyja (Mrs A.S.C. Ross): vii
Oxford English Dictionary, The (*OED*); entry for *jury*: 119 and *22*; *The New English Dictionary*, Supplement (1933), 30 *84*

Page, R.I.: 84
Palgrave, (Sir) F.: 8; 115–16

153

Palgrave, F.T.: 116
Parker, Matthew, Saxonists of his time: vii
Pfeifer, W.: x *8*
Philippson, E.A.: x *8*; 82; 96
Phillips, G.: 133
Phillpotts, (Dame) B.S.:100; 109 *343*
Pizzo, E.: 106–7
Pollock, (Sir) F., and Maitland, F.W.: 119; 120; 121; 137; 147 *85, 86*
Pons, É.: 4–5; 61 *176*
Pope, Alexander: 123
Price, M.B.: 63; 77; 96
Pye, H.J.: 116–17

Quarterly Review: (1812) 25

Rask, R.K.: 29 *81*
Rau, M.: 11; 63; 69–70
Repp, T.G.: 138
Richardson, C.: 30
Rieger, M.: 53–4
Ritson, J.: 27
Rühs, (C.) F.: xi; 138–9

Savigny, F.C. von: ix
Sayles, G.O.: 65
Schauffler, T.: 65
Sedgefield, W.J.: 100
Shelley, P.B.: 5
Shepherd, Geoffrey: xv
Sieper, E.: 51–2; 55; 57–9; 97–8; 108
Simrock, K.: 90–1
Sisson, J.L.: 29
Skeat, W.W.: 8
Smith, M. Bentinck: 11; 19; 49; 70–1
Stanley, E.G.: (1963) 'Hæthenra Hyht in *Beowulf*', 44 *120*; 76 *215*; (1964–1965) 'Search for Anglo-Saxon Paganism' (first publication), xi; xiii–xv; (1975), xi; xiii; (1981) 'Scholarly Recovery of Anglo-Saxon Records', vii *1*; (1981) 'Glorification of Alfred', vii *2*; 113–14 *2*; 115 *9*; (1987) *Collection of Papers*, vii *1, 2*; 113–14 *2*; 115 *9*
Stenton, Doris M. (Lady): 121; 137; 144

Stenton, (Sir) Frank M.: 136; 139
Stephens, G.: 77–9
Stolberg, F.L. (Graf) zu: 7
Storms, G.: 82 *244*; 83
Strunk, W.: 73
Sweet, H.: 38–9; 40; 73; 94–5
Symons, B.: 11

Ten Brink, B., see Brink, B. ten, above
Tennyson, Alfred (Lord), 31
Thorpe, B.: xiv; 29 *81*; 90; 119–20
Timmer, B.J.: 75; 109
Tolkien, J.R.R.: vii; 43; 44; 45; 49
Toller, T.N.: 101
Toswell, Jane: viii
Turner, Sharon: 24; 114

Uhland, L.: 8

Vilmar, A.F.C.: 20–3; 24; 30; 40; 63; 67; 74; 80; 81; 88; 101; 108
Virgil: 3
'Voltaire' (i.e. Arouet, François Marie): xii; 113

Waller, A.R.: 3–4
Wardale, E.E.: xiv; 4; 5; 41; 52; 55–6; 61; 78–9; 102–3
Weber, G.W.: xiv
Weidinger, Svenja: xii
Whitelock, D.: 109
Wilda, W.E.: 139
Wilkins, D.: 115 *11*; 118 *19*
Williams, B.C.: 62–3; 82; 97; 103–4
Wise, F.: 116 *13*
Wolf, A.(P.): 96 *299*; 107
Wolff, F.A.: 42
Woolf, R.: 73
Wordsworth, Wm: 4; 24
Wormald, Patrick: xi–xii; 119; 122 *29*; 142 *75*
Wrenn, C.L.: 44
Wright, Thomas: 10
Wül(c)ker, R.P.: xi *10*; 29; 63; 103 *330*

Zachariä (von Lingenthal), C.S.: 126–7; 147

III. General index

Ælfsige, bishop of Chester-le-Street: 141
Æthelred II, the Unready: 137; 144
Alcuin: 14
Aldhelm: 15; 52
Aldred, glossator: 141
Alfred the Great, king of the West-Saxons: 100, 134–5; institution of trial by jury ascribed to his time, vii; xii; 113, 115, 136. See also Index I, s.v. Alfred
alliteration, alliterative metre: 55; 69; 72
Alphege, St: 28
Ambrose, St: 14
Angles, Saxons, and Jutes: 8
Anglo-Norman England: 137
Anglo-Saxon poetry: 18–19. See Index I for individual poems
Anglo-Saxon royal genealogies: 62
Anglo-Scandinavian currency: 142
apperception: 130–1 and *48*
Assize, great Assize of Henry II: 134
Augustine of Canterbury, St: 24
Augustine of Hippo, St: 14
authorities, the: 125 and *35*.

Baldr: 78–9
Bayerische Akademie der Wissenschaften: vii–viii
beasts of battle: 17–18; 75; 79–80
Bellona: 19; 68; 69; 79; 89
biblical exegesis: 14
Boniface, St: 14
burials and cremations: 20; 31–2; 57; 98

Carolingian law: 123; 136–8; 143
ceorl: 119–20
'Christian epic(s)': 40; 66; 95
civil liberty, civil liberties, liberty: vii; 7; 26; 113–17; 121–2; 132; 134; 136; 146–7
comitatus, kingship, royal power: 22; 58; 64; 75; 76
compurgator, see oath-helper
conscience in legal process, inwardness of those involved in legal process: 113; 124; 129–30; 134; 147

constitution of England: 7; 34; 114; 133; 146
constitution of Norway: 138–9
conversion of the Anglo-Saxons to Christianity: 24–8; 80; 84; 98–100
court of law, court of justice: 124–5; a learned institution, 127 *40*

Danelaw, Five Boroughs: xi; 137; 139; 141; 142–4
Danes under Anglo-Saxon kings: 143
Dark Ages: 3
Death personified: 91; 105; 107
democratic element in Germanic constitutions: 127 *41*
descriptive poetry: 38–9
disintegration of Old English poems: 40–63; 102–3
drunkenness: 72
dryhten: 55–6; 97
duel: 129

elves: 71; 110
English language and its history: 7–8; 34–5; 38; 68
ent: 97
epic formulas: 16–17; 21; 60. See also oral formulas, below
epic period: 68
epic poetry, Germanic and Anglo-Saxon: 11; 19; 45–6; 47; 50; 58; 69; 73; 74. See also 'Christian epic(s)', above
essential liberty (Hegel's *subjective Freyheit*): 130–1
executive: 125

fæge, see fate (Wyrd), fatalism
fasting before legal process: 145
fate (Wyrd), fatalism: xiv; 20 *49*; 38; 53; 58; 61; 62; 71; 81; 85–109; *gewyrd*, 86–7; *wyrd* collocated with *fæge*, 86; the word *wyrd* evidence of heathenism, 96–8; 108. See also s.vv. Fortuna, Norn(s), Providence, Weird Sisters
feudalism: 133
Fortuna: 85–6; 88; 105
franchise, see civil liberty, above
Frankish law: 128; 138

155

free will: 100
French Revolution: 132–3
Frigg: 78
Furies: 85

gender and personification: 88
Germanic (and Proto-Germanic) age and shared heritage: x–xi; 18; 27; 52; 137–8
Germanic Antiquity and antiquities in Old English poetry: 5 *10*; 15–18; 28; 40; 43; 48; 50; 63–76; 84
Germanic antiquities in Old Saxon poetry: 20–2; 40. See also Index II s.v. Vilmar, A.F.C.
Germanic language(s), Teutonic, *deutsch*: xi; 7–8; 20; 84
Germanic law: 35; 137–9; 143
Germanic poetry: 15–18; 27
Germanic ritual: 97; 99; burial ritual, 51; 57–8; 98
Germanic spirit: 69
giants: 62; 71
Glorious Revolution (1688): 113; 132–3
Götterdämmerung: 54
Gregory the Great, St: 24
'Grimm's Law': 29 *81*
grið: 118; 144
Gundulf versus Pichot: 114
guð personified: 20; 91

Hel: 78
Henry II: 132; 133; 134; 147
Herodotus: 5
Heroic age: 3; 47–8 *133*
heroic poetry, heroic song: 11; 43; 76
hild personified, a goddess: 19; 69; 89; 91. See also *woma* listed s.v. 'words', below
Homer: 42
homilies and Old English verse: 44–5; 60; 63; 69
horse (Baldr's or Christ's) dislocates foot: 78

Icelandic law: 139
inwardness (*rein innerliches*), see conscience, above

judges: 123; 125; learned in the law, 127

judging not the same as testifying, as delivering the truth: 123–4
jury, trial by jury: xi–xii; 111–47; juries now composed of men and women, 147; jury of accusation (*Anklagejury* or *Rügejury*), 118; jury of proof (*Beweisjury*), 118–19; 126; 134; jury of trial, trial jury (*Urteiljury*), 118–19; 122 *29*; grand jury, petty jury, 121–2 and *29*
juryman, juror: 123–4 and *33*; representative of the people, not of authority, 124–5
justices in eyre: 133

kingship, king or lord and comitatus: 22; 58; 64; 75; 76; the king sits in judgement, 72; king's thegn, 117
Kronos: 81

lawman: 124 *23*
learned (or not learned) in the law: 124; 127 and *40*; 147
legal antiquities in Old English poetry: 64
legal reform in nineteenth-century Germany: 127; 132
legislature and executive: 125
liberty, liberties, see civil liberty
Loki: 78

magistracy, executive authority: 123; 125 *35*
Magna Carta: 115–16; 122
marches, borderlands: 70
mariners of England: 56
Mars: 68; 79
mearcweardas: 69–70
melancholy, Germanic; elegiac mood and gloom in Old English poetry: 3; 38; 39; 43; 50–2; 81; 94–6; 102; 106
metod, metodsceaft, meotudwang: 99, 101–2
metrical impressions as evidence of interpolation: 44–5; 55
minstrel, see *scop*
mythologizing etymologies: xiv; 19–20; 69; 77; 79; 88–9

Napoleonic Wars, Napoleon I: viii–ix; 6
national character, identity, and

consciousness: 68; 71–2; 80; 114; 126–7; 133
nature in Old English poetry, natural order, natural description: 3–5; 11; 39; 59; 62; 68–9; 71; 78
Niflheim: 71
Nimrod: 81
Ninus: 81
Norman Conquest: vii; 7; 113; 117; 119; 120; 136
Normandy: 136 and *60*; 138
Norman kings; their legal institutions: 120; 136; 145
Norns; Urð, Verðandi, Skuld: 87–9 and *274*; 90; 92–3; 94; 109
Northumbria, its language: 141

oath: 113; 114; 120–1; 124; 129; 137; 143; 145; 147
oath-helpers (compurgators), not jurymen: 114–15; 117; 118; 119–21; 126; 129; 132; 133; 137. See also judging, above; and words, below
Odin, Othin, see Woden, below
Old English: 7–8; 67–8; 77
Old High German poetry: 16; 27
Old Norse poetry: 16
Old Saxon: 8
oral formulas, poetic formulas and motifs: 21; 60; 81; 91
ordeal, God's judgement: 120; 129; 134; 145

Parcae: 85; 87–8
patriotism, German (*Vaterlandsliebe*): viii–ix; 132; English patriotism, 115–17
peers, judgement by one's peers; peers of litigants deliver the truth: 115–17; 122; 124; 135
personification: 88–9; 109. See also s.v. mythologizing etymologies, above
poetic imagery: 68
poetic vocabulary: 18–19; 21; 33; 60; 73; 75; 81; 91; 109; poetic language distinct from that of prose: 68. See also oral formulas, above
predestination: 86; 99; 100
providence, divine; fate and providence: 56; 58; 85; 92; 98–102; 105; 109
public (or open) and oral trial: 127; 129 *44, 45*; 131 and *48*

Ramsey versus Thorney: 137
recognitor, recognition: 121; 133
reeve sits in judgement: 72
Roman law: 143
Rome under Domitian: 64
royal power limited: 64–5; 117
rules of proof, of evidence: 130
runes, rune-magic: 83–4

sagas: 109
Saturn: 81–2
Scandinavia: 139; Scandinavian influence on Anglo-Saxon institutions and laws, 137; 143–4; Scandinavian loanwords in III Æthelred: zu Wantage, 141; 142 and *75*; 144
Schöffe: 124 and *33*; 133
scop, gleoman, minstrel: 11; 21; 48–50; 53; 60; 68; 95
sentence and verdict: 125 and *35*
Settlement, Anglo-Saxon: 8
sins: 105
sovereign as judge: 125
sum-catalogues: 62
sylvan deities: 75–6

thegn; king's thegn: 117; 135; thanes of the Wapentake: 115; 136; 139; 142–3
Thǫkk: 78–9
Thunor, Thor, Donar: 62; 82; 83 *246*
þyrs: 97
Tiw: 82
transubstantiation as expressed by the Anglo-Saxons: 26
travel in Anglo-Saxon England: 141
truth in legal process: 113; 114–15; 121; 123–4; 129; 134; 147
twelve men in legal process: xi; 113; 114; 115; 117; 118; 120–2; 124; 130; 135; 137; 139; 145 and *83*; 147
twilight of the gods: 54

Ultrices (Furies): 85
unanimity of verdict: 120; 130; 147

Valhalla: 71; 77
Valkyrie: 19–20
verdict, 'guilty' or 'not guilty': 115; 118; 120; 125 *35*; 129; 134; 135
Verdun, Treaty of (843): 35–6 and *98*
vicinage from which jurors are drawn: 113; 118; 122; 124; 134 *55*; 135; 147;

vicinetum where court of law is held: 133
victory: 77; 109

Wantage, birthplace of Alfred the Great: 134–5; 140–1; 144
warfare and a warlike spirit in poetry: 11; 17; 20–21; 27–8; 39; 50; 52; 58; 66–7; 69; 72; 73; 74; 75; 79. See also beasts of battle, above
warning, OE *warnung*: 86; 105
Wayland: 52
Weird Sisters: 88, *269*; 89; 98
white god: 78
William the Conqueror: 7
Wish, supposedly a Germanic god: x
Woden, Othin: x; xiv; 17–18; 19; 62; 68; 70; 79–80; 82–4 and *246*

wolf: 70. See also beasts of battle, above
words (Old English, unless otherwise specified): *bæl*, 20; *broga*, 19; *compurgator* (MnE), 114 and *6*; *egesa*, 19; *empanel* (MnE), 138 *63*; *frið*, 144; *grið*, 144; *hild* (see also *woma*, below), 19; 91; *oath-helper* (MnE), 114–15 *6*: -*scrifan, forscrifan, gescrifan*, 98–9; *sweg*, 19; *twelfa sum*, 145 *83*; *Unready* (MnE sobriquet of Æthelræd II, 144 and *79*; *verdict* (MnE), 124 and *34*; *woma, hilde woma, wiges woma*, xiv; 19–20; 68; 69 *199*
Wyrd, see fate, above

Yggdrasil: 109

WITHDRAWN